A Delius
Companion

A Delius
Companion

Edited, with a Preface by
Christopher Redwood

JOHN CALDER
LONDON

Typeset in 11 point Plantin by Woolaston Parker Ltd., Leicester

CONTENTS

LIST OF ILLUSTRATIONS

INTRODUCTION

Few compilations of this kind have been less deserving of the encumbrance of an introduction than the present tribute to Eric Fenby. It needs no *Imprimatur*: its contents are already winged, ready to fly to those whose love for Delius's music makes them avid to read more about him. It goes beyond the traditional idea of a *Festschrift*—"a publication celebrating an event or honouring a person", for its contributors, dead or alive, do not ride a series of disparate musical hobby-horses to mark an anniversary, but are united in their common interest—Frederick Delius, the man and his music. This goes, too, for Delius's own essay, for he never concealed the love he bore his own music: it suffuses, I think, his strictures on *The Present Cult*, which he would have been unlikely to modify had he been writing today.

It was a similarly pervasive love for Delius's music, now shared by ever-increasing numbers, that moved the young Eric Fenby in 1928 to offer his services as amanuensis to his fellow Yorkshireman, the ageing, blind and paralysed composer, and so brought about a collaboration unique in the annals of music. In gratitude for that gesture and for its musical fruit, these writings about Delius and his music, old and new, have been assembled here by Christopher Redwood to honour the young man from Scarborough on his seventieth birthday on behalf of us all.

FELIX APRAHAMIAN

EDITOR'S PREFACE

The music of Frederick Delius was slow to gain recognition in the country of his birth, as Lionel Carley shows in his essay "Hans Haym: Delius's Prophet and Pioneer". By the 1920's, however, encouraged by the popularity of his two recent compositions for small orchestra, "On Hearing the First Cuckoo in Spring" and "Summer Night on the River", and subsequently by the success of "Hassan" with his incidental music, his following had become enthusiastic. So much so, indeed, that when he returned to France after his last visit to England in 1929 for the momentous Beecham festival of his music, he was able to say: "Place my chair so that my eyes may be directed upon the shores of England, which has given me the recognition that I have not obtained anywhere else." His death in 1934 was followed by the inevitable reaction, which lasted until well after the end of the Second World War. Since then a new generation has grown up; one that missed the adulation of the 'twenties and has been able to form a more coolly balanced judgement of his contribution to music. This has included several scholars who have devoted painstaking efforts to research into the life and music of Delius, and it was my original intention to collect together in a single volume the most valuable of the post-war essays on these subjects. However, Felix Aprahamian reminded me of the large number of articles dating from an earlier period which were far too valuable to be lost in the dusty archives of the journals in which they first appeared, often obscure and in several cases no longer extant. I therefore decided to widen the scope of the book to include a balanced selection of pieces written during the composer's lifetime and since his death.

My chief debt is to the Delius Trust, without whose help this publication would not have been possible; more particularly I wish to thank them for permission to quote from letters in their possession and from the music of Delius. My gratitude is next due to Felix Aprahamian who encouraged the scheme from the start and made valuable suggestions. Having been personally acquainted with nearly all of the contributors, he was also of great help in compiling the personal details given at the end of the book. I must thank Mr. Robert Threlfall and Dr. Lionel Carley, respectively Musical Adviser and Archivist to the Delius Trust for their help, and Mr. Stephen Lloyd of the Delius Society who drew my attention to the piece by Gerald Cumberland. I am also grateful to Mr. Edward N. Waters, Chief of the Reference Department, Music Division, The Library of Congress, Washington D.C., who obtained a copy of the essay by John F. Runciman for me. Finally I would thank my wife for her patience and forbearance while the project was taking shape; simultaneous gestation in husband and spouse is uncommon and not without its difficulties.

The publishers of the books and periodicals in which these essays first appeared have generously granted permission for their reproduction; I apologise for omitting to request this formality in the one or two cases where it has proved impossible to trace the owner of the copyright. The State Photographic Archives, Strozier Library, Florida State University, kindly supplied the illustration opposite page 166. Miss Evelin Gerhardi of Bonn, West Germany, took the photographs opposite pages 50, 51, 109 and 131; Mr. Marshall Johnson took that of his wife opposite page 108; Mr. Norman Cameron took the picture of Sir Thomas Beecham and Eric Fenby opposite page 67; the photograph of Eric Fenby on the same page is by Mr. Roger Fenby. The illustrations opposite pages 190 and 191 are the property of the Delius Trust, and that opposite page 167 of the Grainger Museum, Melbourne. The postcard reproduced opposite page 13 is from the collection of Adrian C. Harland.

CHRISTOPHER REDWOOD.

Wimbledon, 1975.

Delius in about 1897.

GREZ-SUR-LOING. — Le Pont de la rivière

Édité J. Teland à Moret, cliché Cotun

The bridge over the River Loing at Grez, from a postcard of about the turn of the century.

Fritz Delius, Composer   by John F. Runciman

It is often stated that following the 1899 *London concert, which Delius promoted at his own expense, nothing more was heard of him in the land of his birth until the autumn of* 1907, *when both Piano Concerto and "Appalachia" were introduced to the capital. The article below, neatly dating from midway between these two events, gives the lie to such a tale, and shows Runciman to have been one of the earliest English critics to achieve a balanced perception of Delius's work. It was from this essay, incidentally, that Philip Heseltine quoted (mentioning the author but not the source) in his* 1923 *study of the composer.*

Some 50 miles south of Paris, on the skirts of the forest of Fontainebleau, there lies a tiny village very well known to me. Grez-sur-Loing is built along one side of the River Loing. It may contain a couple of hundreds of inhabitants, tillers of the soil and poachers mostly, but, excepting on fête days, you might stand an hour in its long main street and not see half a dozen people. It has a post office and even a telegraph; there are two butchers and three groceries; there is one hotel. But the place seems deserted, asleep. In the Middle Ages it was fortified, and there are still standing the ruins of the castle in which naughty Queen Blanche was imprisoned. The church, too, is said to be ancient, but as I have not read the guide I cannot swear to it. The village burst into active life again when artists from all quarters of the earth made their way there to labour in valorous emulation of Rousseau and Millet, for only some 16 kilometres on the other side of the forest stands the world famous Barbizon. Grez is prettier than Barbizon, for besides the forest it has the river, deep in places, silently flowing, but here and there decorated with tiny islands covered with rushes. The painters painted there, and flirted, and ate and drank, and then they went leaving the place silent as before. Robert Louis Stevenson stayed there some time, and wrote about it, and called it Gretz. But the "Gretz" of his day is only a memory. The Chevillon

Hôtel has a grey look of decay, and save in August, when a few of the rampant bourgeoisie come and spoil the calm with their squalling children, it has hardly an occupant. I have been the only client sometimes for weeks at a stretch. No better spot could be found by anyone desirous of inventing, say, a flying machine or an opera, and here Fritz Delius, indifferent to the flying machine problem, but intensely occupied with the opera, has set up his rest.

Some readers may remark that they don't know who Fritz Delius is. Very likely not; I am going to tell them. They will have to hear about him some day, and it seems to me it is well worth while hearing about him now. Let me begin in the approved style, with a description of the man. He is about forty years of age, taller than one at first thinks, lean, wiry, strenuous in every movement, a fine face with piercing eyes, hair a little thinner than it was and turning from brown to grey. Every movement he makes is rapid, decisive; he is a prodigious walker, bicyclist and swimmer; soft and kindly in speech, he will yet sit up all night to do dialectical battle on any subject under the sun or from beyond it. Every morning he rises early, swims if the weather is passable, then sets to work. In the afternoon he sets forth on a walk or a trip on his bicycle. In the evening he works again and then to bed. That is his life there, a life varied only by excursions to Germany or Paris or England. If I do not supply details about what he has for breakfast, lunch and dinner, it is because his tastes are simple and he eats much as other men, and because I want to leave something for the paragraphists to glean later. Also I want to get on with some account of the musician.

Delius, in spite of his German sounding name, is an Englishman. He was born in Bradford, started the study of music when in charge of an orange plantation in Florida, and last went to Leipzig for a couple of years. There he worked with Jadassohn and Reinecke—two teachers to whom he reckons himself under no very special obligations. Afterward he lived in Paris, finally settling down at Grez. Among his works are, first, a set of songs published by Augener, in London, some years ago. These are occasionally sung, and though not comparable with his later music are highly interesting Then there are four lyric dramas: "Irmelin", finished in 1891; "The Magic Fountain", finished in 1894; "Koanga", finished in 1897, and "The Garden of Paradise", finished in 1900. These, or some of them, I will discuss presently, but let me complete the list of his achievements. There is a fantasia for orchestra, "Over the Hills and Far Away"; a symphonic poem (which he says is "after Ibsen"), "Auf dem Hochgebirge"; "The Council of the People", Norwegian suite for orchestra; "Zarathustra" (das Trunken Lied), for baritone solo, men's chorus and orchestra; "Paris" ("Ein Nachtstück"—the song of a great city), for orchestra; "Life's Dance", symphonic poem. This is a pretty fair batch, but there are in addition a piano concerto written for Busoni and a large number of songs—among them a Danish set with accompaniments for orchestra, and some settings of poems by Nietzsche.

Many of these things of Delius have been publicly performed, and more are down on the programmes of the near future. Some years ago he gave a concert in London—St. James' Hall —with a fair sized orchestra conducted by Hertz, late of Breslau. The programme included the "Zarathustra Night Song", "The Dance Goes On" ("Life's Dance"), a selection from "Koanga", some of the Danish songs and "Over the Hills and Far Away". The criticisms—mine not less than the rest—were amusing to read. The truth was that we didn't know what the devil to make of this music; and most of us were frank enough to say so. That there was intention, real mastery of notes; that every sound proceeding from the orchestra was meant by the composer; that there was no bungling, not from beginning to end an unanticipated effect—all this every competent critic knew. But the strains sounded unpleasant in our ears; the melodies made no seductive advances; the harmonies were harsh, raucous; the orchestral colours seemed purposely raw, often repulsive. We were baffled. Had some Ernest Newman been about to collate our articles and notices he would have found nothing like the diversity of opinions that was shown in the case of Richard Strauss. Rather he would have found no opinions at all— merely open confessions that as yet we had formed no opinions. Now this did not mean a damnation of Delius and all his works, nor did it reveal critical cowardice. Personally, I am supicious of the music that comes smiling to meet you, that seems to claim you as an old acquaintance. It generally is an old acquaintance. And I distrust the critics, professional or amateur, who rush to hail everything new as the greatest "long results of time", just as much as I do those who will have it that nothing new can possibly be good. Work worth understanding takes time to understand. I flatter myself I can see as far into a stone wall as most musicians and as quickly; but I should consider myself a donkey if I allowed myself to be hustled into an instantaneous admiration of a Strauss or a Delius. We have had warnings enough of the folly of such brainless proceedings. Where are those who went mad over Mascagni as a great composer, over Perosi—nay, over art achievements far above anything attempted by those two men: the "Otello" and "Falstaff" of Verdi? They are mightily glad, I suppose, that their glowing paragraphs are forgotten, buried in back numbers of unread journals. To understand music, new or old, you must be soaked in it; when you have been soaked long enough you get to know; and when you know absolutely nothing, neither the neglect of the world nor the scoffs of newer fangled pressmen can have power to shake your conviction. Only when deep down in yourself you know, when your intuition has grasped all there is in a piece of music, can you set your intellect to work to find plausible reasons for your faith. This is my defence of slow criticism and my justification of the "not proven" verdict brought in about Delius in London. More recently Busoni gave some of these same things in Berlin. But your German critic is nothing if not cocksure. Some of them remarked that here was mere anarchy and the apotheosis of ugliness; and then asked bitterly: "Have we really got so far that Wagner sounds like Mozart?"

This last is surely triumphantly fatuous. Yes, my gentle, long eared brother, if the day has not come it certainly will come when we shall have "really got so far that Wagner sounds like Mozart". There was a time when Mozart sounded like Wagner, and magnificent emperors found that in his music there were "too many notes". Mozart replied that there was just the right number; Wagner might have said the same in answer to the earlier criticisms of his music; Delius might say the same today. Though his scores are complex, complex as those of Richard Strauss, when one has taken the time and trouble to understand them, all is perfectly clear; there is no ugliness, no anarchy, nothing but order—logical order, to the point of severity—and beauty and expressiveness. But before offering my own criticism, let me say it is possible that I am biased, for Delius is my intimate friend; yet on the other hand be it remembered that in art matters friendship usually makes one a more exacting judge. At any rate, I have been afforded ample opportunities of studying his music; and the conclusions I have arrived at are simply those I could not help arriving at.

The early songs may be dismissed briefly with the remark

that they are valuable not so much for themselves as indications of what was coming. In the set of Danish songs we have the real Delius; the poet's emotion passed on to us after suffering a sea change at the hands of the composer. They are full of Scandinavian feeling; full, also, of Delius's own dreaminess. For this man, alert, keenly intellectual though he is, is at bottom a dreamer. The melodies seem at first a little trying to the voice, but boldly tackled by a singer who has musicianship as well as a voice they are soon found to be nothing of the sort. Of the whole set "Irmelin" and "Wine Roses" are most likely to become popular. Next let me take the concerto. I don't like concertos, and Delius himself remarked that it was unlikely he would ever write another. But such as the thing is, it is well done. Some of the themes—notably the second of the first movement—are strikingly beautiful; and the finale, without being riotous, is full of all conquering energy. From the pianist's point of view the piano part seemed to me admirably written; and as Busoni is going to play it, I take it he thinks the same. This is one of the smoothest of Delius's compositions. There is no glibness; but as his purpose has been to write a beautiful thing, there are none of the dramatic touches that abound in his other works. As soon as Busoni plays it we shall see.

Of the operas I know three. "Koanga" was to have been mounted at Breslau some time ago, but those who know anything of the everlasting delays that make the opera composer's heart sick will understand how easy it has been for the management to put off the performance so far. The parts given in London—in the concert hall, of course—were very effective; and, without being theatrical, or at least melodramatic, the whole thing is powerfully dramatic. But for sheer loveliness, expressiveness and high mastery of the technique "The Garden of Paradise" is immeasurably beyond it. The plot is based on a story by some Swiss or German novelist. It is the story of "Romeo and Juliet" transferred to peasant life; the parents quarrel about a piece of land which is allowed to run wild, and there is a mad fiddler who comes out of a fir wood there to take an important share in the events that happen. The wild tunes of this fiddler and the sound of the wind in the firs pervade the opera, giving it an atmosphere unlike any other known to me. The fir wood is as important in "The Garden of Paradise" as is the river with its swan in "Lohengrin"; the sea with its storm in the first act of the "Flying Dutchman"; it pervades the music as well as affording a lovely scene on the

17

stage. Finest of all is the last act, with its passionate tenderness and the exaltation with which the lovers go off to drift down the river—where, no one knows. "The Magic Fountain" contains some fine music, but is not nearly so dramatic as the others. "Irmelin" I have never seen.

The symphonic works I must deal with very shortly. "Over the Hills", an earlier one, attains to the atmosphere wanted, but is a trifle crabbed at times; "Auf dem Hochgebirge" is full of noble things; while the "Zarathustra Song", so harsh at first, grows amazingly on one after a while. But all show a superb mastery of part writing and the orchestra; the themes are strong, pregnant; and many of the passages, uninviting at the first hearing in outline and colour, are afterward found to be full of the spirit of beauty. Delius commenced late and he has developed slowly; but already he has done enough to justify me in calling him the biggest composer we have produced for many a long day. Seeing that he is cosmopolitan he can scarcely be claimed for England; but at least he was born here. I do not expect, do not want, anyone to accept him as a heaven sent genius merely on my recommendation; but with a full sense of the responsibility of the situation I say that those who will take the trouble to hear his music and try to understand it will find themselves well paid for their pains.

("The Musical Courier", 18th March 1903.)

Pen Portraits of Musicians – Frederick Delius
by Gerald Cumberland

There is nothing in the world so deceptive as a photograph; it gives you but the outward semblance of things and hides all the intimate and revealing beauties that lie beneath the surface. The human eye can see below the surface: the lens of a camera cannot. But a photograph is merely a piece of cold science; and science as it is understood today is never strictly true.

Now, look at a photograph of Frederick Delius, and what you will see is a lie. Delius is not *that*. What is it that you see printed by the sun on that piece of cardboard you hold in your hand? It is a monk. The head is slightly bent, the left hand being raised to the chin to support it; the eyes are gazing downwards, the lips being slightly parted; the lines of the face all fall downwards, from the nostril, from the eye, from the corner of the mouth; the hair near the ears is grey. This is the face of a man who lives in the cell, in the cloister; the face of a man who fasts; the face of a man who looks out upon the world without curiosity, without passion and without interest. Even the palm of his hand, half closed, is strangely wrinkled, like that of a man whose skin has been made to hang in folds by constant chastisement of the flesh.

This photograph may be somebody else—it certainly is not Delius. Before I describe the actual man to you, let me tell you something of his life.

Delius was born near Bradford, Yorkshire, forty-six years ago, his ancestors having emigrated to England from Germany some generations earlier. Yorkshire is a musical county and the people there know how to sing; but it has not what is loosely called "an artistic atmosphere". Neither has England—at least, not the kind that Delius likes to breathe. So he has not lived in his native country since his youth and probably will never settle down here again. "England is too parochial", he said to me once, laughing. At the age of twenty-one, he went to Florida in quest of health, money and romance. Orange planting seemed to him a noble and a free way of earning his bread, so he crossed ·the seas full of enthusiasm. But he could not escape from his art. As a youth, it had pursued him, claiming his close attention at all times and seasons; and now, in Florida, it captured him once more, so instead of planting oranges he studied music. It was impossible that it should have been otherwise. Then, at the end of two years, the open spaces and the free life of the Southern States were exchanged for the regular routine and the hard mental labour of the Leipzig Conservatorium, where he studied for two and a half years. From Leipzig he went to Paris, where he has lived for many years. He has married and his wife is a painter of considerable talent and reputation. Fortunately for his work, he has not been under the necessity of earning his living; he has been able to devote to composition the best of his time and his energy; thus what would otherwise have been spent on mere money-getting has been put to more glorious and more valuable uses.

A glance at a list of the works of Delius will show something of what manner of man this is. He has written two music dramas, a piano concerto, several large choral works and a number of tone poems for grand orchestra. Latterly, he has been attracted to the works of Walt Whitman, Nietzsche and Ernest Dowson. He is modern in his sympathies, taking a passionate interest in all new developments of artistic endeavour and in each new phase of thought. He lives *in* the world, in the midst of its most strenuous activities. Few men are so eager to absorb all the experience and emotion that life can give as is Frederick Delius. He has a positive lust for life; his days are lived with zest, his experiences are tasted with gusto. There is nothing of the monk in this keen eyed, sharp tongued man, with his constant flashes of wit, his confidence in his own power and his fervent yet buoyant attacks on all that is poor and meagre in modern art.

I first saw Delius in the Philharmonic Hall, Liverpool, listening to a rehearsal of his English rhapsody "Brigg Fair". He sat near me and I vaguely wondered who he might be. I certainly never associated him with the composer of the work to which I was listening. He had a curiously old fashioned appearance, caused by the way that he wore his hair, by the cut of his clothes, by the cast of his face. But I know nothing of the fashions of clothes and of hair; so I am unable to say definitely in what way he differed in his appearance from the average man. Old fashioned however he certainly looked; and he seemed to me like a man whom Dickens might have thought of, though he was not at all conspicuously odd (as most of Dickens's men are). I could see him emerging from some old gabled building in a far off town and walking along country lanes immersed in his own thoughts. Or perhaps he was a quick brained solicitor, very respectable and quietly prosperous. But these impressions were gathered from his profile when in repose; the actual man proved a very different creature.

In the evening "Brigg Fair" was played; and, though I had heard it in rehearsal during the afternoon and though I listened to it with sympathy in the evening, I did not understand it. On being presented to the composer later on, I told him that I did not like his work; that it seemed to me confused and incoherent; that it did not appear to have either beginning or end. For answer he stepped back a pace, examined me steadily from top to toe and smiled softly to himself. "Not understand it?" he exclaimed; "well, I daresay *you* wouldn't! What sort of music is it that you *do* like? Wagner, Strauss, Brahms? H'm, h'm! But you know my music isn't at all like the music of these men; you must get used to it before you condemn it. But *Strauss*! He's simply dished up Wagner with twice as much devil and not half the inspiration; and Brahms is stodgy German philosophy, all congested from lack of exercise and dry through want of rain. Wagner, of course, is a different matter altogether; music has not advanced a step since the Ring. *Changed?* Oh, yes, it's changed; but I'm speaking of advance. Strauss is not an advance, nor is Max Reger. Reger, as a matter of fact, has run back to the eighteenth century—tortured and shocked by the irresponsible prophets of modernity. We have no really great men living today; the heroes came to an end with Wagner. Debussy? Very extraordinary, of course, and full of interest; but we were discussing *great* men. Debussy is not great, nor is Sibelius, nor is Puccini, nor is MacDowell. People have lost the ability to feel greatly; great primal emotions are dead, dry thought is the only thing that has a chance nowadays. But thought is only the framework: its useful, indeed its indispensable, skeleton. Emotion is the flesh and the blood of music; and modern writers have no great overwhelming feeling. They are too bewildered by the complexity of life to feel anything deeply. They want something new, something startling; and so they go in search of abstruse intellectual problems, quite heedless of the fact that it is the simple emotions of ordinary human nature that work all the revolutions of the world. Nothing is so wonderful as elemental feeling; nothing is more wonderful in art than elemental feeling expressed intensely. But music today is sick for want of feeling; it is full of doubt, dismay, self distrust, blatant self assertion."

Much more was said in a quick vehement way, using startling expressions and terms of contempt and of condemnation which would not look well in cold print. Many of the great men of the past were dismissed with a few words of amused tolerance. Beethoven's Nine Symphonies, I remember, were subjected to a remorseless criticism—a criticism that I suspected at the time was indulged in a good deal for the fun of the thing and because it was unorthodox. But his extravagance of view was at least consistent; for a month or two later, when in Birmingham, I discovered that Delius had been insisting on precisely the same points of view in that city.

Six months later, I heard in London Delius's "Appalachia"; later still, his "Sea Drift" in Manchester. Having studied pianoforte versions of these works beforehand, I was able to understand them: my attitude of luke warm curiosity changed to one of ardent admiration. The Manchester concert, at which "Sea Drift" was played, was a sheer disgrace to that professedly musical city. From the point of view of orchestra, chorus, soloist, conductor and the works chosen for performance, it was one of the most important concerts ever given in Manchester. People had come from Paris, London, Birmingham and Liverpool to hear it; yet, as a matter of actual fact, there were more people taking part in the concert on the platform than listeners in the audience. Nevertheless, Delius's "Sea Drift" aroused tremendous enthusiasm, the audience making up in applause what they lacked in numbers.

"You liked it?" said Delius, and then he stepped back a pace, examined me quietly and steadily from top to toe and smiled softly to himself. "Well, I daresay you would!" he exclaimed. And I laughed as I remembered what had happened in Liverpool when I had heard "Brigg Fair" and had told him of my want of appreciation.

("Musical Opinion", July 1909.)

EDITOR'S POSTSCRIPT:
In the interests of historical accuracy it is only fair that the above essay should be followed by the letter which Delius wrote to the Editor of "Musical Opinion" the following month:

Sir—My attention has been drawn to an interview with myself written by Mr. Gerald Cumberland and published in the July issue of *Musical Opinion*.

When I met Mr. Cumberland I had not the least idea that I was being interviewed; and the opinions that he attributes to me are so intermixed with things that I am quite certain that I did not say and their meaning is so exaggerated by the light in which they are made to appear that I must disown any responsibility for the whole article.

I should like at the same time to protest against the fashion of interviewing as here practised. Had I known that an interview was intended or that any casual thing that I might say would have been made use of as here done, I should have refused any conversation with Mr. Cumberland.

Will you kindly insert this letter in your paper?

Yours, &c.,
FREDERICK DELIUS.

Palsgaard, 8th August 1909.

To this the author rejoined:

Sir—I am obliged to you for the copy of Mr. Delius's letter dated 8th August 1909, from Palsgaard. If I have misrepresented Mr. Delius, I can only express my regret. Still, in justice to myself, I feel compelled to say that my article embodied nothing of importance that did not actually pass his lips; and, if necessary, I am confident that I can bring forward independent witnesses to verify my statements. Fortunately for myself, the views I attribute to Mr. Delius were expressed in the hearing of at least two other people.

My article was not an "interview"; and the practice of recording the sayings of men of genius has received the sanction of the most honourable journalists and men of letters in all civilised countries for at least three centuries. If I had waited until Mr. Delius's death, there might have been reason in protesting "against the fashion of interviewing as here practised", for after death one cannot correct any errors of statement. But, fortunately for the world of music, Mr. Delius is still alive.

Yours, &c.,
GERALD CUMBERLAND.

Manchester, 20th August 1909.

23

English Opera in Berlin: A Review of the World Première of Delius's 'A Village Romeo and Juliet'
by Edward J. Dent

German literature of the nineteenth century can show few works of fiction more charming and delightful than Gottfried Keller's short story, "Romeo und Julia auf dem Dorfe". A simple tragedy of village life, it is both powerful and poetical, without ever lapsing into either sordid realism or the artificiality of Arcadia. Two Swiss peasants, Manz and Marti, cultivate fields separated from each other by a strip of land that has long lain waste, and gradually become a wilderness of stones and bushes. This waste land, which serves only as a playground for Sali and Vrenchen, the two children of the peasants, when they come every day to bring their father's dinner, belongs rightfully to a drunken creature known as the Black Fiddler. But the Black Fiddler has no means of proving his identity as the grandson of the old village trumpeter, and Manz and Marti are the only persons who could swear to his parentage. It suits their interests better to try and turn the Black Fiddler out of the village, and gradually, year by year, to plough their furrows deeper into the waste land, until they have each annexed a good part of it. But eventually, as each becomes aware of the other's encroachments, a quarrel arises. For the two peasants this feud becomes the all-absorbing passion of their lives, and sets them both on the road to ruin. Manz is at last reduced to keeping a miserable tavern in the neighbouring town, while Marti has been forced to part with everything except his dilapidated cottage and a scrap of garden. The children are children no longer. They have been separated by force, and seldom see each other; but the old feeling of friendship is strong, and one day Sali finds Vrenchen alone at her father's cottage, and persuades her to come to their old playground, the Black Fiddler's piece of waste land. Here Marti discovers them. Furious at the sight of his daughter with the son of his enemy, he strikes her; Sali picks up a large stone, and fells him with a blow that deprives him of his senses. When

25

he recovers, he has lost his memory and his reason, and has to be placed in an asylum. Vrenchen is left, and the cottage and last scrap of garden have to be sold to pay Marti's debts. As she sits alone in the empty house, and makes her coffee for the last time, Sali comes in. Although he and Vrenchen are now quite certain of their love for each other, they regard marriage as impossible, on account of the quarrels of their families. They agree, however, to go and dance at a neighbouring fair, and to spend one happy day together before the girl is obliged to go out and earn her living as a servant. At the fair they are recognised by the villagers, and treated with such contumely that they make haste to leave, and proceed to an inn called the "Garden of Eden", where there is also dancing, in less select company. The Black Fiddler leads the musicians, and the dancers are a motley crew of vagabonds. Darkness falls; Sali will not leave Vrenchen to pass the night there alone. "Come with us," says the Black Fiddler; "your fathers cheated me out of my property, but I bear you no ill-will, and we will all be your friends!" Half indifferent, half against their will, they let him perform a mock ceremony of marriage, and after a scene of wild merriment, the party starts in procession, led by the Black Fiddler, to see the happy pair home. They dance at midnight through the village where Sali and Vrenchen once lived, and up the hill to the waste land; here Sali comes to his senses, and holds Vrenchen back while their vagabond escort pursues its way up the river bank. Is this the end? Must they now go home their separate ways? The tide of passion is too strong; they can only love and die together. At the bank is a boat loaded with hay; Sali lifts Vrenchen on to it, pushes out into mid-stream, and lets the boat drift. When the sun rises, the boat is lying against the bridge of the town, and, a little below, the people find in the water the dead bodies of the two lovers.

Such is a rough outline of the story which Mr. Frederick Delius has chosen as the basis of his new opera, produced at the Komische Oper in Berlin on 21st February. It is a story which naturally attracts a composer, first by its steady development of the passion of its hero and heroine, and secondly by the picturesque surroundings which environ them. The short summary given above can make no pretensions to suggest the wonderful charm of detail, the perfect finish of workmanship, the strength and reticence of Gottfried Keller's art. It will be seen, however, that to convert such a story into a musical drama is no easy matter, even allowing for the facility with which rapid changes of scene are effected in modern opera-houses. Mr. Delius, who has himself written the book of his opera in English, seems to have adopted the general principle of assuming that his audience are familiar with the story, as, indeed, may well be expected of audiences in Germany, and has treated the drama practically as a long series of love-duets between his Romeo and his Juliet. The opera is preceded by a prologue, in which we see Manz and Marti ploughing. The children bring their dinner in a little go-cart, as Keller describes, and the Black Fiddler also makes his appearance. The prologue ends with the quarrel of the two peasants. The first act shows us Vrenchen outside her cottage; Sali comes to see her, and suggests that they should go to the waste land. The scene changes to the waste land, where they continue their duet, until interrupted by Vrenchen's father. In the second act Vrenchen is sitting by her deserted fireside; Sali again comes to see her. They sit down on a bench and fall asleep; and here Mr. Delius takes the liberty with Keller which is hardly satisfactory. According to Keller, Sali dreams of their wedding, and especially of their dancing at the wedding feast; Vrenchen dreams that she is pursuing Sali through a thick forest, happy only when he turns to look back at her. Mr. Delius makes his two lovers both dream the same dream, in a very conventional fashion. The stage becomes dark, mists descend from the ceiling, and in the distance we hear a chorale; then silence, and the voice of the pastor speaking the words which join them in matrimony. After another hymn from the chorus, the mist clears away, the stage becomes light, the lovers awake, and agree to go to the fair. The first scene of Act III shows us the fair with its booths, and Vrenchen and Sali buying the big gingerbread cakes which are so characteristically described by Keller. Sali buys the girl a big cake in the shape of a house, and Keller says of her that "she looked like a saint of the middle ages, holding the model of her church in her hands." They are driven away by the crowd, and the scene finally changes to the outside of the "Garden of Eden", with the river at the back. The Black Fiddler and his vagabond comrades are drinking on the balcony; Vrenchen and Sali enter by the road. When the others leave the stage the lovers remain behind, and the manner of their death is vaguely suggested by the musical cries of the boatmen on the river, as Sali rushes off with Vrenchen in his arms.

To the reader who is familiar with the original, this libretto must seem to have renounced almost all the features which give the story its characteristic charm. Yet the complaint is hardly justifiable. We can afford to sacrifice many of the details which define the atmosphere of the literary work, when the composer can suggest with his music an atmosphere which perhaps may not be the same, but still one that is equally inevitable, with an equal or even stronger power of acting upon our emotions. "Atmosphere" is, indeed, a very strong point with Mr. Delius, and to the hearer who is unacquainted with Keller's tale the opera may be deficient in incident, but certainly not in interest. Two scenes only are decidedly unfortunate. The first of these is the prologue, in which Mr. Delius has compressed into a short scene of action a series of events which, in the original, are spread over some eight or nine years, and which it would have been better to have narrated, either in the course of the first act, or possibly in a prologue such as Shakespeare himself prefixes to "Romeo and Juliet". Children are sufficiently unsatisfactory on the ordinary stage; in opera it is almost impossible to make them convincing. Hänsel and Gretel are exceptions; but Hänsel and Gretel are not only drawn by their composer as child-types with masterly musical characterisation, but dominate the whole opera to such an extent, that the grown-up characters appear as abnormal and fantastic to us as the fairies. In Mr. Delius's prologue Sali and Vrenchen are not child-types; they are mere accessories to a scene, the sole object of which is to explain the hostile relations of Manz, Marti and the Black Fiddler. The children's parts are, however, sufficiently prominent to require capable singers; and it was perhaps unavoidable that they should be represented by two ladies who certainly sang well, but who bore no resemblance to the hero and heroine of the later drama, and did not look in the least like children. Indeed, whereas Vrenchen at seventeen or so was slim and dark, Vrenchen at eleven was of the type that we associate with Brünnhilde.

The other scene that appears somewhat regrettable is the dream scene in the second act. The conventional sentimentality of the whole idea is foreign to the idyllic atmosphere of the rest of the opera; moreover, its musical treatment is hardly clear enough to indicate its intention, while at the same time the musical side of the affair is as unsuited to Mr. Delius's methods of composition as the dramatic aspect is to the story. Let us at any rate be thankful that we were spared a transparency with a Gothic church and chorus of priests and peasants! Yet we were not spared a sudden ray of limelight which descended vertically on the heads of the sleeping pair. Such faults of taste are especially surprising at the Komische Oper, which is generally remarkable for its admirably artistic stage management. Gottfried Keller's story and Mr. Delius's setting of it are both far too natural and poetical to be treated to melodramatic Parsifalisms of this kind.

Apart from these two scenes, the libretto may be regarded as well constructed. It has, at any rate, the very great advantage of concentrating the attention on the story of the two lovers and the ever-increasing force of their passion in the face of their tragic destiny. It was interesting to confront the opera with Shakespeare's tragedy, which was revived about the same time at the Deutsches Theater, a theatre which represents the highest artistic ideals of the modern German stage. Here, out of pure reverence for Shakespeare, the love-story of Romeo and Juliet seemed almost to be pushed into the background, so determined was the management to do full justice to the minor characters and to those characteristically Shakespearian scenes which in England are considerably mutilated out of respect for Mrs. Grundy.

Mr. Delius has already the reputation of being first and foremost a musical colourist. In this opera he has been to some extent influenced by modern French tendencies. The main musical interest is in the orchestra, which flows on, intangible and elusive, full of half-suggested phrases, while the voices are treated more in the manner of speech than of song. Yet the composer is indisputably northern: no one could mistake his music for that of a Frenchman. His characters do not address us in the *parlando* of Debussy and Hahn, although they avoid the rhetorical declamation of some English and German composers. His music is above all things genuinely and sincerely poetical. There are times when the listener becomes oppressed by the continuous stream of sound, in which the musical themes seem to disappear almost before they have risen to the surface; there are times when one longs to hear a character on the stage find expression in a broad and vocal phrase. Yet it is partly by this very means that the composer manages to surround his work with its peculiar atmosphere. The stage setting was well designed for the same purpose. Herr Hans Gregor is a virtuoso in the art of making the greatest possible effect out of a small space. The Komische Oper is anything but roomy, and from the balconies one could almost shake hands with the actors. Nevertheless, Herr Gregor reduced his stage still further by setting his scenes behind an inner proscenium, specially built up, thus throwing the whole picture some three feet further back. The scenery, painted from the designs of Herr Karl Walser, was simple, and of a quite remarkable beauty; indeed, at the first performance the cornfield and its mass of poppies (Act II, Scene 2) was greeted with a spontaneous burst of applause. Even on this small scale the fair was well suggested without being cramped. Thus the whole opera took place, as it were, in a dream, as an opera should always do: it is when realism is attempted that we are shocked by the unnatural conventions of the musical drama. "A Village Romeo and Juliet" is an opera (Mr. Delius rightly calls it an idyll) without sensational effects. The whole work is characterised by a quiet tenderness which is the result of self-restraint, not of weakness. Where symphonic development is needed, Mr. Delius is not wanting in power; we find themes effectively treated in this way in the music which leads up to the dream scene, and in many places where the curtain is down. Moreover, Mr. Delius possesses a vein of melody which is decidedly original, and one regrets that it is so sparingly employed. The wild strains of the Black Fiddler form a striking example of musical character- isation; and for haunting beauty nothing surpasses the lament of Vrenchen at the beginning of the second act.

The performance was, on the whole, a worthy one. The two principal characters were well represented by Herr Willi Merkel and Frl. Lola Artôt de Padilla; Herr Desider Zador was a fantastic exponent of the Black Fiddler. The orchestra was under the direction of Herr Fritz Cassirer, who showed a sympathetic insight into the delicate beauties of Mr. Delius's complicated score.

("The Monthly Musical Record", April 1907)

The Approach to Delius   by Paul Klenau

Everyone interested in music today is acquainted with the name
of Frederick Delius. Frederick Delius is famous, and his fame
is of the kind that has within it the seed of immortality. So long
as our musical culture and our musical history endure, Delius
will rank among the great masters. His fame has nothing
sensational about it—his music is not popular like the music
which is sung today or will be sung tomorrow, nor does it enjoy
the problematical popularity of the music which, for a year or
two, is described as *le dernier cri*. It has created no school, as did
the music of the polyphonic or atonal composers; it is not
revolutionary; it establishes no new system. No, his music is a
natural product, a manifestation of a cultured personality of the
highest order.

All creative work is at once new and old, for in Art there is no
such thing as something new in the sense of being "heaven-
sent". Art, regarded as a whole, is a stupendous edifice, and
whoever does not consciously co-operate in the building has no
concern therein. The composer who, today, discovers tones
which our ear is incapable of assimilating can only be described
as an "outsider". Nor can he who frames musical laws which
our ear cannot discriminate expect to be taken seriously. The
continuity of the forms of art cannot be broken. In this respect
everything that is created is old, is based on tradition, and has
grown organically, as every tree and every flower have grown.
Only what is personal is new in art, but the personality itself
springs from old soil, draws its nourishment from substance
already existing, employs those forms which have already been
created in order to produce fresh combinations, and thus
creates new forms, new complexities of expression.

Such an innovator is Delius. His works are unconventional to
the highest degree, and yet they grow integrally as a splendid
branch in the coherent structure of the tree of culture. The
effect of his music was revolutionary only so long as the sources
from which it was drawn had not been grasped. The peculiar

quality of his personality and the power of his original genius were bound to have an alienating effect at first. Now that we have become familiar with this personality, we see clearly that the structure of his art is rooted in the past, as is all great art. Did not Bach and Handel learn from their predecessors and from their time ? And Beethoven, that great revolutionary, does not his music grow out of the work of Bach, Mozart and Haydn ? It is exactly the same with Delius. The achievements of Wagner, Berlioz and the romanticists were duly recognised by Delius, and, together with Debussy, Dukas and Ravel, Delius has created an art which is usually described as impressionism in music. To Berlioz and Wagner we owe the fineness and variety of instrumental music—an achievement of such importance that its reaction upon the entire structure of musical composition was inevitable. Upon the succeeding generation devolved the task of developing the cultivation of this new territory in music. This applies to Delius exactly as it applies to the German and French impressionists. But whereas the French frequently find satisfaction in genre pictures (is there any better example than Debussy's *L'après-midi d'un faune*—that "show" piece of French musical impressionism ?), Delius paints with a greater breadth of vision. In this connection I would refer to one of the finest pieces that Delius has ever written, the *Nachtlied* from *A Mass of Life*. It makes one think of landscapes by Constable.

Nothing has been left at the stage of mere superficial pictorial representation. Nothing therein is objective (I call music objective when it endeavours to imitate natural sounds: twittering of birds, croaking of frogs, post-horns, cow-bells, etc., etc.). It is the deep peace of the night, the feeling of the darkness, the profoundly moving effect of the night, that we find depicted here. But the motion is so powerful, so specific in its nature, that it cannot be just any emotion, but only that quite definite emotion that stirs us at the sight of the starry heavens, in *experiencing* the night.

The reference to Constable is not made at random. Constable's paintings are thoroughly English—so, too, is the music of Delius. If Constable's paintings are compared with the Dutch landscapes (and such a comparison is perfectly justifiable and natural), it will soon be seen how great is the difference. The same thing will be experienced if Delius's music is compared with German or French music. Delius's music is altogether non-German, altogether non-French. He has, certainly, learned something from the study of German music—indeed, this impressionist frequently shows a certain predilection for a German method of working. There is, however, an essential difference of character between his music and the German music. What landscape painter would not have drawn inspiration from the Dutch masters, and what musician would not from the German masters? But that which Delius adopted (from Wagner especially) has been so thoroughly permeated by his own personality that it has acquired an entirely fresh significance.

I should like to insert here some brief reminiscences of personal conversations with Delius. I have often met him. Best of all I liked to be with him in his house at Grez-sur-Loing, where he lives in an environment that looks as if it had been created by his own hand. Not by chance did this man, who seems to know every place in the world, choose this spot, where the scenery is of enchanting loveliness (Sisley, the finest and greatest nature lyricist of French impressionism, lived for years at Grez).

Driving along the dusty highroad from Bourron to Grez, one passes through a grey stone-paved street, with low grey houses on either side. At the end of the street is an ancient grey church, the tower of which is a dilapidated grey ruin. The carriage stops in front of a large gate. And here occurs the miracle that always reminds me of the Arabian Nights—the gate flies open, and through the gate you look into a garden whose riot of colour and profusion of flowers is beyond description.

Here Delius has made his home.

Delius, the man, is ever the great impassioned lover—and Nature is his beloved. His tall, spare figure, with its angular, abrupt movements appeared, in this environment, to be absolutely pervaded with happiness—happiness which his wonderful wife understands how to cherish, while sharing and intensifying it in sympathetic devotion. There was yet a third party to the alliance—their pet raven, to whose opinion these two original individuals attached much value. The spontaneous display of sympathy or antipathy on the part of the raven played, consciously or unconsciously, an important part in their appraisement of a visitor. The raven used to cock its head on one side, thus acquiring a great resemblance to its master. Then (generally sitting on the arm of the chair or on the shoulder of one of its "foster-parents") it would watch the interloper with its bright, intelligent eyes. If pleased with the visitor in question, it would give expression to its feelings by deep, melodious, guttural sounds. If it disliked the guest, it would dart, quick as lightning, to peck at his foot.

In this environment, the writer could talk with Delius for hours at a time. Not only about music. Oh, no! There is no subject relating to mankind in which he is not interested. At a time, for instance, when it was the custom to speak disparagingly of the composer Grieg, Delius had not the least hesitation in expressing his admiration for the genius of this little Norwegian. "As a harmonist Grieg is particularly excellent," he would cry, and would then cite passages from his songs. For Munch, the Norwegian painter, Delius has a great admiration. In Helge Rode, the Danish writer, he took the greatest interest. In general, he feels akin to the Scandinavians. He was fond of spending the summer in Norway and Denmark. What mainly draws him to Denmark is J. P. Jacobsen.

On the other hand, he could often express his aversion in the most comical terms. Once, for instance, talking of Brahms he said to me, in his quaintly accented German, "Brahms, wissen Sie, lange Pfeife und Bier" ("Brahms, you know, long pipe and beer"). Sometimes he even railed against Beethoven: "Too much philosophy", he would say. But of Bach his admiration knows no bounds. All these utterances are highly characteristic of Delius. His great love for counterpoint embodied Bach. This love for counterpoint is a quality which separates Delius from most of the impressionists. For in his music the contrapuntal work is often interconnected in the strangest way with the harmonic modulations. His dislike of Brahms was a dislike of all classicism. (In this respect the impressionists have been romanticists.) The violence with which Brahms consciously plunged into historical tradition was little to his mind. The tie that bound him to Grieg was folk-lore, the close kinship to nature. Indeed, folk-lore was a study which he himself pursued and loved.

In Delius's utterances, however paradoxical they are at times, there is nothing of chance; everything is permeated by his personality, and everything is in keeping with his personality.

When Delius is present at productions of his works, it is a most peculiar experience to observe him. At the very outset he is quite overwhelmed by the beauty of the sound. He seems in the first instance to be satisfied with any *tempo*, any reproduction. But this is only a transient phase. In proportion as the rehearsal progresses, his critical sense grows increasingly stronger, until it reaches a pitch of incredible sensitiveness. He hears everything—even the slightest deviation from his rich melodious and rhythmical designs. The slightest dragging or hurrying of the *tempo* completely spoils, for him, the picture he has formed of his music. And this picture is one that is fixed, down to the smallest detail. I have been able to observe Delius during rehearsals of his works, and I have had a sensation as if, on these occasions, Delius the listener were being transformed into the creative musician. It is as if the original conception were at first hidden by a veil, and as if this veil were gradually lifted until the conception impresses itself upon him with compelling clarity. I have been present at rehearsals where, as the work proceeded, nothing satisfied him, and where he spoke in no measured terms of the lack of understanding in regard to his music. On the other hand, however, it was touching to see him when he perceived that the performers had grasped the spirit of his art. I have often discussed with him the *tempi*, etc., of his compositions and have found him sometimes (especially at the piano) very vague in his statements. On one occasion (at the concert in celebration of his sixtieth birthday, at Frankfurt) when I asked him about some passages, he replied: "Interpret it as it appeals to you; you may do so, for you understand my music." When one has gained his confidence, he is easy to get on with. Many people have misunderstood him, because he is unable to state in words what he desires to be done.

And yet, as already mentioned, I know no composer who has so pronounced and so clear an idea of his music as Delius. What appears to be a certain contrariety is part of his nature. The altogether unconstructive essence of his music cannot, in fact, be determined intellectually. Only the person who is capable of "experiencing" Delius's music and who, out of this experience, endeavours to give it form during the reproduction will hit upon that which is the essential in his music. The more architecture a musical work contains, the easier it is to give with cool deliberation full effect to the structure. In proportion, however, as a musical composition operates by pictorial media, it must be re-created by living it at the moment as if it were a great improvisation.

As regards the cultural attainment and distinctiveness of Delius's music the following fact is highly characteristic: If the internal thread breaks during the performance of his music, the listener is repelled and the effect fails; but if the inner tension

35

The Present Cult - Charlatanism and Humbug in Music   by Frederick Delius

In 1920 Philip Heseltine persuaded Delius to write down his views on contemporary music for his journal "The Sackbut". The essay was reprinted in "The British Musician and Musical News" at the time of the 1929 Festival, along with a postscript taken from a more recent interview which had appeared in "The Daily Telegraph". This had consisted of a statement made by the composer to an official of the Columbia Gramophone Company by way of thanking the British musical organisations who had arranged the Festival.

As Sydney Grew, the editor of "The British Musician", stated in his introduction. "It gives a picture of musical conditions in England in the years following the war, when a number of writers filled the country with propaganda on behalf of certain modern composers, some of whose names are hardly known today. The chief interest of the essay, however, is in its indication of Delius's philosophy of music and his manner of thinking . . . [He] was fifty-seven when he wrote this article. He was still little known in England, and his art is such that the modernist propagandists of 1920 might have ridiculed it. Yet it will be observed that there is no bitterness in what he says, however strong his disgust with what he has to condemn."

The time has come when every musician of serious aims should declare, in the interest of the public, what is his attitude towards the current attempts on the part of Russian impresarios, Parisian decadents and their press-agents, to degrade his art to the level of a side-show at a fair. The musical public—especially in England—is very innocent and trusting in the face of loud-mouthed quacks who employ every device of street-corner oratory in order to palm off their shoddy wares; and therefore I consider that every serious musician owes it to the public to raise his voice in warning and protest when he sees them being taken in and imposed upon by a clever gang of self-seeking mountebanks.

There is room in the world for all kinds of music to suit all tastes, and there is no reason why the devotees of Dada should not enjoy the musically imbecile productions of their own little circle as much as the patrons of the musical comedy enjoy *their* particular fare. But when I see the prophets of the latest clique doing their utmost to pervert the taste of the public and to implant a false set of values in the rising generation of music-lovers by sneering at the great masters of the past, in the hope of attracting greater attention to the *petits maîtres* of the present —then I say it is time to speak openly and protest. In the end, of course, all art finds its own level and takes its due place in the estimation of the world; and everything that is shallow, catchpenny, sensational and insincere sinks into oblivion from which no propaganda can rescue it. But why, in the meanwhile, should a whole generation be confused and contaminated by the specious claptrap and humbug of a crew of little men who have deliberately set out to make the worse appear the better cause? Genius is not a mushroom growth. Inspiration does not come without hard work any more than a crop of corn. There is no short cut to glory. No great work of art has ever come into the world save as the fruit of years of earnest, unremitting endeavour on the part of its creator; and no great artist ever blasphemed his ancestors.

Music is a cry of the soul. It is revelation, a thing to be reverenced. Performances of a great musical work are for us what the rites and festivals of religion were to the ancients— an initiation into the mysteries of the human soul. A man who walked into church without his trousers would be promptly turned out: and anyone who meddles with art in a similar spirit of disrespect should be treated in the same way.

How does music stand today? Is the world full of men of as much importance as Bach and Beethoven, Chopin and Wagner? If we are to believe some of the composers themselves, or rather, their trumpeters and tub-thumpers, we have amongst us not the equals but the superiors, the *superseders* even, of the old masters. After a thousand years of evolution, music is just beginning to become articulate! Already some music-publishers have put up electrical sky-signs and others have had recourse to their literary equivalents. The average man of the present day is so accustomed to have his mind made up for him by advertisements, posters and illuminated signs at every street-corner, that he comes to believe implicity anything he reads often enough on the hoardings. If this is the case with patent medicines, it is also the case with art, and we find that propaganda and advertisement carry all before them.

This is an age of anarchy in art: there is no authority, no standard, no sense of proportion. Anybody can do anything and call it "art" in the certain expectation of making a crowd of idiots stand and stare at him in gaping astonishment and admiration. Imagine a wonderful cathedral which has stood for centuries as a monument of an age of intense faith and devotion to high ideals: now there comes along a little Johnny and sticks a bowler-hat (call it that, for politeness' sake) on the top of the spire, proclaiming his exploit as the crowning achievement of art. "See", he says, "there's something higher than your old cathedral"—forgetting that his addition will only be seen when a searchlight is thrown on it.

Great men must be denied and great achievements scoffed at in order that the little ones may become conspicuous. There must be a complete transvaluation of values. Art has been "serious" too long: now let us play the fool, in season and out of season, let us deny everything, turn all our values upside down. On this principle, a beautiful face is no longer as "interesting" as a grimace. But the interest of a grimace is *purely negative*; it depends entirely on its relation to the natural face. It is only the incongruity of the grimace with the normal features of human kind that causes merriment—the exaggeration of certain traits to the exclusion of others—a false perspective, a wrong proportion. The musical concomitant of a grimace is necessarily negative: it is only a pretentious development of the time-honoured tradition of the bang on the big drum when the clown falls down.

Music does not exist for the purpose of emphasising or exaggerating something which happens outside its own sphere. Musical expression only begins to be significant where words and actions reach their uttermost limit of expression. Music should be concerned with the emotions, not with external events. To make music imitate some other thing is as futile as to try and make it say *Good morning* or *It's a fine day*. It is only that which cannot be expressed otherwise that is worth expressing in music. . . . There is a certain section of the reading public consisting of people who join a circulating library and always demand "the latest" novels or other books. This section, needless to say, has no literary pretensions whatever. There is a corresponding section of the musical public which always

39

demands "the latest" rather than "the best": but its æsthetic pretensions are as great as its lack of taste and musical understanding. For the "latest fiction" public, Shakespeare is out of date and unreadable: for its musical counterpart, Bach is a fossil and Beethoven a mummy. But whereas no student of literature would take the "latest fiction" crowd seriously, the corresponding gang in music—by means of assiduous advertisement and propaganda—has become a real danger to the ever-growing section of the public which demands "music" rather indiscriminately, as a necessary part of a cultured education, and accepts unquestioningly whatever is recommended by critics who have no qualifications with which to recommend themselves. Only carry on the advertisement campaign long enough and vigorously enough and you will hypnotise people into believing that black is white and that there is no more excellent music in the world than the creaking of cart-wheels and the cries of cats.

Music that needs "explanation", that requires bolstering up with propaganda, always arouses the suspicion that if left to stand on its own merits it would very quickly collapse and be no more heard of. The present Franco-Russian movement in music is entirely founded on denial—denial of harmony, of coherence, of intellectual lucidity and spiritual content—denial of music, in fact. Of course I shall be told that people said exactly the same thing about Wagner, and that after thirty years of active musical life I am not sufficiently cultured and that my sensibility is not yet sufficiently developed to appreciate the subtleties and novelties of the latest clique of composers. Exactly the same defence might be put up in favour of the jumblings of a child of four at the piano.

The chief reason for the degeneration of present-day music lies in the fact that people want to get physical sensations from music more than anything else. Emotion is out of date and intellect a bore. Appreciation of art which has been born of profound thought and intensity of experience necessitates an intellectual effort too exhausting for most people of the present day. They want to be amused: they would rather feel music with their bodies than understand it through their emotions. It seems as though a tarantula has bitten them—hence the dancing craze: Dixie, Dalcroze, Duncan and Diaghilev—they are all manifestations of the same thing. In an age of neurasthenics, music, like everything else, must be a stimulant, must be alcoholic, aphrodisiac, or it is no good. We do not hear the word "vitality" at every turn except from people who are aware that vitality is the one thing they are most in need of, the one thing they must at all costs get supplied to them from outside. (Reader, next time you attend a performance of the Russian ballet, don't let the stage absorb your whole attention. Have a good look at the audience, and you will see that it would require the pen of a Rops or a Beardsley to do justice to it.) But let them at any rate see clearly what kind of a cesspool they will go dancing into if they follow the line of this latest fad.

There is no longer any respect for music as such. It can only be tolerated, it seems, as an accompaniment to something else —a dinner or a dance or what not. An impresario, shrewd enough to see what the public wants and to give it to them at the right time, comes along with a resuscitation of the old Italian ballet from St. Petersburg, proclaiming a *new* form of art compared with which all past achievements are as nothing. Led by the nose, the public and, worse still, many of the young musicians flock around him, and the critics cannot find enough adjectives of adulation for his shows.

A ballet is all very well in its proper place, as a pleasant after-dinner entertainment; but we don't want ballets to every-thing, and to proclaim the ballet as a form of great art—*the* art form of the future, in fact—is sheer bunkum. But the English public seems to have an insatiable appetite for ballets, and the demand for such works having speedily exhausted the slender stock of living composers' ideas, the scores of long-dead musicians are pressed into service. No one is immune. Bach fugues are employed as exercises in muscular mathematics and Beethoven sonatas "interpreted" (!!!) by every hysterical, nymphomaniacal old woman who can gull the public into seeing "a revival of the Greek spirit" or some other high-falutin' vision in the writhings and contortions of her limbs.

What is the effect on young people who may perhaps hear some great work for the first time in such an environment? The music will inevitably become associated in their minds with hopping and prancing and jigging, and in the end they will themselves be unable to hear it without twitching and fidgeting.

There seems to be a very prevalent belief that any Tom, Dick or Harry has the right to tamper with a work of art, even to the extent of altering it beyond recognition and forcing it to serve a purpose its composer never dreamed of. In this direction irresponsible "editors", "adaptors" and "transcribers" are as much to blame as the dancing cranks. It is time a law was passed to keep good music from violation.

By all means become dancing dervishes if you want to, and dance in a delirious *cortége* right into the lunatic asylum: but don't try to justify your procedure in the name of art, nor degrade the works of great artists in doing so. Above all, don't spoil works of art for other people who may not want to dance in the same direction. We do *not* all go the same way home. Let us try to preserve a little clearness of vision so that we may see things in their proper perspective. The art of Marionettes is good enough for some people, but let us not confuse little painted puppets with great men.

("The Sackbut", September 1920.)

POSTSCRIPT

Delius admits that he is a self-taught musician (the official said yesterday) and says he owes a great debt to the negro music which he first heard when he was working on an orange grove in Florida in the 'eighties. His orange plantation was on the River St. Johns and Delius used to sit at nightfall on the wide verandah, smoking and listening to the beautiful, harmonious singing of the negroes. After hearing only such choral music as *The Messiah* and *Elijah* in England, this natural music made a deep inpression on him. To quote his own words: "I loved it, and I began to write music seriously myself. Night falls quickly there, and the native voices, always in harmony, sounded very lovely. It was mostly religious or gay music, but by no means like the negro spirituals sung by one man or woman, which are so often broadcast from London today. It was much more harmonious. I felt that here was a people who really felt the emotion of music, as I feel now that this mad jazz has nothing to do with the negro. Jazz is an invention of so-called Americans who have taken rag-time and pretend that it is negro music. This awful invention has had a shocking effect on Europe.

"What could be worse than the spectacle of serious musicians trying to imitate jazz? To imitate jazz is as bad as imitating the 'atonal' music invented by Schönberg and company. Worst of all, I see that the young English musicians are being influenced by what I call this 'wrong note' school of music. The only way for any man to write music is to follow the line of his own feelings and not imitate foreigners or anyone else. Such ugliness as is heard in some of the modern music now being written in

England and Germany and France can only reveal an extremely ugly soul. It is atrociously monstrous and ugly.

"In my opinion, the adherents of the 'wrong note' school are merely sensationalists. Stravinsky himself is a very good example of a clever man writing excellent ballet music, but he, too, is affected with this craving for sensationalism. He became more and more sensational until at last he shouted to his followers, *Go back to Bach!* and wrote the dullest sort of Bacho-Handelian music, which, if he had produced it earlier, would have been completely ignored. Music never went back to anything—if it did it only showed that it was on the wrong road. All you have to do if you wish to write music is to go on and follow your inspiration—if you have any. But there is very little inspiration in music today. It always has been rare. Since Bach—in the past 150 years or so—the world has had only a dozen composers of genius, all of whom produced bigger-sized music than is being written today. Yet today we are expected to hail dozens.

"We are living in a bad epoch for the arts. A craze for sensation has affected the young. They wish to become celebrities at 25. A journalism of the arts is in progress and it is having a deplorable effect on English music. But none of these young geniuses will produce anything of permanent value until he has found himself. They must dig inwardly and get rid of all the dross and find the pure metal—if any. If not, they would be better employed digging their gardens or doing some really useful work."

("The Daily Telegraph", 5th October, 1929.)

43

Delius: Landscape Painter of Music
by Richard Capell

Let us make the approach by a roundabout way, by way of a casual tour of the rooms of a great picture-gallery, the National Gallery or the Louvre.

At first there are virgins or saints by Duccio and Simone Martini on a background of gold. In a room or two farther on the gold has turned to sky and to hills—and the hill-top cities and the winding rivers of Umbria and Tuscany are perceived in glimpses behind the thrones and the personages. But still not Perugino or Leonardo or even Giorgione paint landscape wholly for landscape's sake.

Farther on we come upon Claude, Ruisdael, Gainsborough, Richard Wilson and on to Turner, and the landscape becomes the thing and personages incidental or absent. Still it is a man-moulded landscape, and Nature had obviously had to submit to the rules of composition. Now, in a generation or two, there arrive on the scene Monet and Pissarro and all the impressionists of the 1880's, and the artists appear to be submerging themselves in Nature, to be reflecting—as far as oil-pigments and canvas can reflect—the play of light and lambent atmosphere. Later still the gold background or something like it comes back, but this has nothing to do with our case.

What is our case and what has all this to do with music? Is not the static art of painting evidently concerned with ever-lasting Nature, while ever-moving music, existing in time and not in space, must deal with the fluctuations of human feeling and not representation?

Yes, but there are moods of ours when we have the illusion of time at a standstill, moments of dreamy meditation when the mind seems one with Nature's immobility. The young Siegfried listens to the sempiternal rustling of the forest and forgets sword and dragon. The travel-worn Parsifal returns and, looking with tears in his eyes upon the flowering fields, is lost

45

in the sweetness and calm of the morning. We measure music by our own pulse; but music in these moods slows down to such another pulse-rate that it seems not mortal but Nature's expression: landscape music.

It was Wagner's invention, so far as anything in art is any one man's invention. His landscape music was, however, incidental—he had his hands full of other things. There was more to be found along the path.

Where was the starting-point of Delius's most rare, most individual art? One may suggest that it is in the meditations just referred to in the second act of *Siegfried* and in the third act of *Parsifal*. Wagner had little time for the sighing forest and the meadow "wearing white for Eastertide". Great affairs were calling, and he passed on. Delius has lingered there all his life, finding what Wagner had not time for; in a word, he is a landscape musician.

Delius's life-long preoccupation with harmonic colour gives the listener to his music the sensation not so much of being carried along on a stream as of floating in a pool of sound. It may be that the musical texture he most delighted in required the static subject, or it may be that the music did indeed arise from passionate contemplation on the bosom of Nature, on "the aftermaths of soft Septembers, the blanching Mays".

Dramatic action was ruled out—it did not lie in his way— and this brings us to admire the artist's integrity, his renunciation of what was not rightly his to do. But the disinterested spirit of the man is made so clear in every page of his work that the thought of anything but disinterestedness is absurd.

Then, if another phrase can help the attempt at definition, there is the freedom of Delius's feeling for beauty; the freedom from theory that allows him all the beauty that instinct and taste can apprehend; in which again he is like the French impressionists as against the austere post-impressionists, all so theoretical and fanatically renunciatory.

Delius has been taxed with monotony, but, after all, a gallery of Turners would look dull in a bad light. It is not true that Delius has been a neglected composer, that is, not in the last twenty-five years; but the Beecham Festival of two years ago was needed to bring home in the fairest conditions — under a conductor unique in his devotion and comprehension—all the variety of Delius's work.

It is the composer's fortune to have had in Beecham an

interpreter who knew how to bring out the melody (which, Wagner said, is the principal business of a conductor) so well that a Beecham performance of *A Mass of Life* a few weeks ago set Mr. Neville Cardus talking of it as "the most beautiful choral work ever written".

A Mass of Life is not likely to make Nietzscheans of English choral singers. Delius has left out nearly all of Zarathustra's pagan sermons: his sensibilities and ecstasies were the matter for the musician. And now Nietzsche, like Walt Whitman, strikes us as an imperfect poet whose words might, so it seems, have been simply meant for completion by Delius's more lovely art —by his landscape, now cool and mountainous, and again gorgeous as the lotus-eater's land—by the tenderness, the tranquillity and the love which his music adds to the bare text.

There are, then, the idyllic England of *Brigg Fair*, Paumanok's tragic shore in *Sea-Drift*, the flowers and heavy odours of *Summer Garden*, the keen and lonely air of the *Song of the High Hills*, and so on and on, but always with unity in the variety, a unity due to the intense, passionate feeling in the meditation.

Whatever its different moods, this music is all of a piece, all of it the essentially natural expression for an uninfluenced mind. The only considerable exception is the curiously Lisztian piano concerto in C Minor, an effective work in its way but hardly Delius at all—the composer's only excursion from Barbizon into mundanity!

To justify the linking of Delius and Wagner (a connection, mention of which is sometimes as much resented as that between Sibelius and Tchaikovsky) one may point to the Parsifalesque phrase on the *Village Romeo* intermezzo. It were wrong all the same to make much of the reference to Wagner. We come back to it that the real affinity is with the painters.

His music is peculiarly aristocratic in a vulgar age. The music of Mozart and the eighteenth-century Italians had unmatched aristocratic manners and form; there exists today a school, the Schönbergian school, of intellectually aristocratic music. Delius is aristocratic in his feelings, so preternormally sensitive; in his shrinking from contact with the mass of men, and his lifelong avoidance of all things common and ugly. He composes a symphonic poem, "Paris", but it is Paris from afar, its noises a distant roar and the city's lights reflected a glow in the night-clouds.

47

His characteristic melody, as that of the Violin Concerto, for instance, evades the metrical shapes of ordinary human song; it is a wandering, elusive melody, which used to make audiences at first say that Delius's music was vague and formless. It is not a melody with which one goes away whistling or to which one fits words. It is this very detachment from the rhythms and metres of speech and verse that sets the listener's fancy seeking after non-human images, such as boughs bending in the wind. When it comes to setting words to music Delius seems half pre-occupied; the fit is hardly ever very close. In *A Mass of Life* if does not seem to matter greatly what words are being sung, and the lack of vivid accentuation in *A Village Romeo and Juliet* brings about an effect of a dream rather than drama.

And as with Delius's melody so with his harmony. Classical harmony was based on the association of human voices, a human contact. This late-romantic harmony is full of more casual and more delicate contacts—of leaf on leaf, and of the wind among the reeds.

Much of the beautiful wild land still remains unknown to almost everyone. Of the familiar masterpieces I would name two as most particularly lovely and beguiling: *Sea Drift*, a haunting song of grief in solitude; and *The Song of the High Hills*.

("Radio Times", 4th December 1931.)

Frederick Delius in his Garden by Philip Oyler

The privileged few who were welcomed to the home of Delius without special invitation were not surprised that he and his wife should have chosen to live in Grez-sur-Loing, and that they should have selected the house which they did, for though in itself it has no features of special interest, its setting is an inspiration to all who are affected by the sight of beautiful things. For those who would like to know some few intimate details upon which the eager eyes of the composer looked often and lovingly, this sketch is written by one who knows each tree in the garden, from the weeping-ash that reflects itself in the lily-pond, to the giant ash that overhangs the river and has two massive iron bands attached to a tall plane to prevent it from falling by its weight into the water.

But before we enter the garden let us come to Grez in the way by which visitors invariably come. We take the express train from the Gare de Lyon in Paris and alight at Fontainebleau after an hour's quick run. Passing the palatial hotel—the *Savoy*—where the ex-King of Spain has a permanent suite, we take the great high road that leads through the famous forest south to Vichy and the Mediterranean. On our way we pass under a beautifully designed aqueduct which conveys water to Paris, mount up through fine pines to a stone cross on high ground, where Napoleon met the Pope, descend again to the little village of Bourron resting under the hill on the southern border of the forest, and then after a mile's run in the open country we sight Grez on our left, or that part of the village which is visible from the high road.

It is only about eight miles from Fontainebleau station, and the approach disappoints a little, for the first two or three houses outside the village are modern and atrocious in every way; but these past, the joy begins, for one enters the village itself, where no change has been for many generations except the installation of electric light (which is everywhere in France).

We wind down through narrow paved streets to the Poule

49

d'eau (Water-hen) which was the centre of the noted artist colony in the past, turn to the right and have the old church facing us. We go in this direction, notice the ruins of an ancient fortress on our left and stop at the last house before reaching the church, for this is the house of Delius. It presents to the road an extended plain front with three storeys, the top one having dormers. It is distinguished from the other houses by being much longer, by having all its window shutters painted green instead of the prevailing grey, and by having at intervals rambler roses climbing up it and adding, when in bloom, some pleasing masses of colour against the solid stone walls.

There is no bell, so we take hold of a large wrought knocker and hammer loudly on the double massive doors, for these give entrance to a courtyard and not to the house itself. While we await the arrival of someone, it should be explained that in the districts of France which have often been subjected to invasion through the ages, one sees no farms (unless fortress-farms) between village and village—nothing but unspoiled country, rich in corn or fruit or woods. The villages themselves present a means of defence and in them there are still the farmhouses, stables and cattle-pens, and the doors and door-ways have to be high enough to admit cart-loads of hay and corn. Sometimes these doorways are at the side of the house, and sometimes in the middle of it, with rooms above as is the case of Delius's house.

We will assume that we have entered the garden, having satisfied the doubts of Madame Grespier, a loyal French woman of long service with the family, who opens the large doors just wide enough to see with one eye who is there. It is she who scolds her mistress if she leaves her purse about, bakes excellent bread and other good things, makes the electric pump go when the electrician swears that it is completely worn out, holds on to the cellar key as though her very life depended on it. God bless her! She has let us in knowing that we have a free pass.

And what do we see? Not much for a moment. We have been standing in deep shade on the north side of the house and as we go out on to the other side, our eyes are dazzled by a rich sunlight falling on the courtyard. When they grow accustomed to this, they are amazed at a mass of flowers, so vividly intense, that one wonders what they are. We approach to satisfy our curiosity and find that they are roses of all sorts and annuals covering the ground completely between them. Owing to the nature of the soil and the fact that the climate is hotter in

Delius's garden from the West.

Polish home for orphaned and handicapped children

summer and colder in its short winter than in England, the herbaceous border is not a great success here. Many things refuse to grow at all, or grow in a very feeble way, and others have such a short flowering period that it hardly justifies them occupying the ground for twelve months to provide a few days' delight. One must adopt other methods, and that is why one sees so often in French gardens nothing but bedded out plants in formal plots.

But this would not satisfy the taste of Mrs. Delius and she has solved the problem in her own way. Finding that the slugs upset her arrangements when the seed was broadcast, she imposed on herself the task of sowing in frames and transplanting afterwards, leaving the gardener the duty of keeping them watered. The result is a riot of colour throughout six months of the year, for the annuals, regularly watered, seem to delight in the hot sun and bloom as one never sees them in England—petunias, salpiglossis, cosmos, phlox, nicotiana, marigolds in the most astounding luxuriance, with here and there a madonna lily growing amongst them and looking down upon them as a sort of benediction.

There is a reason—unusual indeed—for the especial luxuriance which these annuals exhibit and here is the story. The Marquis de Carzeaux, from whom Delius bought the property, had an extraordinary way of amusing himself. He was fond of horses and kept a number of them. The lower parts of the west wing of the house were stables in his time. He disliked gardens and would not have one. Having large quantities of manure and no garden to put it on, he covered the ground with it till it was some feet thick, and he spent a lot of his time driving a four-in-hand round and round that which is now this beautiful garden. The great trees were there, of course, and the pond, but these were sporting obstacles, no doubt, from his point of view.

When we have satisfied out eyes with this feast of colour, and look around us, we find that the house has wings at each end that project southwards, thus forming the courtyard, and that where the wings end, old stone walls continue, and indeed lead right down to the river Loing below, giving perfect seclusion. Moving out of the courtyard, where climbing roses spread in profusion on all sides, we notice on the east, and barely a hundred yards distant, the towering ruins of a Norman castle round which the jackdaws are ever circling and in which they find ideal nesting places. On the west, and even nearer stands the old church with its noble twelfth-century tower, beautiful in its stern simplicity. On either side, too, one sees the roofs of old houses, barns and sheds of many shapes and sizes, but all covered with mellowed brown tiles that seem to have deep purple shades in them, a most pleasing combination with the grey stone walls, and entirely satisfying to the eye.

Continuing down the path, we have to stop a little to miss an overhanging branch of an elder. It is growing out of the wall and is so gnarled in its antiquity that it reminds one of the twisted olive trees growing in the rocks of the south. Though the elder is a tree for which one has not much sympathy, since at times it can be almost a pernicious weed, this one in its great age has taken on a character that commands respect, especially in winter, when all the muscles of its limbs are visible. It will be allowed to die a natural death, having furnished an exuberant crop of fruit for countless seasons and providing nightly the roosting place of Koanga, the family tame jackdaw.

Beyond this the path forks, and both parts descend with pleasant windings till at length they reunite at the landing place by the river. Whichever one takes makes no difference. They are equally beautiful with fruit trees of various kinds growing on either side in luscious grass, with here and there a large clump of peonies. But it is really impossible to keep to either path. Between them in a little natural valley is a pool of enchantment, furnished by a never-failing spring of clear water. On its northern bank a weeping-ash—a Chinese variety—stands like a dignified guardian; at its southern end bamboos grow in luxurious profusion to fifteen feet high and more, while yellow iris fringe its sides, and, if one approaches quietly, a pair of water hens will be seen at home. The hand of man has had very little to do with this lovely spot, and perhaps that is why it promotes a delight which one does not feel in beholding an artificial lily pond, no matter how rich in aquatic flowers.

Certainly it is not easy to pass on, yet when we do it is only to arrive at another beautiful place, a roughly circular lawn between the pool and the river. Here again there is an extra-ordinary natural charm. A beech with polished boles and of great height keeps guardian, this time at the northern end, apple trees are along the sides, and forming the border between it and the river, rise gigantic plane trees with the sun shining on their flaked boles—simple indeed all of it, but majestic in effect, a sight one could never forget.

And so to the river Loing, a wide, silent current with magnificent trees overhanging it on the village side, and pleasant meadows opposite. We sit on the bank awhile and admire the grandeur of the great trees above us, and turn round to look at the garden from the opposite direction. There in the foreground is the lovely lawn and beeches, to the left we see the eastern end of the church peeping between branches of apple trees, in front and middle distance the bamboos and various flowering shrubs form a thick screen which guards the secret of the enchanted pool, and to the right we have glimpses between the trees of the ruined castle.

There is a peace here—the peace of ages, and time passes softly and silently like the river beside us. Yes, it is a haven indeed of greenery in this summer sunshine, but when the trees are just breaking into leaf in the springtime it is perhaps still more fascinating, for where we see now the mown lawn and the lush grass under the trees and along the pathways, there are to be seen swathes of snowdrops, crocus, daffodil, periwinkle, violet, cowslip, primroses, and pink low-growing delphinium. It is easy to guess that Mrs. Delius has been responsible for this, but one would not guess that these were mostly wild flowers, but daffodils with large trumpets like these grow wild hereabouts. Near the neighbouring village of Recloses on the hill there is a large wood, in one valley of which there are more flowers in early spring than one could ever imagine. They grow so closely packed that, if one leaves the footpath, it is in places quite impossible to stand without treading on flowers. Spring comes slowly in England and there are many weeks between the blossoming of daffodils and cowslips. But in this sheltered valley spring comes in with a rush and the result is astounding —indescribable even, if one has not seen it.

To this valley Mr. and Mrs. Delius made for many years a little pilgrimage with trowel and basket and from that inexhaustible supply transferred some specimens which have found themselves so much at home in this half-wild garden that they are trying to cover the ground completely.

As we are by the river we may as well get into the boat and push out. What magnificent old ash trees overhang the water! The giant planes have taken so much room that the ash trees have had of necessity to grow out horizontally from the bank in order to get light, and one has had to be secured to a plane, having ignored its centre of gravity. But what lovely reflections they make in the mirrored river! And what an interesting row of silver-stemmed poplars on the opposite bank. Planted by Delius? Impossible, they must be fifty years old at least. But they are not. He planted them in 1910, and the moisture which their roots get, and the many months of warm sunshine each year combine to produce that extraordinary rapidity of growth.

If we landed on the opposite bank and looked through them at the old bridge only two hundred yards down-stream, we should regret that Delius could no longer see what a delightful picture his trees have made. But let us paddle slowly upstream and admire the adjoining gardens with terraces and sloping lawns leading down to the water's edge, and past the little mill surrounded with flowers. Here the river has made islets and we steer among them and hear the roar of many waters, to the sound of which the village sleeps its quiet nights; for the weir is near, the water is churned, and when we have rounded the next promontory we shall be unable to proceed any further for we have come to what is locally known as the End of the World.

("The Music Student", July 1934.)

Frederick Delius: Some Personal Recollections
by C. W. Orr

When I first went to live in London, at the beginning of 1915, I had heard little modern orchestral music. The town in which I had lived till then was, and still is, hopelessly unmusical, although renowned as "a centre of education". There were a few celebrity concerts during the winter months, and from time to time the local Philharmonic society toyed shyly with Handel and Mendelssohn, rising on one occasion to the giddy heights of a concert performance of "Martha". For serious music one had to rely on the Three Choirs Festivals, which had at least taught me to love Elgar, for whose music I developed a passion that has lasted ever since I heard Kreisler play the Violin Concerto at Worcester in 1911. But with the exception of some of the Strauss tone-poems, which I had heard during some brief visits to London, I knew practically nothing concerning the composers whose names were already famous throughout Europe. I had heard some of Debussy's chamber music and a little of Ravel; but Stravinsky, Sibelius and Schönberg were for me merely so many reputations, and Delius nothing more than a name. On the other hand, such modern music as I had heard had aroused my curiosity and enthusiasm, and my taste in this direction was shared by a friend, older than myself, who though forced to live in C—, did not suffer from the provincial musician's hopelessly narrow judgement. During our country walks together we talked of little else but music, and I fear dismissed many of the classical composers as showing up badly against Wagner, Elgar and Strauss, with their glowing orchestral colours and bold, chromatic harmonies. This attitude, I regret to say, led us into professing what I suspect was a somewhat affected disdain for the solemnities of Beethoven and the solidities of Handel. These heresies, however, were not encouraged by the music-master with whom I was studying harmony and counterpoint: an excellent musician of the conservative type, but one who viewed Wagner with suspicion and contemporary music with acute horror. I still remember how he

55

showed me an innocuous arrangement of "Cherry Ripe" by that mild revolutionary, Cyril Scott, as an awful example of the utter degradation of music; and he never ceased to warn me against taking the broad way that leads to chromaticism, unresolved discords and musical destruction generally. (Atonality was a horror not visualised by either of us.) These warnings only confirmed me in wrong-doing, and I arrived in London resolved to hear as much modern music as I could digest, and possibly more.

The war had shorn the musical season of some of its former glories, since there were naturally no German artists, and even modern German music was taboo. Nevertheless, there was plenty for a musically starved student to enjoy. Sir Henry Wood was giving his fortnightly Symphony Concerts, the L.S.O and the Philharmonic Society were in full swing, while Sir Thomas Beecham was acting as a kind of glorious free-lance. Amongst his other activities then he was conducting a series of concerts at the Palladium, and it was at one of these that I first heard some of Delius's music. I had gone specially to hear "L'Après-midi d'un Faune," and the group of Delius pieces to be played immediately before it aroused in me no anticipatory excitement. They were the now familiar "Two Tone Poems for Small Orchestra" and a March from the "Folkeraadet" Suite. Of the programme as a whole I remember little, but the silent intoxication with which I listened to "On hearing the first cuckoo in spring" is still fresh in my mind. The little work is now so familiar that it is difficult to convey to a sophisticated reader the state of bewildered enchantment in which I was left at its conclusion. I can only say that the quality of delighted surprise with which one's mind greets a work of art that is new, and at the same time one towards which one feels at once entirely sympathetic, was present for me here; and those who have had similar experiences will understand my feelings perfectly. I believe every admirer of Delius would agree that this piece is the acid test of any listener's receptivity to his very individual harmonic idiom; for me, at any rate, it was a case of love at first hearing. Then and there I determined to go to every concert at which a work of Delius was announced to be played.

Fortunately, there were frequent performances of his music during that winter and the following spring and summer; and in fairly quick succession I heard "Brigg Fair", "Dance of Life", "In a Summer Garden", the first "Dance Rhapsody" and the

"North Country Sketches" (these last at their first performance). My enthusiasm grew with what it fed on, and even Elgar
had to give place for a time to the worship of this new divinity
revealed to me. It was an admiration quite uncritical, which is in
some respects the happiest way of enjoying music; but it was
none the less sincere, like so many of the idolatries of youth.
Meanwhile, I had got to know the composer by sight, as he frequently came on to the platform to acknowledge the applause—
a thin, slightly stooping figure, with the face of some ascetic
Catholic priest. To such lengths was I carried by my hero
worship that I would hang about the concert halls after a performance in order to see him come out; and it was thanks to this
(and the boldness of inexperience) that I achieved a self-intro
duction to the great man. It occurred after a concert at which
May Harrison and Hamilton Harty had played the First Violin
Sonata in its revised version, and I found myself immediately
behind Delius and his wife as they left the Æolian Hall together.
Without any very clear idea in my mind as to what I proposed
doing, I followed them up Bond Street, into Oxford Street and
finally into a restaurant, where I chose a table as near to them as
possible. I waited a few moments, and then, walking boldly over
to where he sat, I heard myself say: "Excuse me, but are you
Mr. Delius?" (Fatuous question!) On his replying "Yes I am,"
I stammered: "Oh, then, I wanted to tell you how much I love
your music." Banal and stupid as the words must have sounded,
I think he must have felt they were the expression of genuine
feeling, for he greeted me warmly, introduced me to his wife and
invited me to sit down with them.

Of our conversation then I remember little, save that I was
impressed by his easy, unaffected manner, with nothing in it of
the condescension of a great man towards a nonentity. I remember the quiet charm of his wife, and her smiling encouragement,
which helped to put me somewhat at my ease and enabled me
to conceal an inward elation under what I hoped was a fairly
calm exterior. Some weeks later he invited me to spend an
afternoon with him at Hampstead, which concluded with a visit
to the Promenades, where we heard the "Dance Rhapsody".
Thereafter, save for the time during which I was in the army, I
saw a good deal of him whenever he was in town, and kept up
an intermittent correspondence with him while he was abroad.
The recollections that follow are a kind of telescoped edition of
his conversations and letters, and may, perhaps, give some idea
of his attitude towards music in general, which, like his own

work, was entirely independent, and quite uninfluenced by what happened to be the fashionable judgements of the time.

First, as regards his views on the technique of composition. I think they may be summed up in a reply he wrote in answer to a question I had asked him about his early studies:

"You ask me whether I found any difficulty in composing when I began. It is rather hard to answer. I always found intense pleasure in composing; but doing theoretical exercises was a painful drudgery, and I don't know even now whether this drudgery was any use. I believe that harmony is entirely a matter of instinct, and that exercises in harmony are quite useless. On the other hand, counterpoint is extremely valuable, as it teaches you to use your brains and make the most of your material. Learn to write fugues and double fugues, and you will thus acquire a certain facility and mastery of your means. . . . Work as hard as you can if you feel you have something in you to express: you will thus gradually acquire a technique of your own, and it is the only way to acquire one that will be of any use to you. Simply work as much as possible; study the scores of the composers you love, and never mind about the music you don't like, however clever it may be. Give vent to the expression of your feelings in your own way, and you will then eventually find it. Cleverness counts for little, in my opinion: the French composers, for example, are all far too clever when they are young. Your technique ought to develop with your ideas. No composer whose chief idea is to be brilliant and startling ever lasts . . . If you devote yourself to music, there is only one way to attain to anything at all, I mean any originality, and that is by working right through your influences. Everyone has been influenced at first, and you will only find your real self after getting rid of great masses of other people's. . . . Music is a way of expressing one's feelings; and one ought to follow one's own inclinations entirely, otherwise one will never attain to any intensity of expression or emotion—*the two essential things in music.*"

And in another letter, written during my student days at the Guildhall School of Music, he said:

"Beware of the so-called 'broad tune' and writing diatonically, and for goodness' sake don't try and write in the style of Beethoven; you will end by producing banal things."

Which brings me to his attitude towards composers of the past. Like those of every really individual composer, his sympathies were decidedly limited. I imagine that no great creative musician can ever listen quite dispassionately to other men's work, whether they be his contemporaries or his predecessors. His own mental make-up is bound to predispose him as strongly in favour of one kind of music as it will antagonise him towards another. The indifference of Berlioz to Bach and Wagner's contempt for Brahms did not arise from a wilful misunderstanding: it was a hostility inevitable once we take their musical natures into account. Thus, what Mr. Ernest Newman wrote of Busoni applies with equal force to Delius, so far as his antipathies were concerned: he "was bound to react unfavourably to certain composers, for the simple reason that not only could they contribute nothing that would enrich his own blood-stream, but they might pump into it (if he did not reject them) elements that in his case could only act as poisons". It is not surprising, then, to find that Delius—whose style was harmonic rather than contrapuntal, and whose temperament romantic rather than classical—drew his musical sustenance from just those composers most akin to him in this respect. His own self-confessed favourites were Chopin, Wagner and Grieg: "These three have all given me great thrills, especially Chopin and Wagner. Grieg also in a smaller way: his music at its best is so fresh, poetic and original—in fact, just like Norway". With Grieg, he had much in common, both as man and musician. They were both passionate lovers of Nature: not as a mere background, to be enjoyed in the intervals of creative art, but as part of their actual musical inspiration. Moreover, there are certain harmonic passages in Grieg (see, for example, the last six bars of the song "Am Strome") that might have been written by Delius at almost any time in his career. These three composers are undoubtedly his musical ancestors. From Chopin and Grieg he learned to use harmony as a fluid medium, and to intensify his melodic line by that means; while from Wagner he acquired a delight in orchestral colour, and the device of using the voice, not as a self-supporting entity, but as an integral part of the musical tissue. For Beethoven he did not care greatly:

"Beethoven's music has never given me the great thrill, though he was, of course, an intellectual giant. I like the Symphonies and some of the chamber music, but his choral works I find tedious. I am also indifferent to Mozart and Haydn, and prefer Bach by far, who always interests me."

He loved Schubert's songs, but I never heard him speak of the chamber music. Brahms he thought academic and heavy,

"He works his subjects to death," he once said, and Schumann he disliked for what he called "that Teutonic sentimentality". Of non-German composers he once wrote quite warmly of César Franck:

"I think a good deal of Franck. The Symphony and the Sonata I consider works which will live",

though in another and later letter he all but cancels this out:

"Perhaps I don't admire Franck as much as you do. I like the first movement of the Sonata and some of the Symphony, and that is all. I never find him quite original, and influenced greatly by Wagner, Schumann and Grieg. . . ."

which must be one of the most extraordinary judgements of Franck ever written!

But it is his opinions of some of his contemporaries that best illustrate the limitations of his temperament. I once wrote to him enthusiastically about the Elgar A flat Symphony, and got this reply:

"Of Elgar I only know *Gerontius* and *The Apostles*; both of which I think very dull; *Gerontius* much influenced by *Parsifal*. I know nothing else but some trivial works, and should much like to see the Symphony you speak so highly of. Do me a favour and send me the miniature score if you will—I should not like to do Elgar an injustice."

This I did, but failed to convert him. He writes:

"I fear I am not as enthusiastic about the Symphony as you are. But that means nothing whatever—music is entirely a matter of temperament and taste. I find Elgar's musical invention weak; whenever he gets hold of a good theme or nice harmonies they remind me of Parsifal or Brahms. He never seems to have outlived his admiration for the Good Friday music; he has it also in *Gerontius*. His manner of composition is also Brahms's. And then the Symphony is very long, and the orchestration thick and clumsy, as is also Brahms's, and the musical matter in the last three movements very meagre. I heard the Violin Concerto in London, and found it long and dull. Sammons played it."

Of the young British composers of the '20's he used to speak warmly of Percy Grainger and praised the songs of Peter Warlock (Philip Heseltine); but the others he felt were too much influenced by the French school, though he thought Goossens had great talent. For the French composers of the day he appeared to have only a luke-warm admiration. Here is another extract from one of his letters:

Delius's study with his Ibach grand piano. In the background is the bust of the composer in his mid-fifties by Riccardi.

" 'Cleverness' counts for very little in my opinion. The younger French composers are all far too clever. Debussy wrote his best things before he was 30, and gradually got more superficial and uninteresting. His best work is *l'Après-midi*; parts of *Pelléas* are very fine and there is great dignity in the work. These I consider works that will live, but none of the others. Of Ravel, the String Quartet is one of the best, and also a piano piece *Le Gibet*. But without Debussy Ravel would not exist."

Elsewhere he wrote:

"We must always remember that although Debussy dwindled into a mannerist it was perhaps an idiom that was not capable of development. But all the same it was of great originality. . . . The other French writers don't count; they all resemble each other."

Of Stravinsky he said:

"Grieg had more music in his little finger than Stravinsky has in his whole body."

Writing from Germany after the war he said:

"They play a lot of Mahler here. I find him long, dull and pretentious"

—not an unexpected criticism, one feels. As to the atonal school of Schönberg and his disciples—he could not bear them. "You can't make music out of theories," he used to remark; "when a man has to write about his methods of composition you may be sure he has nothing to say." His criticism of this sort of music never varied: he found it lacking in any genuine emotional impulse. In one of his letters, he says: "In music, which ought to be the expression of emotion, only that which is based on emotion is capable of development, and nothing based on technique or on anything objective will develop into anything but mere intellectuality." It is not necessary to say that he had no objection of chromaticism as such—his own music would be sufficient refutation of such an idea; but he felt that it must be used as a means, and not as a fascinating toy for clever young men to play with.

Nevertheless, it is only fair to add this postscript to these critical Jeremiads of Delius. At the end of one letter, after indulging in some stringent criticism of works for which I had expressed the greatest admiration, we went on:

"But do not let anything I say influence you in any way. Always stick to your likings—*there are profound reasons for them.*"

61

So much for the musician. Of the man, as distinct from the composer, I can only write as I knew him. An enemy of pose or insincerity in others, he was himself absolutely free from affectation or eccentricity. Indeed, I think his chief characteristic was a hatred of anything that suggested these twin vices. I remember two amusing examples of this. The first was a description he gave me of a charity matinée to which he had been invited, and which was organised in aid of the Russian aristocrats who had been exiled through the revolution. These poor down-and-outs, who did not know where to turn for the next £1000 note, were present in force—the ladies garlanded with expensive jewels, and every *emigré* looking remarkably well-fed and prosperous. Delius's comment was very typical: "I went in hating Bolshevism as much as anyone, but I came out feeling like a Communist. Why, do you know, my dear chap, Jelka and I were the only two who went home by bus!" The second example was when a young musician was trying to interest him in a quartet by one of the "advanced" school. Delius listened to the rhapsodic praise of the work, and then said: "Well, play me some of it, dear boy." The young man (whom I will call X) demurred, on the grounds that it was impossible to play for two hands. "Then let's do it as a duet," said Delius promptly; "you take the first and second fiddles, and I'll do the viola and 'cello." But X, who was either unable or unwilling to submit his idol to this stringent test, made some excuse and left Delius master of the field. "Don't try to take me in with that sort of talk, dear X," he said, "I am too old to be bluffed in that way!"

It was just this ingrained commonsense and balanced judgement that made it impossible to imagine Delius as a beer-drinking Bloomsbury æsthete or an absinthe-sipping café-crawler of Montparnasse. *A propos* of that curious tribe, he said to me once: "I'm no Bohemian, nor ever was. I like my meals at regular hours." He responded modestly to genuine appreciation of his work, and suffered patiently (but not gladly) the gush of certain feminine leaders of London "musical" society—those vaporous females who could hardly distinguish B flat from a cowslip. But I believe he was happiest in his country home at Grez-sur-Loing, with a few intimates for company: he frequently told me how glad he was to return there after any prolonged stay in cities. I think he preferred living in France because there it is possible to live informally and comfortably; but he was under no illusions as to the French national character. He had lived there long enough to appreciate the finer elements in the French nature, but he could not bear their eternal chauvinism in art and politics, to say nothing of an even less engaging trait—their avarice and close-fisted habits: of which he once remarked, "a Frenchman would never accept your hospitality for fear he would be expected to return it."

I do not think he had strong political leanings, though he followed the events of the day with great interest. He loathed the pre-war militaristic Germany, of which he had some illuminating anecdotes, and was delighted at the ultimate victory of the Allies. Nevertheless, he condemned the Versailles Treaty from the first as, at best, a stupid makeshift, and at worst, a monstrous injustice. His reading was wide and varied; his particular admiration being for Nietzsche, Walt Whitman and Dostoevsky. The latter's "The Idiot" he thought specially fine. I never heard him mention the English novelists, though he must have been well acquainted with them; indeed, Philip Heseltine, in his study of the composer, states that at one time Delius had contemplated a libretto on "Wuthering Heights". He was keenly interested in painting, especially the French school, and possessed a fine Gauguin painting of Tahiti, which hung in his music-room.

Like Busoni and Elgar, he was supremely fortunate in his wife, who in addition to being a superb linguist, was a talented painter, but who gave up her career to be his *alter ego*. It cannot be all roses and honey to be married to a great composer, but I think that Jelka Delius asked no more of life than to be allowed to submerge her whole personality into that of her husband, and to further his interests in every way she could. I trust, and believe, that she felt rewarded by his devotion to her, and by the love and admiration she inspired in everyone who knew her.

I saw Delius at Grez in the summers of 1926 and 1928, when he was a mere physical wreck of what he had been. But though disease had done its worst to the body, his mind was as fresh and alert as ever. That this man, blind and paralysed, the face shrunken and withered, the body wasted to a pitiful mask, should have so far overcome these heartrending disabilities as to continue to compose, is surely one of the most heroic manifestations of a brave soul's defiance of Fate that the world has seen.

("Musical Opinion", August 1934, with additions from "Making Music", Summer 1955.)

Beecham on Delius

It would be unthinkable for a book of this nature not to include a contribution from Delius's greatest champion, Sir Thomas Beecham. The problem is, of course, that the maestro's views on the composer are well known, first through his 1943 autobiography "A Mingled Chime", and later through his full-length biography of Delius published in 1959. Here, however, are two less well-known articles by Beecham, the first from the "Evening Standard". In it, the conductor makes an eloquent plea for recognition of Delius by the award of the Order of Merit, and the piece elicited so much interest that the paper sent a reporter to visit the composer. Despite the latter's habit of leg-pulling the Press, the interview secured and published six nights later is full of interest, and is therefore also included here. (It should be added that Delius was never awarded the Order of Merit, as his contemporary Elgar was, but he was made a Companion of Honour two years later.)

Beecham's second article dates from 1953, when it appeared in "The Daily Telegraph". He was about to conduct the première of Delius's first opera, "Irmelin", at Oxford, and besides commenting on that work he makes some interesting remarks about the composer's early music in general.

Delius, the Neglected Genius
by Sir Thomas Beecham

A few weeks ago I was dining at a friend's house, and among the subjects of conversation was the Order of Merit. Of those present most knew nothing and only a few anything at all about it. An eminent politician declared it to be the highest honour the Government could confer on a man who had brought uncommon distinction to his craft or calling, but he was able to remember the name of only one recipient, an ex-Prime Minister.

An application to a popular book of reference revealed the curious fact that there were over half-a-dozen vacancies in the Order, which suggested that the advisers of the Government were unacquainted with any outstanding personality to whom it might be offered. At least such was the view of the eminent politician, and clearly he ought to know.

I am not of that optimistic tribe that sees the world of today flooded with genius; but I think that the pessimism of the official outlook would have sent a chill to the heart of Jeremiah himself. And on the way home my mind was haunted by thoughts of a great Englishman, one of the most remarkable of this or any other age, upon whom his country has never bestowed a single mark of recognition.

As it is likely that there are millions to whom his name is unknown, I may say that Frederick Delius is not one of those flamboyant figures who contrive to be constantly in the public eye in one fashion or another.

There has rarely existed a man of equal consequence who has so assiduously avoided publicity. To him the arts of advertisement mean no more than to an Arab in the desert. He lives alone and far from the haunts of men. But this has not hindered him from developing into one of the most singular and picturesque figures of our generation, from creating a fair portion of its loveliest music, and from being (in the opinion of many) the greatest musician England has borne since the death of Purcell.

There are few things more reckless than prophecy about the arts or artists, and the annals of criticism overflow with examples of the devout faith of one decade transformed into the irreverent doubt of the next. But I propose to ignore the warning of experience and to assert boldly that when the historian of fifty years hence comes to sift the wheat from the chaff of latter-day music, Delius will be found with a heavier account on the credit side of his artistic balance-sheet than any other living composer.

A select company already knows this of a certainty, and each succeeding year adds to the number of those who suspect it. But his popularity is likely to grow more steadily than sensationally, for his music is the very counterpart of the man.

In comparison with that of a great contemporary, Richard Strauss, it is as the voice of Wordsworth when first heard beside that of Byron. The storms and struggles, the joys and sorrows of our everyday life are not its main preoccupation. It has much of the aloof and observing spirit that Goethe admired and coveted above all else, and it is less the spokesman of the passions of humanity than the interpreter of the moods of nature from the oppressive and lonely grandeur of the Scandinavian Fells to the soft and soothing calm of the English countryside.

Sir Thomas Beecham, Delius's friend and champion.

Eric Fenby in 1976, seated at Delius's Ibach grand piano, which he now owns. Behind him is a painting by Jelka

Sir Thomas Beecham in conversation with Eric Fenby at the composer's reinterment at Limpsfield, Surrey, on

It is this contemplative rather than dramatic strain which has delayed a fuller understanding of him, for even in art it is not easy for a man to make himself heard nowadays above the cackling clamour of mediocrity unless he shouts at the top of his voice all the time.

It has also made him unusually difficult of interpretation, and I cannot think of a composer who has suffered more severely from inadequate or perverted readings.

I went to the first hearing in London of one of his later works: it lasted a third of the time longer than intended. The audience was plainly disappointed and bored, and no wonder! But in spite of these disabilities the fame of his music as well as the love of it grows apace, and more quickly in foreign lands than at home. On the Continent he obtains more performances than any other English composer, and in this way he has assisted to rebuild the credit of our music more effectively than a dozen lesser gifted musicians I could mention who could have rendered better service to their country by resisting the dangerous temptation to cross the Channel.

And as my memory recalled and traversed half a dozen of his masterpieces, the picturesque breadth of "Appalachia", the sombre brilliance of "Paris", the tender pathos of "Sea Drift" (the finest example in all music of the "Arioso Recitativo"), the simple charm of much of the "Village Romeo and Juliet", the "Mass of Life", and those exquisite fragments the "First Cuckoo" and "A Summer Night on the River", the more I wondered what was the purpose of a bauble such as the Order of Merit if not to be offered in humble thanksgiving to a man who has gladdened the world with this vision of beauty.

But our way of judging and rewarding genius has ever been mysterious, as I was reminded later on that same night when my work of preparation for a concert that was imminent evoked the image of another Master who lived and laboured amongst us two centuries ago.

For thirty years the mighty Handel strove to scale the rock of British hostility and indifference, only to fall back at the end exhausted and vanquished. The greatest dynamic force known to musical history was driven to ruin, paralysis, and blindness. The public, when satisfied that the creator of eighty operas and oratorios could write no more, indulged in the luxury of a brief revulsion of feeling and buried him in Westminster Abbey.

But fate, powerless to inflict further injury on the man himself, pursued the children of his brain with unchanging malevolence. Ever since his death the musicians of this country, assisted by the barbarous taste of the public, have done everything imaginable to promote a complete misunderstanding of his works, which today lie buried deep beneath the crushing weight of a tradition that has become the scorn of Europe.

I often read that we live in an age which with all its faults is kinder and more merciful than any that has gone before. Posterity will be a better judge of this than ourselves, but I am willing to admit that we have a different method of dealing with artists who do not instantaneously tickle our superficial palates. The aristocratic society of the eighteenth century persecuted them, which may have been unpleasant: the democratic community of the twentieth ignores them, which is fatal.

Wide apart as the Poles in every other respect, these two composers meet on the common ground of affliction, for the same physical calamities which darkened Handel's declining years have overtaken Frederick Delius. Well over sixty years of age, he, too, lies helpless, paralysed and blind; and unless the gods intervene to restore his sight the voice of this sweet singer will now be mute until the day of his death.

Even the loftiest spirits are not insensible to a token of national regard, and in the hour of tribulation they may be partly solaced by it. An act of grace and justice is within the dispensation of our rulers. May they be minded to accomplish it before the ultimate night descends upon their great countryman.

("Evening Standard", 13th January, 1927.)

A Visit to Frederick Delius
by an Evening Standard Correspondent

The tribute paid by Sir Thomas Beecham in the "Evening Standard" to Mr. Frederick Delius, the British composer, has caused him much pleasure; but the indignation of Sir Thomas over England's neglect of him is not shared by the man who "on the Continent obtains more performances than any other English composer."

I found Mr. Delius broken in health, almost completely paralysed, and threatened with total blindness. Yet his mind and spirit remain as serenely tranquil as the idyllic environment in which he lives. He dictated his last composition to his wife more than a year ago. He has not left his quiet retreat at Grez-sur-Loing since March, 1925, when he went to Wiesbaden for a great production of his works.

The composer's last visit to London was in 1923, when he attended the première of "Hassan", for which he wrote incidental music.

I told him Sir Thomas Beecham had stated in an article published by the "Evening Standard" that the Order of Merit would be a fitting reward for his life's work. This plainly pleased and embarrassed him. His innate modesty was evident in his reply. "Naturally one doesn't pursue or bid for such honours."

No trace of bitterness or even discouragement was revealed by Mr. Delius.

"England has a predilection for mediocrity," he explained, in a gentle apologetic tone. "Emotion isn't liked there; it isn't good form".

After leaving the Paris-Lyon railway station at Fontainebleau, I had arrived at the little village on the banks of the Loing.

We passed the "Poule d'eau", the quaint little artists' hotel, where Strindberg lived and worked for two years, and where Robert Louis Stevenson met his wife. Then we came to the house in which Delius had lived since 1898. It is flanked on one side by an ancient church, and on the other by the ruins of an old castle.

I was received by Mrs. Delius, the composer's artist-wife, who laid aside her brush and palette five years ago to devote all her tender care to her husband.

My first inquiry of Mrs. Delius concerned her husband's present state of health.

"He says a veil seems to cover his eyes sometimes," she informed me. "Then he cannot see at all, and he must rest his eyes for several days. He is unable to walk, and cannot use even his arms and hands much."

The war is blamed for his infirmities. When the Germans reached the Marne the heavy gunfire of the opposing armies shook the Delius home day and night. Along with the rest of the village's population, the composer and his wife had to flee to Paris.

Delius, at that time past fifty, was working intensely on an elaborate score, which had to be dropped. Badly shattered nerves quickly terminated in a physical breakdown. Five years ago he developed a strange case of paralysis, which has since baffled many specialists.

Mrs. Delius asserted that food carefully selected for vitamins and fresh air have helped her husband to recover a little of his strength in the last year. She prepares the food, and an Austrian valet carries him from his room upstairs to a wheel-chair below.

I first observed an eight-valve radio set in the big room in which we were sitting. Mrs. Delius said a clear reception of the London, Berlin, and Vienna programmes regularly afforded keen enjoyment to the composer.

Before they came to this home nearly 30 years ago, Mrs. Delius said her husband had an apartment in Paris. "He found the atmosphere here more favourable to composing," she added, "and we have stayed on happily. He has always lived apart from the world, but his music is entirely English. It would not be impossible for him to leave his retreat again. Should there be an important presentation of his music in England tomorrow, I would get him there to attend."

From a great window in the salon I looked down the sloping garden to the river. A small boat was tied up in a neat little shed.

"He loves the garden and river," said Mrs. Delius. "They never failed to inspire him in the past." She reminded me of one of his compositions, "A Summer Night on the River", which was written in the small boat I saw.

She showed me the music room upstairs, where two pianos were installed without crowding the available space. This studio also looks out on the beloved garden, where a quartet from the nearby music academy at Fontainebleau serenaded the composer last summer with his own music.

On our return to the salon, our conversation turned to Sir Thomas Beecham, and his advocacy of greater recognition for Delius in England.

"I think Mr. Delius discovered Sir Thomas," said Mrs. Delius. "Their friendship began in 1907. Sir Thomas is a beautiful conductor, and interprets perfectly the music of my husband. He has twice conducted his music in concerts at Covent Garden. Once, when the score had been lost, Sir Thomas conducted throughout from memory.

"It is true, as Sir Thomas says, that Mr. Delius is much more widely appreciated on the continent. In Germany and Austria no fewer than twenty big organisations play his music, as compared with only three in England. In America Percy Grainger, Damrosch, and the Boston Symphony Orchestra have made his works known."

Just at that moment Mr. Delius himself arrived. He was borne downstairs in the arms of his valet, and I shook hands with him after his wife had snugly bundled him in blankets in his wheel-chair.

"You were perfectly right in getting an interview with me from my wife—she knows more about me than I do myself," he declared, laughing gaily.

I walked beside his wheel-chair as we took the road to Bourron, a neighbouring village. He spoke of the surrounding scenery.

"I never was a town-man," he explained, "and I'm unhappy unless I'm in the country."

About Sir Thomas and the Order of Merit, Mr. Delius felt that he couldn't properly say a great deal.

"Sir Thomas is a wonderful friend," he affirmed. "We have had many talks, but this matter of English appreciation of my music, of course, was never discussed."

("Evening Standard", 19th January 1927.)

An Unknown Opera of Delius's Youth
by Sir Thomas Beecham

"Irmelin", Frederick Delius's first completed opera, was written a little over sixty years ago. What I mean by saying that it was his first "completed" opera is that during the two years preceding the beginning of his work on "Irmelin" he had experimented, none too successfully, with libretti based on Bulwer Lytton's novel "Zanoni" and Ibsen's historical drama "Emperor and Galilean".

The composer was just thirty at the time, and had already written a considerable quantity of instrumental, choral and vocal music, hardly any of which has been published.

In the case of any other musician this might be surprising: but in that of Delius it may be recalled that after the passage of another ten years, not one of his major works had found its way into print.

For this reason the average musical amateur might be excused for concluding that Delius wrote little of interest before the beginning of the present century. Of those works with which the public is most familiar, such as "Sea Drift", "Appalachia", "Brigg Fair", "A Mass of Life", "A Village Romeo and Juliet", together with the two miniatures, "On Hearing the First Cuckoo in Spring" and "A Summer Night on the River", all were written when their author had run into his fourth decade.

It has been too readily assumed by some commentators on this music that, because most of that portion of it written between 1888 and 1899 has not received the benefit either of performance or publication, it must on that account have defects of immaturity which influenced the composer against its issue or production. But this is by no means the whole truth of the matter.

During his later days, when he was incapacitated for further creative work on any sustained level, his thoughts frequently turned to the days of his springtime.

More than once he spoke to me of his two earlier operas, "Irmelin" and "The Magic Fountain", and when I asked him if he would like to see them produced the answer he gave me ran something like this:

"When you are satisfied that all or most of the works of my best period have been made well-known to the public through performance and publication, I should offer no objection to the appearance of any of those earlier pieces of mine which in your opinion would detract nothing from such prestige as my name may have acquired."

If we give more than a casual glance at the general body of this composer's work, we shall at once recognise that the theatre never ceased to occupy his thoughts. During something like twenty years he wrote six operas, whose playing time exceeds in duration that of all his other compositions taken together; and nearly his last effort of consequence was also a stage work, "Hassan", for which he wrote a large amount of incidental music.

For this reason I suggest that it is worth examining, with a closer interest than has yet been given to them, some of his operas which so far have never been heard in this country; and it is to the two earliest of them that our curiosity might usefully be directed and, I venture to say, without disappointment.

The term immature can be justified only if we think of the first twenty-five works of Beethoven as unripe, when compared with those that followed them. The early piano sonatas fore-shadowed little of the splendours of the "Waldstein" or "Appassionata", nor does the Second Symphony anticipate anywhere the dramatic magnificence of the Third and the Fifth.

But we have not ceased to love and to play them; and the same may be said of the youthful flights, symphonic or operatic, of many other composers. To me, in any case, the first Delian period has a very lively interest, and the two operas which I have mentioned are the peak points of it.

Although I intend to bring forward at some time or other

"The Magic Fountain" as well as the last opera of all, "Fennimore and Gerda", it is only "Irmelin" upon which I now ask leave to comment.

The libretto, which unites two stories of different origin, was written by the composer himself. The legend of Irmelin, a king's daughter who rejects the marriage offers of a hundred noble suitors, is Northern and early mediæval. That of the Princess and the Swineherd belongs to the less dateable period of the fairy-tale.

To this alliance Delius has added a new element of the sort to be found in all his other operas—save one.

This takes the shape of a force, either in nature or destiny, which tends to make the human actors in the drama of almost secondary importance.

Here it is the Silver Stream. Before the curtain rises its course has unhappily been lost by Nils, the Prince-swineherd who consequently has been reduced to a condition of degrading servitude under Rolf, a robber chieftan. Eventually he rediscovers it and is led by its friendly influence to Irmelin, who at once recognises in him the lover of her dreams.

In "The Magic Fountain" is to be found the same subservience of the hero and heroine to powers stronger than their own: in "Koanga" we have the semi-mystical influence of Voodoo, and in both "A Village Romeo" and "Fennimore" we view the slightly disconcerting spectacle of unfortunate creatures struggling without avail against superior forces unseen.

But, although vanquished, the victims do not surrender without some show of resistence. Occasionally it is heroic, more often pathetic; but invariably romantic and poetic.

As for the music, the writing for voices is smoothly singable, and that for the orchestra reveals an easy plasticity and wealth of colour, demonstrating that Delius had nothing here to learn from any other composer living at the time. An appealing freshness permeates the whole piece, the style and content of which are unmistakeably those of the creator of "Sea Drift" and "A Mass of Life".

Lastly, "Irmelin" is the only one of Delius's six operas which has a satisfactorily happy ending, thus making it suitable for a performance at a moment when all of us hope to be taking part in joyful celebrations.

("The Daily Telegraph and Morning Post", 21st March 1953.)

73

The Art of Frederick Delius
by Constant Lambert

The purely musical emotion of Delius's work makes any appreciation or analysis of his art somewhat difficult. This, at first sight, may seem a little paradoxical, for Delius is often superficially classed among the "tone poets", "musical impressionists", and the like, and it is true that the greater proportion of his work is inspired outwardly by some poetical idea or actual poem. But, whatever its inception may be, his best work as it stands may be called purely musical in that its effect is not really dependent on any superficial realism or empty formalism. By purely musical emotion I certainly do not mean the cerebral fabrication of musical material that passes for "pure music" in certain by now rather *démodé* intellectual circles, but an emotional expression that could not be obtained in any other art.

The emotional quality of Delius's music is intensified by the entire absence of conventional and accepted technical formulæ, and although this complete lack of any academic device results in an amazingly direct appeal to the ordinary listener, it is often a bar to his appreciation by the more sophisticated musician. Thus, one cannot say of any work by Delius (as one might of one by Ravel), "Even though this does not appeal to you, you must admit it is consummately well done," for, with Delius, technique and inspiration are not two separate entities but an indissoluble whole, and craftsmanship, as such, simply does not exist for him. For this reason his least satisfactory works are those in which he has bound himself to the more severe classical forms. The best of Delius is to be found, not in his concertos and sonatas, which are in a sense comparative failures, but in the exquisite series of works for chorus and orchestra (it would be a mistake to describe them merely as settings of poems) which includes "Sea Drift", "Appalachia", "Songs of Sunset", and the "Song of the High Hills". It is in these that Delius finds his free-est emotional expression and, strangely enough, his most satisfactory formal expression. Only when he essays a set form do we find ourselves tempted to agree with those critics who condemn his work as formless.

Technique and thought being so delicately fused in all his best work, it would be as foolish to waste time over pedantic criticism or analysis of the actual structure of his compositions as it would be to seek for influences in the music of a composer so intensely personal. All that one can do is to attempt some appreciation of that rare, emotional quality, half melancholy, half contented, at one moment a reflection of the strange, inhuman beauty of elemental nature, the next moment a poignant expression of the transience of human emotion, which is the dominant characteristic of Delius's art.

Many writers have laid stress on the great influence of Nature in his work and have almost classed him as a Nature poet in music. Some of his titles ("In a Summer Garden", "On Hearing the first Cuckoo in Spring", "Summer Night on the River") certainly tempt one to such a classification, but it would be the greatest mistake to look upon him only as a musical landscape painter. It would be safer to compare his works to landscape with figures in which both elements are perfectly balanced. Unlike either Wagner on one hand, or Debussy on the other, there is no scene painting in his music. Wagner's scene painting is, of course, magnificently but a little self-consciously done. We seem to feel a certain theatrical swagger behind his sunrises and river scenes. "This'll fetch 'em" we can almost hear the composer (with justice) say. Debussy, like a Chinese poet, presents us with some exquisitely wrought and decorative detail from which we fill in the implied emotion. But with Delius the human passion and its background of elemental nature are inextricably woven, and in this he reminds us of the best pages of Conrad rather than of any plastic artist. I am thinking of "Sea Drift" and "Appalachia", where, to my mind, his art reaches its greatest height, and in particular of passages like the outburst of the chorus to the words: "Shine, Shine, Shine!" in "Sea Drift", or the entry of the solo voice in "Appalachia". Such moments strike too deeply to bear analysis.

As I said at the outset, it would be wrong to look upon Delius as a "literary" composer because one can relate his music to definite scenes and emotions. He never allows himself to be shackled by either dramatic or pictorial considerations and it is significant that the emotional climax and finest passage in his opera, "The Village Romeo and Juliet", is the orchestral intermezzo in which no word is sung and (in its original form at least) no action takes place. The purely dramatic scenes, such as the quarrel of the fathers, are by contrast singularly poor. This intermezzo is even more typical of Delius than his purely symphonic pieces. It has the almost unbearable melancholy and nostalgia of so much of his music, and yet the mood cannot be described as pessimistic. There is a vein of sensuous beauty which runs through even his most tragic moments and saves them from bleakness or austerity.

It is this sensuous melancholy that is the most English quality in his music, which, for the rest, is not so national in feeling as some would have us believe.

There has recently been a tendency to hold up Delius both as a pure Englishman and as a purely national composer. As every one knows, he is of mixed descent, and his music is equally free from a national label. He might more accurately be described as a Nordic composer, for his mentality is of a peculiarly un-Latin kind, and one cannot imagine his music having much appeal to the essentially practical and clear-cut French mind. One has only to think of the end of "Appalachia" and then to compare its romanticism with the widely different romanticism of his friend Gauguin, as displayed in the marvellous "Nevermore", to realise the gulf between them.

("Apollo", November 1929.)

Delius: A Personal Reaction in the Form of a Letter   by Edwin Evans

My dear . . .

You do not lack assurance. Being, lucky man that you are, several hundred miles removed in a southerly direction, you ask me to convey to you my impressions after listening to the Delius Festival. You appeal to me as never having been either a whole-hearted enthusiast or a detractor, and being therefore likely to give you something that will contrast with the rapturous and rather sentimental outpourings which the Festival has occasioned. The fact that you have read the published accounts of it fortunately dispenses me from marshalling a lot of detail. That, say you, reduces the task you so lightly place upon me. My dear man, it is a hundred times easier to relate a succession of facts—a journalist's daily job—than to collate the essence of them in one interpretation. What you are asking is really that I should inform you what I think of Delius, and that, let me tell you, is an extremely difficult task. The very nature of his music creates impressions which are seldom easy to define or to trace to their musical sources. Moreover, are we not told almost weekly by a certain critic that such personal reactions are of value only when they are his—or, at least, when they are based upon knowledge which he alone possesses, which is much the same thing in the end? I am surprised that you should ask for anything so valueless, but since you do ask, I will do my best.

One's collective impression of a composer is rarely simple or direct. It is a partly subconscious ciphering of many factors, and depends to a considerable extent upon the value one assigns to each of them. I do not know whether you have ever had the onerous experience of being an adjudicator at any kind of musical competition. If you have, you will have acquired the knack of allotting points for certain qualities. But in the end the relative importance you assign to these qualities will decide your judgement, and probably no two adjudicators assess that relative importance in precisely the same terms. Now, far be it from me to arrogate for criticism any functions even remotely

79

resembling those of an adjudicator, but its processes present a certain analogy. Two critics may be in close agreement concerning the relative degree in which a composer excels in a number of different attributes, but be at variance as to the relative importance of those attributes themselves, and therefore differ completely in their appreciation of the music. That is generally the reason why you so often find two musicians whose knowledge and authority you respect giving opposite opinions on the same music. It is not that one apprehends less than the other—as it might be among the smaller fry—but that each assesses differently what he has apprehended.

Now, whatever difference of opinion there may be among such people concerning Delius is almost entirely of this type. There is general agreement concerning his qualities, good and bad. Even his warmest admirers are prepared to admit—except, perhaps, at festival times—his shortcomings. But they regard these as affecting only details, or matters of secondary importance, and as therefore so completely outweighed by his virtues that it is evidence of a mean and pettifogging nature to mention them. It is, for instance, rarely denied, except by fanatics, that Delius's writing is often defective in a practical sense, that sometimes even a certain amount of editing is necessary before the first performance can be given. That happened, if I remember rightly, in connection with the String Quartet. Of course, so far as performance is affected the flaws, once removed, are forgotten, but there are other, more permanent signs of a lack of technical scruple. Now it is perfectly rational to dismiss this idiosyncrasy as merely illustrating the contempt of true genius for procedure, and claim that, after all, if the message is delivered it does not matter much that it should not be couched in musical calligraphy. I have no quarrel with those who take this view, but among my personal reactions is a kind of intuitive distaste for work which leaves its creator's hands in that condition. I am not sure that such technical insouciance is really compatible with the attributes of mastery in music. I cannot bring to mind that any of the great composers, however contemptuous of mere rules, was similarly neglectful of the last link between creation and realisation. This personal feeling frequently comes between my enjoyment of Delius's music and my judgement. It may, as I say, be a personal reaction, but before it is dismissed on that ground as valueless I invite you to consider to what extent its nature differs from that of the view with which it is in disagreement. Surely both are personal reactions, and therefore, if our friend is to be believed, equally valueless. Since the facts are not seriously disputed, it cannot be a question of knowledge possessed on one side and lacking on the other. In this I have taken an extreme type of the kind of divergence I mean. And, please observe that I do not claim to be right. No infallibility for me, thank you! I am only explaining how I am personally affected by one particular factor in a problem depending upon many. I discount it, of course, but the mere fact of having to discount it affects the outcome.

Lest you think I am tilting the scales, let us now turn to something on which there is general agreement: the poetical quality of Delius's musical thought. Here is no ground for dispute. In this sense Delius is profoundly and magnificently musical, one of the most musical of all the thousand and one composers now living, so musical in fact, that it is the more irritating to be conscious of what I have described above. And, what is more, it is in the poetical quality of his music that Delius comes nearest to being English. I have always been inclined to resent the laboured efforts to claim Delius as an ornament to British music. They seem to imply a confession of poverty which I refuse to endorse. But there is something about Delius's music which suggests that at one time, most probably in adolescence, he was profoundly influenced by English poetry. This has been remarked upon, and an affinity claimed with Keats. There is also some analogy with the poetry of the Pre-Raphaelite period—with its lusciousness, not its tendency to pseudo-archaism. But to me this element is even more clearly allied to English landscape painting. In French landscape painting—to take the opposite extreme—the norm is objective, and the sentiment is more often than not sophisticated, a product of deep-rooted culture. In the English equivalent it is the norm that is sentimental. The tendency is so deeply ingrained that when the *fauves* of Chelsea attempt to paint a landscape objectively you can almost see on the canvas the effort they have to make to curb their congenital instincts. To take typical instances, there is sentiment in Constable and in Corot, but in the former it is natural and represents the mutual relations of the facts as they appear to his unconscious mind. In the latter the facts are placed in mutual relations which are the conscious product of a mind steeped in a culture which has been continuous from classical paganism. Now, except only that it is more lusciously expressed, for which his ancestry may be responsible, the sentiment of Delius's tonal landscapes is of the English kind. He does not place the factors in sentimental relations to each other. To him, as to Constable, they are themselves the sentiment. This is to me their greatest charm. Because I have at times sought to redress scales which have been weighted on the Teutonic side I am sometimes credited with a bias in favour of the Latin attitude, but my only prejudice is against exclusiveness—against the claim that this is music and that it is not, or that is not music because its fundamental impulses are not those of this music. That is what I have contended against for so long, and the difference between me and those who disagree with me is not that we honour different shrines, but that my pantheon holds more shrines than theirs. For reasons which I have tried to make clear, the Delius shrine in my pantheon may be less conspicuous than theirs, but those tonal landscapes of his have long ensured my fidelity to it.

Another aspect of his art on which there is general agreement is the richness of his harmonic colouring. It is as rich as the most sumptuous brocade ever woven. It also has the continuity of brocade. Its contrasts are generally no more than the play of light makes upon the draped folds of a length of brocade. To some these contrasts are not enough, and they charge Delius with overworking his patterns. But the five-note chord to which Saint-Saëns permanently attached an expletive, with its attendant elevenths and problematical thirteenths, offers a much larger number of permutations than the four-note chords of chromatically-disposed sixths and ambiguously diminished sevenths which served the same purpose with the earlier romantics. We are speaking now of harmony alone. In this, Delius's variety is necessarily greater than theirs. But thanks to it his palette is kept consistently keyed to the more luscious hues. If monotony ensues, it is the monotony of Gerhardt's legato, or of conversation with an intelligent woman who is invariably charming—in other words, too much of a good thing, and the remedy for those who find it cloying is to take it in smaller doses. The richer the fare the sooner, in each individual, is the point of saturation reached, but that point is not the same in each individual. I find that I can stand, without waning enjoyment, quite a lot of Delius's richness; and I shall not be told that this is a personal reaction, because our pontiff shares it, and it is only those he does not share that are personal to such as experience them.

The question of form, however, tends again to divide us. That Delius is nearly always faithful to his material hardly reconciles us. With this kind of writing it is always easy to include bits of recurring material. I read the other day that, at a certain point of Strauss's *Heldenleben*, twenty-four themes are simultaneously present. It may be so. I shall certainly not trouble to verify the statement because, but for the number of instruments employed, I can see no reason why there should not be two hundred and forty. The lines swing from harmonies erected like the telegraph posts you pass on a railway journey, but, unlike the telegraph lines, they may be crossed and form contacts without apparent detriment to the communication. A handful of themes can thus be used to give consistency to the texture without necessarily producing form. When Delius is deliberately formal, as, for instance, in the piano concerto, he usually overdoes it, which does not argue a good natural conception of form. Otherwise his style is too fluid to produce points of sufficient salience to give comfort to a listener who needs to hang his attention upon them. He rears edifices which have no corner stones, or at best inconspicuous ones. The effect is to invite greater passivity from the listener. The stream down which he drifts has the most alluring banks, but few landmarks, and these unobtrusive. But it is a winding stream whose graceful curves are not planned without a sense of direction, if such is necessary to your happiness. Often it is quite sufficient to feel that you are definitely getting somewhere. But I confess that sometimes curiosity as to the stages of the journey remains unsatisfied, and then my personal reaction is that the music is formless, for a form so elusive is scarcely form at all. Even in the sense in which a painter employs his quantities Delius's form is too often unsatisfying to me, and no amount of recurrence in his *motifs* is capable of furnishing a remedy. This factor affects the reactions of all but the most enthusiastic listeners to Delius's music, but its influence upon their final judgement differs, as I have explained, with the importance which each one of them individually attaches to it. Not being one of the extreme enthusiasts, I find that it counts adversely with me. I happen to have a relish for the stages of a journey, whatever its goal.

There is, however, one point which divides us still more sharply: Delius's polyphony. Now this is a factor which is not determined by knowledge. I defy anybody to criticise contemporary counterpoint on a strictly technical or morphological basis. The traditional procedure so admirably codified in its final form by Taneyeff no longer has unchallenged authority, and the laws of the new dispensation are as yet empirical, evasive, and open to contradictory interpretation. Not even Dr. Kitson could cite chapter and verse for saying which modern counterpoint is skilled and which merely arbitrary. But, as a personal reaction, I find the dissonant "linear" counterpoint of Central Europe aurally satisfactory, whether susceptible or not of the explanation offered, among others, by Ernst Kurth; and the *fausse note obligatoire* of the French seems to me no more than the purposeful deformation of a skilled draughtsman. I cannot justify either on the basis of demonstrable knowledge, and I venture respectfully to doubt whether any pontifical authority can do so either, but, though intrigued, my ear receives an impression of conscientious craftsmanship. Such as it is, I do not get the same satisfying reaction from Delius's counterpoint. Of course, I am not referring to his part-writing in harmonic textures. That is another matter, in which there is considerably more licence. But where the intention is contrapuntal, as, for instance, at the beginning of the variations in "Appalachia", the effect on my ear, I am sorry to say, is simply that of rather slovenly writing.

If that weighs somewhat heavily with me, I attach less intrinsic importance than even the enthusiasts to what Cecil Gray, for instance, calls the autumnal over-ripeness of Delius's art, for this attribute of his music is a chronological factor for which he is not personally responsible. History willed that he should belong to the decadence of a movement—the one unwittingly inaugurated by the sons of Bach, and of which the final scenes have been enacted before us. That an artist should belong to a decadence always appears to me fortuitous. He might equally well have been born at any other time, when he would have used his gifts differently. If I never grovelled before Strauss, as even pontiffs did once, it was not because of his Byzantinism, which, like Delius's luxuriance, is characteristic of the decadent stage, but because his grandiose presentation of essentially commonplace ideas came near to being a method of obtaining applause under false pretences, which my intelligence resented. Latterly, the weathercock has swung round so far that I often find myself committed to defend the good in his music from the effects of reaction. The megalomania of Strauss, the niggling of Reger (which, though its opposite, has also a Byzantine equivalent) and the *Üppigkeit* of Delius are all well-known symptoms of approaching dissolution in an art-phase which has run its course. What matters in a personal estimate of any of them is not the hour of their appearance, but what they made of the world as they found it. It takes a strong man to squeeze yet more significance out of a tired medium, and in that sense I esteem Delius a strong man. Certes, his music is autumnal, for his whole career has fallen in an autumnal phase, which he reflects as only a subtle artist could. And if his own emotions sometimes appear, in the light of more recent tendencies, to exercise too great a fascination upon him, allowance has to be made for the emotional exaggeration and introversion to which musical romanticism had led. It would not be just to attribute to him, a late arrival, responsibility for a tendency which was already inherent in the Romantic Movement at its inception and the germ of its ultimate disintegration. It is characteristic of all romantic movements, of whatever art or period, that, once set in motion, they must gather momentum until they culminate in excesses. Born thirty years later, Delius would have been more frugal, more reticent. Would that in itself, other things being equal, have been to his personal credit? I think not. Nor do I think it to his discredit that he shared some characteristics that were rife in the generation of musicians to which he belongs.

With that I conclude the confession of my personal reactions to Delius after having attended four of the six festival concerts devoted to his music. It only remains to say that the performances were such as to be completely authoritative. For particulars of them I refer you to the accounts given in the leading papers, which I understand you to have within reach. Delius is indeed a fortunate man in having Beecham for his champion. There are many contemporary composers of rank who have not yet had in London even one performance as illuminating as the many he was given. I sometimes wonder how much the inferiority of comparatively unrehearsed performances has contributed to bring about the conservative reaction which has endured here for six years. Delius's reputation has now been redeemed, and stands clearly upon the attributes of his music. Perhaps some day as much will be done for one or two others.

Yours,
EDWIN EVANS

("The Sackbut", November 1929.)

Delius: His Method and his Music
by Neville Cardus

It would be very easy to incur the wrath of Mr. Ernest Newman in writing about Delius. More, perhaps, than by any other composer, a musical critic is tempted by Delius to produce literary "flummery"—vague meanderings about translucent harmonies, dawns that shimmer, and white pools of peace. Even Mr. Philip Heseltine, best of all of Delius's commentators, allows his subject to lead him into purple but musically inarticulate passages such as this: "In this music ["Sea Drift"] we seem to hear the very quintessence of all the sorrow and unrest that man can feel because of love. It is the veritable drama of love and death. . . ."

The critic's difficulty with Delius is to give to the lay public, without the aid of musical illustrations, some idea of the style and the poetic significance of a composer who is quite unlike any other in his technical means of expression and in his emotional reactions to the art of music—his use of it as a means of self-expression. To discuss a work of Delius purely qua music would not get us all the way; on the other hand, we are not the wiser when we are told that Delius is a mystic. A man might be beatific with mysticism and yet write bad music, just as a man might exploit cadences of descending sevenths (as Delius does) and yet fail entirely to force his music upon our attention. Difficult the task indeed; but at this time of homage to Delius some effort must be made by all of us to show exactly where Delius is different from the rest of the great music-makers, and why his music is not only different but beautiful.

To describe to the layman Delius's technical apparatus, his style of expression, is almost impossible, for the simple reason that, as I have suggested, there is nothing else in music to which we can compare it. During the last half-century and more, music has developed along two main tracks, and Delius has avoided both. We can call these the tracks of symphonic and of illustrative music—music "absolute" and "programme" music. On the one hand we have had development (or derivations) from the classical forms. The first condition of these classical forms is thematic statement, contrast, transformation, and a final synthesis—the rhythm and harmony being products of the melodic idea and sequence. It is fairly well known that Delius has written few if any masterpieces of music in which a classical formalism is observed. As I will try to explain later, Delius is a writer whose music lives less in contrasts of thematic material (which of course are indispensable to the "absolute" forms of music) than in a homogeneous continuity or enlargement of melodic phrase and harmonic texture. Had Delius written nothing but his works in sonata or concerto form we should not today be hailing him a master.

But while even the layman is aware that Delius's music turns away from the traditional moulds, too many folk (musicians included) jump to the view that Delius is a tone-painter, an "impressionist", a maker of "programme music". The truth is that Delius at his most typical is a writer of music pure and undefiled. If you do not respond *musically* to "Brigg Fair", to "Sea Drift", to the "Mass of Life", to "In a Summer Garden", or even to the opera "A Village Romeo and Juliet", you will get little satisfaction out of Delius. There is no listening to Delius in terms of the realism of a Strauss on the one hand, or on the other hand in terms of the very tangible impressionism of a Debussy. In Strauss there are concrete images, literary and dramatic, to stir the imagination of the non-musical mind; in Debussy the languorous atmosphere of "L'Après-midi" is entirely tangible, and evocative of poetic as distinct from purely musical associations. With Delius it is music or nothing. The words of Whitman, in "Sea Drift", will not help you to enjoyment unless you also can follow the music's essence, its subtle and long-lengthed melodies, its instrumental and vocal combinations, all of which are woven into a texture that can be sensed æsthetically only by the musical faculty, and by no other faculty whatsoever.

If we look at one of Delius's loveliest but simplest works, "In a Summer Garden" (I choose this work because it is one of the best known), we can get a good notion of those traits in his style which are the most important, the most original. A realist, or an impressionist, could hardly have written to such a title without a few touches of realism, or (to suggest a less stark method) "pictorialism". A Debussy would have given us a summer heat and languor which could have been felt physically. There is no tone painting in the "Summer Garden" of Delius;

the wood wind's delicious flutterings at the outset might possibly hint of bird music to many listeners, but they are not essential parts of the texture; they are exquisite decorations upon it. The work begins with a melody which Grieg could easily have composed. Delius makes it his own by quickly drawing it into the tissue of his orchestra, until it is perceived only as we perceive a single strand of a texture; or, rather, we see it as though lapped by waves of sound—washed in them. The melody is lost, but—and here is the secret of Delius's way of sustaining his form—other melodies grow out of it; fragments are used almost as motives; the thought is continuous; the melody is but one factor in a process of musical thinking and feeling which works according to the comprehensive logic of changeful emotion, in which the "what comes next" is spontaneously prompted from Delius's heart and not by a logic taught formally in the schools. The other musical factors—rhythm and harmony—are inseparable from the melodic idea. Harmony in Delius does not support, by blocks, a melodic line, nor is the rhythm an effect of the recurrent stresses of harmonic supports. Delius's melodies—and, contrary to the general idea, his music is full of tunes that can be whistled—possess a lovely trick of dissolving the moment you have heard them, dissolving into a harmony of which it is difficult to name the tonal centre. This, of course, is due to the well-known chromaticism of Delius, and, of course, none of the conventional measured rhythms of music could go with it. As well might we try to measure and fit into bar-divisions the rhythm of changing light. Harmonic variation, as Mr. Heseltine has acutely written, takes the place in Delius of the usual linear thematic developments. But I find it hard to agree with Mr. Heseltine that melody in Delius is dependent upon and conditioned by its harmonic background. In my ears, there is in Delius no one dominating factor, melodic, rhythmical, or harmonic; all of these factors mingle in one another's being; we can only speak of a texture—which, indeed, is the texture of one of the purest musical natures mankind has ever known.

In the whole of the "Summer Garden", as I say, there is no tone painting. It gives us not the scene but the mind and heart of the artist in the scene or rather after the scene and the hour have passed for ever. Nearly all of Delius's music recollects emotion in tranquillity. The sudden climaxes of passion—and we get one of the most beautiful in all music in the "Summer Garden"—are not climaxes caused by excitement of blood or nerve; they do not work us up into a physical elevation or activity. They are the climaxes of a mind moved by the poetry that comes of beauty remembered. Delius is always reminding us that beauty is born by contemplation after the event, not while it is vigorously growing and taking shape before us. It is the "timelessness" of Delius's music that gives us the impression of its all-pervading beauty, for beauty is what is left for us when the show of life has passed on. Experiences have all sorts of values and significances while they are actually happening to us; the poet, after they have ceased actively to set into vibration his common or garden physical sensations, which have, like any other man's, their "use values"—then it is that he is interested only in the beauty that remains. Other composers are more human than Delius, because their music contains the dynamics of life and action felt immediately—now! Delius seems almost always to be aloof from the active life—life which, because it is active, is transitory. His music's most unique quality is what I can only, for want of a better word, call "bloom". And by that I mean an essential peacefulness, a poise won by poetic contemplation.

Delius has so refined his emotional experiences down to sheer musical sensibility that some of us would welcome in a score by him an occasional roughness or even harshness. Even in "Brigg Fair" the flesh-and-blood jollity of countryside revels is forgotten; the music tells us only of the bloom that was on the hour, long ago. A study of "Brigg Fair", from the passage marked *Lento molto tranquillato*, where the tempo changes to 4-4 time, to the close of the climax which leads to the transformation of the main theme into a new melody for trumpet and trombone, with an occasional toll of the bell—a study of this indescribably beautiful passage will bring us into the very heart of Delius the composer and Delius the man. Here, especially, we can look into his rhythmical fluidity, the sign of a musical sensibility that would have been dispersed by the ordinary recurrent rhythms of music.

During the festival which is now being given in London opportunities will occur for discussion of the full-scale works of Delius. After many years of neglect Delius now is coming into his own. Reaction at such a time may easily lead criticism to excesses, at the extreme to the misunderstanding which for years has marked the reception of much of Delius's music. He may not be as big a figure in the music of tomorrow as he seems to some of us to be at the moment. Perhaps in the long run it is the artist of the broad and not only the intense appeal who lasts the longest. At the present time Delius's music is becoming loved, not merely liked, because in an age when most of the arts have little to do with beauty, but have apparently been overwhelmed by the complexity, the cynicism, and even the hastiness and noise of modern civilisation—in this age Delius has made for us a music which is serene and never unbeautiful.

("Manchester Guardian", 14th October 1929.)

My Visit to Delius   by Sir Edward Elgar

Elgar was five years older than Delius and they first came into contact, it appears, around 1907 when they were associated with the ill-fated League of Music. This, with Elgar as President and Delius as Vice-President, was intended to promote the music of younger British composers. The two had never been close friends, Delius's feelings for Elgar's music, as C. W. Orr has shown, being something less than enthusiastic. In the other direction, Delius had described Elgar's attitude to his music as "slightly censorial as if he considered it not quite proper".[1] By 1933, however, age had mellowed both men, and when Elgar was invited to conduct his Violin Concerto in Paris with the fifteen year-old Yehudi Menuhin as soloist, he expressed a desire to visit Delius, whom he had not seen for twenty-one years. Exaggerated reports of the latter's state of health made it advisable to enquire beforehand whether a visit would be welcome. The following prompt reply was received:

"Your kind letter gave me the greatest pleasure, and I should like nothing better than to welcome you here at Grez—In spite of my infirmities, I manage to get something out of life, and I should love to see you."

Elgar left Croydon airport on the afternoon of Sunday, 28th May—his first flight in an aeroplane—and the following afternoon set out from Paris for Grez in a new Buick belonging to Menuhin's father. Before long ignition trouble developed and, rather than keep Delius waiting, they continued the forty-mile trip by taxi, arriving after five o'clock. The visit, which the seventy-six year-old Elgar later described as "a great event for me", was recounted in detail for "The Daily Telegraph", who published it on 1st July.

Elgar could hardly have imagined on that summer afternoon that he would die before Delius, yet in the nine months that were left to him the two corresponded regularly and cordially. Elgar even suggested that Delius should write him a three-movement suite for small orchestra, of the standard of difficulty of "On hearing the First Cuckoo in Spring", which he could play in Worcester. On

[1] Quoted by Eric Fenby in "Delius" (Faber: The Great Composers, 1971).

93

Christmas Day, 1933—only a couple of months before he died—Elgar wrote again:

> "*My visit to you is still a vivid thing in my memory and is one of the things that will endure. The kindness of Mrs. Delius and you to me lifts 1933 out of the ordinary Anno Domini.*"

I found Delius, as the energetic, bold writing of his letter had led me to hope, a very different being from the invalid of some portraits. It is true that illness has robbed him of strength and set a limit to his activities, but the infirmities of the body have not in the least dimmed the brilliance of his mind—the mind of a poet and a visionary.

Delius takes a keen interest in all that goes on. He is very much amongst us: little escapes his alert intelligence of what is of interest or value in contemporary art—music, painting, literature. And he is still writing.

Just now he has finished a composition for soprano, baritone and orchestra to words by Walt Whitman which he is to call "Romance". Delius is a man with a future.

A short conversation shows that he is conversant with the literature of all countries. He had Hergesheimer's last volume, although he shares my belief that there is, among modern novelists, no one great outstanding name.

Delius had been re-reading Dickens, and remarked on his rich humanity and uncertain art; this led to a discussion of the comparative merits of his novels. Apart from the "Tale of Two Cities" and "Barnaby Rudge" (which are historical), and of "The Pickwick Papers", which stands apart, I have always held "Bleak House" is the best of his writings. Delius thought "David Copperfield" might claim the first place, but agreed that the picture of Dora was, to say the least, overdrawn.

Then the talk went round to older writers and I mentioned Montaigne, whose translation by Florio Delius does not know. He became at once tremendously interested.

"Elgar has new ideas," he said to his wife, and, throwing up his left arm outstretched (his characteristic gesture when making a decision), "we'll read Montaigne," he declared.

I inquired what prospects there were of seeing him in London. There is nothing Delius would like better, and he is anxious to be present when his opera is performed. But the journey, the going from train to steamer and from steamer to train, is, for him, too arduous an undertaking. Having flown from Croydon to Paris, I suggested the pleasant alternative, and pointed out how after motoring to Le Bourget he could reach London by aeroplane in less than two hours.

The prospect attracted him. "What is flying like?" he asked.

"Well," I answered, "to put it poetically, it is not unlike your life and my life. The rising from the ground was a little difficult; you cannot tell exactly how you are going to stand it. When once you have reached the heights it is very different. There is a delightful feeling of elation in sailing through gold and silver clouds. It is, Delius, rather like your music—a little intangible sometimes, but always very beautiful. I should have liked to stay there for ever. The descent is like our old age—peaceful, even serene."

My description must have pleased Delius. Up went the left hand; "I will fly," he said determinedly.

I told how the spell of being amongst clouds was suddenly broken by the smell of whisky ordered by a passenger and carried past me—the horrible smell brought my mind to earth.

"Whisky!" said Delius, "the worst smell on earth! But, Elgar, you have not become a teetotaller?"

With vivacity I denied the impeachment.

"Let us then drink a glass of wine together," said Delius. This seemed rather an astonishing proposition; but Mrs. Delius, to whom I looked questioningly, interposed: "Oh, Frederick will join you."

Champagne was brought, and as we drank in the sunshine my old friend talked of present and past friends, of Granville Bantock ("the best of fellows", said Delius) and Percy Pitt, for whose musicianship Delius professed great admiration.

The time passed all too quickly, and the moment of parting arrived. We took an affectionate farewell of each other, Delius holding both my hands. I left him in the house surrounded by roses, and I left with a feeling of cheerfulness. To me he seemed like the poet who, seeing the sun again after his pilgrimage, had found complete harmony between will and desire.

In passing through the pine-scented forest of Fontainebleau on the way to see Delius, I had come to a turn of the road leading to Barbizon. In that far off time little did I dream that one day I should sit at the side of the President of the Republic. After my visit to Grez I decided to go to Barbizon, but when I passed the cross roads the longing had passed away. That belonged to the romance of 1880, now dead. My mind was now full of another romance—the romance of Frederick Delius.

("The Daily Telegraph", 1st July 1933.)

Delius: The End of a Chapter in Music
by Ernest Newman

Elgar, Holst, and now Delius! This is a year of mourning for English music. If the public, as distinct from one's private, grief is less poignant in the case of Delius than in those of the other two, it is because we had already realised that his activity was at an end. Elgar's mind, at the time of his death, was working eagerly not only upon his third symphony but upon the opera he had had on hand for so many years; and there is no knowing what might still have come from a mind so penetrating and boldly speculative as that of Holst. But in Delius's case, though his mind remained astonishingly strong until quite recently, the physical handicap became, in the end, more than he or any man could overcome.

Zur Ruh, zur Ruh, ihr müden Glieder!
Schliesst fest euch zu, ihr Augenlider!

Delius was one of those rare composers whom it is impossible to fit into any of the usual convenient categories: from first to last he was purely and wholly himself. One looks in vain in his music for any "influence" whatever; at most we can detect occasionally a slight similarity between some of his harmonic progressions and those of Grieg, but even here it is not a matter of actual influence, but of a certain congenital correspondence between the two minds in this one small corner of music. For good or for ill, Delius was barred by his very constitution from either profiting by or being damaged by the example of any of his predecessors or contemporaries. Though he studied for a time at Leipzig, Leipzig left nothing whatever of its characteristic mark upon him. Like Berlioz, he must have worked hard during his formative days in a way entirely his own, guided by a sure instinct of what it was necessary for him to take over from tradition in the way of technique, and what had better be rejected as being finally unassimilable by a mind like his, and inapplicable to purposes like his.

It is true that here and there his music prompts the thought that in casting from him what he felt to be alien to him in the

97

conventional technique he threw away also something by which, could he have made the essence if not the doctrine of it part of himself, his own technique might have profited. There are occasions, that is to say, especially in his earlier work on a large scale, when we feel that his hand is not quite subdued to the medium in which it is working, when the notes do not represent with perfect accuracy what it was in his mind to say. But one finally decides that he was right in refusing at all costs the assistance of the standard recipes—the use of which Brahms so liberally permitted himself when he was in a temporary structural difficulty—and in preferring to set down his dreams in his own way, even at the risk of an occasional awkwardness or lack of ideal clearness. Minds like his and Berlioz's have to pay the penalty of their originality; they have not only to find their own individual expression but create for themselves their own individual forms. In Delius's case the problem soon resolved itself into an intensive exploration of his own inner world as it was in the beginning, rather than a spatial enlargement of that world.

No two minds could be more different in orientation than his and Brahms's; but in one respect they were curiously alike. Sink a shaft into any two or three of Brahms's works, dating from his first, his middle, and his last period, and you come upon the same metal. There are minds, such as that of Wagner, that changed their tissue so much in the course of the years that one can hardly believe that their first and their last works were written by the same man. There are other minds, such as that of Brahms, that appear to be full-formed from the first; as life's spiritual experience works upon them they do indeed fill the native mould with a substance of ever greater strength and beauty, but in essence both the mould and the filling remain to the end what they were at the beginning. So it was with Delius. His music is sometimes reproached with being the same in one work after another. To some extent this is true; the same rhythms, the same harmonies, the same exquisite washes of colour, recur again and again: sometimes, even, he unconsciously repeats himself literally, a certain passage in "A Mass of Life", for instance, being an almost literal reproduction of one in "Sea Drift". But with Delius, as with Brahms, though the music remains superficially the same throughout the years, its inner tissue and timbre and clang are subtly modified in one work after another. In Delius's case, perhaps, one requires a special sensibility, and considerable acquaintance with the music, before these fine shades of distinction between works that to the casual ear sound very much alike can be distinguished; but of their existence there can be no doubt.

His music is full of paradoxes. One's first impression of some of it is that it is formless: later one discovers that it has a form, and a perfectly adequate form, of its own. In this respect posterity will do him more justice than is possible to the ordinary listener of today, who has been herded by precept and example into confusing truly organic musical form with the merely schematic: some day it will be recognised that a work like "Paris", in which the nature and the pressure of the thinking evolve their own perfectly congruent shape and articulation from the inside, instead of docilely accepting a standardised scheme applied to the music from the outside, represents a higher achievement in form than is to be met with in many a dozen "classical" symphonies.

Another paradox is that while his music seems to glide along with limbs relaxed, it is often, in reality, extraordinarily vigorous, as many a page in "A Mass of Life" testifies. It is simply that in music of this kind, as in the bodies of the cat tribe, the muscles can put forth the maximum of energy with the minimum of visible effort. Delius's mind in general was one of exceptional strength; and only listeners who are unable to get past the smoothness of the texture of his music to the thought that is functioning within can be under any illusion as to the same strength being there in his music.

If his mind, from first to last, moved within an orbit that seems limited in comparison with that of minds like Wagner's or Beethoven's, it gradually developed the maximum of light and heat within its own orbit. A penetrating and realistic thinker in matters of the intellect, as a musical artist his whole life was devoted to the progressive realisation, in ever clearer forms and ever more poignant expression, of the one primal ideal of beauty, a beauty that is eager in the earlier works, passionate and richly coloured in those of his middle period, and with the sadness of autumn in it in some of his latest works, where he seems to recognise regretfully at last, as we must all do, that this hard world is not to be shaped by the artist and dreamer to his heart's desire. In the music of his final period, with its poignant nostalgia for a beauty that is fast vanishing from the earth, we hear, as in no other music but that of Mahler's, "the sunset cry of wounded kings", the last regretful murmuring of ancient talismans which, in its strange blend of credulity and negation, the distracted new world has for the time being rejected.

With the death of Delius there has died a world the corresponding loveliness to which it will be a long time before humanity can create for itself again. It may be that, as some think, we are now in the first hour before a new dawn in music. But that hour is grey and chilly: and those of us who have been drunk with the beauty and the glory of the sunset of civilisation as we knew it must find our consolation in the melting colours of the cloud-shapes of the music of this last great representative of that old dead world. Delius has summed it all up for us in his moving setting of the no less moving words that Nietzsche puts into the mouth of his Zarathustra:

O man! Take heed!
What saith deep midnight's voice indeed?
"I slept my sleep—,
"From deepest dream I've woke, and plead:—
"The world is deep.
"And deeper than the day could read.
"Deep is its woe—,
"Joy deeper still than grief can be:
"Woe saith: Hence! Go!
"But joys all want eternity—,
"—Want deep, profound eternity!"

("The Sunday Times", 17th June 1934.)

Delius by May Harrison

I have been asked to write about Delius's views on the interpretation of his Chamber Music, but the task is practically an impossible one, so I will instead write of some of the memories I have stored away. To play Delius's music is a kind of instinct —a natural impulse—and he depended more on the instinctive musical feeling of his exponents possibly than any other composer. He once told me that music to him was purely emotional —a series of passing dreams—wherein intellect and actual scholarship should play practically no part. To look for, or expect to find structure or conformity to rule of any kind in his music is a useless quest, for Delius also told me that when, in his student days, he had started to study composition, and to try to conform to rules, his whole inspiration had left him; he *had* to do it his own way or not at all. And so it was, he told me, with his playing, once he started to take piano lessons, he could play no more.

We (my Mother, my sister Beatrice, and I), first met Delius in Manchester, during the War, about 1915 or '16, when Beatrice and I were playing the Brahms Double Concerto with Sir Thomas Beecham at a Hallé Concert. Langford, the well-known critic, came round to the artists' room with Delius during the rehearsal, and great was our joy when Delius told us he had so much enjoyed the performance that it had given him the idea of writing a Double Concerto for us, which he did on his return to Grez, through the following spring and summer.

We saw a great deal of him and his most dear wife, Jelka, during their next visits to England, and they would come to our house two and three times a week for hours at a stretch all through the time that we were working at the Double Concerto —note by note—with Delius.

My Uncle, Charles Charrington (my Mother's brother, who, with his wife Janet Achurch, had been the first to produce Ibsen in England, and also the first to dramatise Thomas Hardy), was living in London then, and Delius enjoyed meeting him, as they had had many mutual friends, both having known Ibsen, Felix Moscheles (an Uncle of Mrs. Delius) and many others, and they both got on extremely well. Delius also loved my father, for whom he had a great regard. Those were happy evenings we all spent together. At this time Delius was very interested in the works of some of the young British composers, and he told me that of them all, he thought Arnold Bax to be far the greatest, both poetically and imaginatively. Just about then I played the first performance in London, with Sir Hamilton Harty, of Delius's 1st Violin Sonata, and Harty in great kindness, spent hours editing and correcting the piano part (MS). With joy and gratitude Delius carried it off then and there from the artists' room to send it direct to the publishers; but by some extraordinary chance, the wrong part got published, and, as far as I know, Harty's wonderful work was irretrievably lost.

Just after the War we moved from London to the country, and for a time had a small house on Ditton Hill, where Delius and his wife would often come and spend long days with us; and Delius, who was always a very small eater, though a thorough epicure, would often forego a meal, and sit in the garden alone, listening to the sounds of nature, as he would listen to his music, with his eyes half-closed and a face from which the spirit had gone—alive and yet not alive—completely lost in sound. And from that was, I believe, evolved the 'Cello Concerto, which he dedicated to my sister. Delius's admiration for Beatrice's playing was very great, and he dedicated all his 'Cello works to her. In her he found a sensitive spirit, alive with the fire and poetry of his own creative imagination.

After this I personally did not see him again for nearly ten years, though he and Mrs. Delius had been to see my people at the time that "Hassan" was produced, which had so greatly distressed him and made him quite ill. At the first performance the audience had talked loudly through all his music, and he could hardly hear a sound of it.

Many years later, when I went for the first time to Grez, it was to a very sad and stricken house, and though my Mother had warned me, the shock of seeing Delius blind and paralysed was so great, that I could hardly speak. But his and his wife's welcome was so warm and dear that I soon felt better.

My Mother and two sisters had already been over to see him some months earlier, and had been the means of having a Wireless set sent over to him, which was to the end of his life the greatest joy, and naturally the only chance he had of hearing his own orchestral works, except of course when he came over to England for the glorious Festival given for him by Sir Thomas Beecham in 1929. My Mother had told me, as I have already said, how changed I should find our dear friend, how still and silent the house seemed with never—what struck her—any laughter heard; so I made up my mind that if I could, I would at any rate try and bring some laughter.

I remember that the first amusing story I told Delius happened to be when he was just about to eat an oyster, and he laughed so much that, to my great horror, the oyster stopped half way, and would *not* go down: I watched with the greatest anxiety, and at *last*, after a great effort, it found its right way down!

The story was one I had been told by a friend from South America. In the summer, he said, in the great heat over there, people often camp out in small huts made of sticks and mud, and with a small bench for a bed. He had a friend, an exceedingly tall man, who was called Long John, and one night when this man was camping out, the hut became so unbearably hot that, in his cramped position on the bench, he stretched out his legs which went through the wall of the hut, and in the morning when he woke, he found that the fowls were roosting on his feet outside!

During my visits to Grez, Delius told me a great deal of infinite interest, especially about his early life in Florida, and of his parentage and descent. Unfortunately, there is not room to put it down here; but one point he emphasized and evidently wished to make very clear was that—though he said I might often be told to the contrary—he was utterly un-Jewish, he had as far as he knew, no Jewish blood whatever, though he was very cosmopolitan, being of Dutch extraction, German and Swedish on his mother's side, and his paternal grandfather having lived for many years in Australia. On this first visit to Grez I played the 2nd Violin Sonata to him with Eric Fenby, who had just then started his wonderful work with Delius and which was giving him new life again. I had never even *heard* that work, and explained to Delius that it would be simply my idea of what I felt he might want, so that when he said to me—"Ah! I am very curious to hear what you will do"—I felt extremely nervous. But at the end he was delighted, and told me that it was *exactly* what he had meant, tempi and all, so it was a great happiness to me to know that my instinct was right. He told me then that he had the outline—only slender sketches—of another fiddle

Sonata, but would not show them to me. My surprise and excitement can be imagined when I received a thrilling letter the following spring from Mrs. Delius, telling me that the 3rd Sonata was just completed, with the aid of Eric Fenby, and inviting me to go for a "nice long visit". I stayed for a fortnight, just at the most perfect time of year, when the weather was glorious, and the Spring had burst into rapture, so that the whole garden was a mass of blossom and a vision of colour. One's heart ached to think of Delius, of all people, sitting blind amidst all the beauty around him, though he would talk of the different flowers, the river and the garden, as if he were looking at them. Fenby and I played him the new Sonata almost every day, as well as the other two Violin Sonatas, and also the new short orchestral work—"A Song of Summer"—which had also been just completed, and of which Fenby had made a splendid arrangement for two pianos, and which Delius seemed to enjoy listening to. On this visit I took over with me the long lost score of "Koanga", which about a week before had been discovered in some cellar by Philip Heseltine.

There were days when Delius was too suffering to be played to, and then he would be carried away to his room, where he would lie for hours in agony. Such fortitude and courage I have seldom seen—*never* a complaint, even when the agonising shooting pains he would get at the changes of the season or the weather would be almost unbearable.

It has been said that he was a colossal egoist, and so he was —but what genius is not? Is it not part of the life of all creative geniuses to be so wrapped up in themselves and their work, their moods and their feelings, that they have little room left for others, either in thought or deed? No one understood that better than Delius's sweet wife, who had given him her every thought since they first had met. One other who had a great understanding of him, both as man and musician, was my beloved Mother. She said to me once that one should not think of Delius as a man—he was not like a human man—but rather like a Creature of Nature, elusive and in a way un-understandable. Certain unnecessary and futile things have been written —and the mistake and pity are great—about Delius's beliefs and anti-religious ideas. To us, in all the years we knew him, he only once alluded to anything of the kind, and then it was to my Mother, the last time she saw him, when he told her that he thought that, when he died, he would become music.

I went a third time, later on, to stay at Grez and this time

Ethel Bartlett and Rae Robertson came and spent the day while I was there. Delius and his wife enjoyed having them, and after Ethel Bartlett and I had played him two of his Sonatas, she and her husband played Arnold Bax's Sonata for two pianos, which Delius was much interested to hear. I stayed on a few days—again in the most heavenly weather—and Delius once again told me many interesting things, and seemed wonderfully well. That was the last time I saw him.

About three months after his death I went to stay with Mrs. Delius for the last time at Grez, and found her slowly beginning to recover from the terrible ordeal she had been through—of her serious operation, and the shock and grief of losing him. I found her very lonely and full of worries and anxieties. She told me that for a year before Delius had died, he had insistently expressed a wish to be buried in the South of England (as some of the little English Churchyards reminded him of Gray's *Elegy*, one of his favourite poems, and upon which his last 'cello work, "Elegy", was based)—not at Bradford, which he said was too bleak and cold, but somewhere in the South—and she was at a loss to know where to go. I suggested the sweet little Church- yard at Limpsfield—(which Sir Thomas Beecham later des- cribed in his memorable and beautiful oration at Delius's graveside as "this fairest spot")—and where our own Mother lay, for whom Delius had had such a real affection and admira- tion. Mrs. Delius thought the idea a perfect one, and she loved the thought of his being among real friends. That was the whole point and reason—among *friends*, and *not*, as Eric Fenby says in his book, among strangers. He had no friends at Grez, and never liked the French, though he lived there.

It was arranged that Mrs. Delius should visit Limpsfield when she came over to England, which she did with my sisters, Beatrice and Margaret, about two months later. She was en- chanted with the place and the lovely surroundings. The Rector of Limpsfield, whose kindness and forethought were all through remarkable, smoothed away every difficulty for her, and when she asked the inevitable question about buying the ground, he replied that there would be no question of that, as it was to be the gift of Limpsfield to a great man, and that they offered him the hospitality of the Church. Mrs. Delius was deeply touched. As is known she was herself laid to rest there only three days after he was brought over, and a few months later our dear father was also laid there.

While I was with Mrs. Delius at Grez that last time, she told me much about herself, of her life as a student of art in Paris, and her first meeting with Delius, of their early life together at Grez, and of the many interesting people she had known. She also told me all about Elgar's visit to Delius, and what a surprisingly happy meeting it had been, how charming and delightful they had found Elgar, and how amazed and struck he had been to find Delius still working, with the help of his amanuensis, and full of enthusiasm, in spite of his affliction and great disabilities. She also asked me to help her go through some of Delius's manuscripts, and sort papers, and I had the privilege of seeing many things which will in time, I suppose, become national treasures.

A great deal has been written about the autocrat in Delius (which after all is not very surprising, seeing that his father was one of the greatest autocrats who ever lived), but little, so far, of his other side, of his great charm of manner, of his beautiful speaking voice and great courteousness, his quick appreciation of, and gratitude for, anything done for him, or given to him, even to the merest flower, and his evident pleasure in the company of those friends whom he liked and found sympathetic. Of the consummate and true artist he was, whose every thought and deed, practically every relationship in life was, in reality, a dedication to the Art he worshipped, much has already been written and is known. Such is, in small measure, the picture we, as a family, remember of Delius.

Of her, his wife, no words can express her love and devotion, her sacrifice of everything—her career, her Art and her every thought which, from the first had been given completely and utterly to help him in every way she could.

These are some of the lovely memories I have of Fred and Jelka Delius.

("Royal College of Music Magazine", 1937, No. 2.)

A Singer's Memories of Delius
by Cecily Arnold

It is strange that so few of the songs of Frederick Delius are heard in concert programmes; even Delius enthusiasts are surprised to learn that he wrote forty songs with piano accompaniment, and that they form a most interesting study of the composer's development. My own interest was aroused in 1930, when, in conversation with a music critic, I was deploring the infrequency of recitals of English songs, old or modern. He questioned if any single English composer's songs would supply a complete and sufficiently varied programme, adding "except, perhaps, Delius". This seemed almost a challenge. I was strongly attracted to the music of Delius and had already studied several of his songs; I soon obtained all that were published, and found them very varied particularly as they clearly fell into different periods.

I prepared a recital programme, arranged as far as possible in chronological order; but finding it impossible to date some of the songs I wrote to Grez-sur-Loing giving details of my programme and asking Delius if he would kindly supply the missing dates. I received a charming and most friendly reply, written of course, by Mrs. Delius as her husband was then completely blind and paralysed. After the recital came another letter congratulating me on the Press notices, expressing regret that Delius himself could not hear the songs, and asking me to take up a small question of translation with the publishers.

The audience had been so good that a second recital was planned, on similar lines. A new song was in the publisher's hands, and they suggested that I should ask for permission to give the first performance in this recital. This was readily granted, but the wish was reiterated that Delius could hear the songs, particularly the new one. I gathered that he often had visits from chamber music players, but rarely from singers. My husband and I thereupon decided to take our annual holiday at Easter, before the recital, and go to France.

Mrs. Delius was delighted, and immediately proceeded to

arrange practical details. A room was booked at a small pension just opposite their house; timetables were sent; and we were commissioned to bring over some records which had been blocked by the Customs when sent as a present from a recording firm. They included Grieg's violin and piano sonata in C minor, played by Kreisler and Rachmaninov, some Hebridean songs with Patuffa Kennedy Fraser, and a South American dance.

We arrived at Grez-sur-Loing on Easter Saturday afternoon, left the bags in our room (brightened that morning by Mrs. Delius with a bowl of wild daffodils from their wonderful garden), and were conducted straight across to have tea with Delius. The blind, helpless composer sat wrapped in rugs with a screen round his chair, able only to raise a feeble hand in greeting. A male nurse was in constant attendance, even having to feed him, yet the brain behind that gaunt, expressionless mask still dominated the situation, and forbade any sentimental pity. He spoke of his school, which was near our home; but he had little time for small talk, and immediately tea was over, I was sent upstairs for a short rehearsal with a young German girl—a relation of Mrs. Delius—who was to accompany me. In about half an hour Delius was carried up to the music room, settled again with his rugs and screen and we began. He received the first song with satisfaction, and then I sang the new one—a setting of Verlaine's *Avant que tu ne t'en ailles*. To my intense relief, he said, "That was beautiful—just as I would have wished it sung: sing it again!" Three more songs followed, and one of those, a haunting setting of Fiona McCleod's *I-Brasil*, also had to be repeated. Then he was tired, and was carried to bed. After supper we saw Mrs. Delius again, and she kissed me on both cheeks, saying, "My dear, he LIKES you!" Poor Mrs. Delius—she sometimes had such difficulty in making excuses to visitors whom her husband did not like, and refused to see again.

I stayed for five days, rehearsing each morning, meeting Delius for tea and then adjourning to the music room for an hour or more of songs. Over tea we talked of his music, of performances he recalled, and of musical friends; but in general he spoke little, though always to the point.

After a song he was sometimes disconcertingly silent for what seemed minutes, but at length a comment would be made—a dynamic altered, or a criticism of my French pronunciation over which he was most helpful; occasionally the accompanist was checked for wrong notes or emphasis, and we would repeat

Cecily Arnold in Delius's music-room in 1932. Above her can be seen Delius's most valuable possession, the Gauguin "Nevermore". To the left of it is a self-portrait by Jelka Delius.

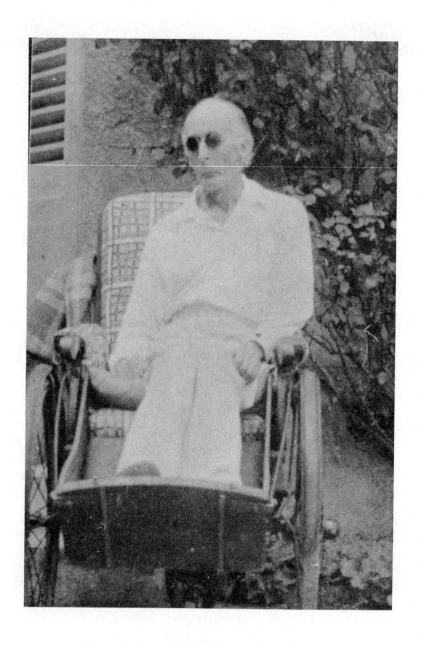

Delius in his wheel-chair in the Summer of 1932.

a section or whole song with revised tempo and dynamics. Altogether he was most kindly, and his adverse criticisms were surprisingly few. I was assured by Mrs. Delius, whom we met after supper each evening, when he was in bed, that he really enjoyed the sessions, and that he had rarely heard anyone for so many days running. I was indeed fortunate that he was well enough at that time to see me every day.

I sang nearly all his songs to him. He evinced no interest in the earliest group, *Five Songs from the Norwegian* written in 1888, his first year in Paris, after Grieg had persuaded his father to let him concentrate on music. He wrote a great deal in this period, but with stern self-criticism allowed little but songs to be published. These are simple strophic settings of various poets, with a strong affinity to Grieg, but with unmistakable gleams of his own individuality. *The Nightingale* and *The Slumber Song* are the most charming, and are occasionally heard.

The next group of *Seven Songs from the Norwegian* contains the well-known *Twilight Fancies*; and others that appealed to me were *Sweet Venevil*, an unusually gay song; *Cradle Song* of Ibsen, one of the loveliest cradle songs; and *The Homeward Way*, typically nostalgic. They were written 1889–90, still in Paris, and are an obvious advance on the first set, showing great variety of mood and treatment.

The next year produced the three Shelley songs, probably the best known. He did not even want to hear these, and had no interest in them. They belong to the period of his piano concerto, and have an exuberance which he never displayed later. After this came the first Verlaine settings in 1895, and these contain much more of the later Delius, particularly *Le ciel est, par-dessus le toit* written when Verlaine was in prison. Delius was very fond of this and has compressed an extraordinary amount of restrained passion into the music.

In 1897 and 1900 came six songs from the Danish of which *In the Seraglio Garden, Autumn,* and *Irmelin Rose* all by Jacobsen, are in three quite different moods, and are very rarely sung. *Let spring time come,* also by Jacobsen and published separately, is perhaps the finest, and most advanced, and this seems quite unknown. It is a short song in which the voice expresses the melancholy of one who can no longer feel hope in the spring, while the accompaniment is full of the joy and excitement of the season. Between these, in 1898, he wrote four Nietzsche songs which are utterly different from any others; the vocal line is stark and the accompaniments bare and simple.

They were designed as a cycle for tenor voice, and were produced six years before the completion of *The Mass of Life*.

All this time he was working in Paris: but in 1900 he settled in Grez-sur-Loing with his artist-wife, and it was there that most of his finest work was accomplished. Only one song, Jacobsen's *Black Roses* was written for some years. In 1908 he turned again to English poets and set Henley's *The nightingale has a lyre of gold*, a beautiful love song that curves up to its climax and falls back again with the inevitability of genius. Fiona McCleod's *I-Brasil* was set in 1913, and as Philip Heseltine has said, this expresses Delius' own philosophy; it was clearly his favourite, and I had to sing it each evening to finish the session. *Four Old English Songs* appeared in 1915–16; of these *To Daffodils* is deservedly well-known, *Spring, the sweet spring* is another gay song, and *So sweet is she* is a most sensitive setting of Ben Jonson's delightful words. The last, *It was a lover*, offers great difficulty to both singer and pianist, but if it is approached as he conceived it, that is not subjectively as a joyous dance song, but objectively as if one were observing the lovers from some hillside with the pattern of fields and cloud shadows all about, it is quite understandable and successful. The rhythmic arrangement of the first few words give the key to the mood of the song, they are almost conversational.

Three more Verlaine songs, *La Lune Blanche*, and *Chanson d'Automne* in 1913, and the last song *Avant que tu ne t'en ailles* (which was, I believe, actually written in 1916 but not revised for publication till 1932) complete the list, except for two charming children's songs, *What does little birdie say?* and *The streamlet's lullaby* published in 1924.

His own preferences were for the Verlaine songs and the English settings (excepting the Shelley songs) all of which are mature and finished works. He was quite uninterested in the songs of any other composer save Grieg, whom he admired very much; and did not even know the original settings of the older poems which had appealed to him. His interest in poetry, and the extent and standard of his reading is proved by the choice of poets of various nations whose works he set in their original tongue. Norwegian, French, German and English were used daily in that cosmopolitan household. He loved the beautiful garden which ran down to the river Loing, with a copse and trees at the water's edge giving glimpses of the fine old stone bridge at Grez. Near the house it was laid out in formal box-fringed beds, but beyond them spring flowers came up in the grass and among the trees with a natural beauty that was unforgettable. A very great deal of Delius's music reflects that lovely garden with the quiet river among the trees. It is no wonder that he felt he could work in such a place, and that Mrs. Delius strained every effort to get it for him.

The last word must lie with Jelka Delius, one of the most selfless and understanding of women, who gave up all personal ambition to provide conditions under which the genius in which she had such faith could blossom. Her care and devotion enabled him to continue even after his body had failed him, and smoothed out many of the difficulties which still had to be faced after the perfect amanuensis, Eric Fenby, had been found. Any personal recollections of Frederick Delius are inevitably bound up with loving and lovely memories of the woman who, while studying in Paris, fell irrevocably in love with "the young composer who went about the woods singing."

("The Music Teacher", April 1950.)

EDITOR'S POSTSCRIPT:

Through the kind offices of Mr. Marshall Johnson, husband of the late Cecily Arnold, I have been permitted to examine correspondence appertaining to her visit which she carefully preserved. To her immediate family she described the events more intimately and more vividly: "Gosh! I'll never have a worse audition!" she told her mother, and to her husband she wrote: "—if only he would say more—but he just sits there after each song and says 'Yes, that's much better' in his slow old way, and we all sit silent, not quite knowing what to do next or whether he wants to say any more, and then just as you are going to start another he may say something— or when you think he isn't listening he will make a remark!"

Before going to Grez, Miss Arnold sent Jelka a list of the songs of Delius, asking if she would check the dates. In returning it Jelka explained that the dates she had supplied were only approximate, and continued:

"So perhaps you would like to know which of the songs he likes best:

'The Nightingale' (Henley)
'I-Brasil'
The Four Elizabethan Songs
'Chanson d'Automne'
and after that 'La lune blanche'. Of the older songs he likes
'The Homeward Way'
and 'Autumn'."[1]

---

[1] I have left this essay exactly as Miss Arnold wrote it, rather than interfere with the text in any way. One or two small errors do need correction, however. The song "Black Roses" is by Josefson, not Jacobsen, and in the sentence that follows 1910 is the usually accepted date for the composition of "The Nightingale has a Lyre of Gold". This is also known to be the year that "La Lune Blanche" was written (beginning of next paragraph), while "Chanson d'Autumne" dates from 1911. (*Editor*)

Delius as I Knew Him   by Robert Nichols

It was very still out there on the stream in the summer twilight
—so still that I could just hear the tiny sounds made by Delius,
blind and paralysed, half-singing, half-sighing some fragment
of his music to himself. He was lying back, a crumpled figure
under a rug, in a special chair set in the middle of the little boat
which, weighed down by Delius, Mrs. Delius, my wife,
myself and the house-boy, was stealing, as if asleep, down the
bosom of the little French river. Overhead the leaves of the
lofty alders softly idled together. Now and then a single leaf
flashed or some sweet sigh, coming one knew not whence and
travelling one knew not whither, set a thousand thousand
leaves shivering . . . and then a leaf would dilly-dally silently
down. One such alit on the rug beside Delius's long, thin
hands—so nerveless, so feeble!—a leaf so green it was like a
flake of emerald in which a sun-star lay imprisoned. Delius did
not see it. It seemed hard that he—he who had loved nature
with a more exquisite passion than any man I have ever known
—he that poet of human love and separation for whom the
presence of nature had been the supreme consolation—it
seemed hard that he could not see that leaf.

Yet my solicitude wronged his serenity. The sound that
issued from his throat didn't, in so far as I could catch it, seem
unhappy, and his face was as calm as the golden light which
illumined his stern and wasted features.

I recalled his face as it had been when I first knew him—the
face of a distinguished technician, severe but debonair. I
contrasted my memory of that face with the face I saw before
me now. That face had been handsome; this was beautiful.
Two qualities were common to both: extreme sensibility and a
signal serenity. One of these had increased and, in so doing,
now revealed, while the evening light shone upon apparent
darkness and disorder, the meaning of the solitary pilgrimage
soon to be accomplished. I pondered that serenity and decided
it was due to his "devotion to something afar from the sphere
of our sorrows", namely beauty.

The characteristic which above all others assures Delius a unique place among the poets of nature is the subtle exactitude of his registration of mood. When, in the First Act of *Walküre*, Wagner celebrates the coming of spring, it is all spring, a whole season and its primitive powers, which he lets loose upon us. Berlioz gives us a particular day in a particular month; for instance, that thundery, sultry, sunlit day—all light and shadow—met in the "Scène au Champs" of the *Symphonie fantastique*. But it is Delius, and Delius alone, who can crystallise for us not a season, not a day, but a particular hour, the hour in which, for instance, a man no longer young, halting beneath the new-fledged alders by the riverside, hears once again the first cuckoo in spring, and, hearing it with a delight in which is mingled sorrow, knows that he does not hear it as in days gone by. It is in fact from some serenely exalted station in memory, which for the pagan is alone outside time, that the composer reaches out to possess himself of the mysterious felicity of one moment which will never be again.

This habit of the creative mind is supremely displayed in Delius's grandest work, the monumental *Mass of Life* and his *Song of the High Hills*. In my view it is quite impossible for anyone—including professional musicians—to arrive at any final just estimate of Delius's status in the history of music until he or she has heard both these works at least three times. They are what the Himalayas are to the map of Asia and, like the Himalayas, they lie at the heart of the territory under survey. That is not to say I think that either—and more particularly the *Mass of Life*—is ever likely to obtain a general popularity. The Himalayas are not for everybody. For it must not be supposed that because so much of Delius's music is of an extreme elegiac tenderness and ethereality that the composer was a soft and gentle and accommodating creature. On the contrary, he was a hard, downright and even dogmatic man with very definite ideas about the cosmos and man's place and destiny in it, ideas just as definite as, if hardly more comfortable than those of Thomas Hardy, albeit of a different cast from Hardy's, since Delius could say with the stoic Nietzsche: "Every complaint is an accusation and every joy a praise."

Two influences moulded Delius, the man: nature and Nietzsche, and these influences are closely blended. For Nietzsche, beside being a sceptical stoic philosopher, was also, and most notably, a great revolutionary poet, whose vision was irradiated by a mysticism that bade him declare "the greatest

events are not our loudest but our stillest hours". Delius, by
virtue of his capacity to communicate the substance of life's
stillest hours, is an exalted and tragic idyllist, the tone-poet of
an extreme felicity, on whom "the burden of the mystery"
hangs heavy because it is never shirked. It is the inevitable
presence of this burden which is perhaps responsible for the
error which declares him an introvert, limp and decadent
romantic. Those who, though acquainted with his major works,
fall into this error are usually those unable to find the courage
to share awhile Delius's fundamental conceptions. He did not
believe that love controls our universe, or indeed that any love
is to be found in it except human love. These conceptions are so
uncompromising as to render him something of an awkward
customer, both to the materialistic optimist, who trusts to be
saved by a plethora of beautiful bath tubs, and to the im-
material pessimist, who renounces this world altogether in
favour of a next and better. Delius tells us that life is beautiful
and brief and bitter and surrounded by mystery, that the beauty
of the mystery is unfathomable and that we would do well to
accept the mystery, first because, if we don't, we shall lose some
of the beauty and, second, because it is becoming to human
dignity to face with quiet resolution the inevitable condition of
any human happiness whatever. He has in fact a very old-
fashioned air: he might be a great Greek tragic poet. Hence the
austerity and serenity of the features I beheld before me in the boat.

Delius was now silent. The evening breeze had strengthened
a little, and the rustle of the alder leaves was continuous and
mingled with the sound of the ripples on the water. It was so
mysterious a sound that it might have been either of the softest
laughter or of a secret sighing. Mrs. Delius, holding the fallen
leaf between her fingers, was gazing at her husband's face with
an air of mingled happiness and anxiety. "They are together
a little longer," I thought, "and this is one of their stillest
moments." . . . Delius had begun to sing again but so low I
could not hear him. "Is it *Sea Drift*?" I wondered. "O past!
O happy life! O songs of joy in the air."

Darkness deepened; I could just see their faces and was
aware that he was still singing. . . . And that is how I like to
remember my friends Fred and Jelka. . . . "He who has once
been happy," said a wise poet, "is for aye out of destruction's
reach." . . . Delius's final message is no different.

("Music Magazine",
ed. Anna Instone and Julian Herbage, Rockliff, 1953.)

The Personality of Frederick Delius
by Percy Grainger

The Australian-born composer Percy Grainger (1882–1961) was a close friend of Delius for many years, and sacrificed valuable time from his own career to help nurse him through his long illness, and to write down his music when his sight was failing. When the older composer died, Grainger wrote a long and valuable memoir for "The Australian Musical News", which he dated "18–20th June 1934." In an accompanying letter to its Editor he wrote with characteristic modesty:

". . . leave out anything you may dislike, though my own opinion is that it is a mistake to cut out all 'disillusionising' elements or to try and make Delius's personality agree with the mood of his music. If true accounts of Delius are suppressed a Delius-myth will grow up that is silly and harmful to a sane view of art and artists. And I would like Australia to have the honour of producing the most true-to-life picture of his personality. This is easy for me, as I was closer to him, in many ways, than the English-born composers were."

Many musicians regard the great man who has just died as the topmost musical genius of his era; different reasons might be put forward for this belief, which unite men holding divergent views on other matters musical.

My own explanation of the strange hold that Delius has on the affections of so many thoughtful and critical musicians is that he is the first great genius that has fully expressed in music the main stir of our period of history, i.e. the emotions underlying colonial expansion and all that goes with it—the "call of the wild", the passion for travel (Delius was a devourer of travel-literature), the hunger for adventure (Delius adored mountaineering), the yearning for "the wide open spaces" (a passage in his "Song of the High Hills" is so labelled) and much inquisitiveness about "native" races (he had a Negro sweetheart as a young man in America).

The spirit behind a large part of Delius's music is at one

with those same forces that drove Segantini to paint the Alps, steered the æsthetic courses of Robert Louis Stevenson, Pierre Loti and Paul Gauguin to the South Seas, and made sea-poets and outposts-of-empire-depicting bards of Kipling, Service and Masefield. For although the amatory yearnings and philosophical introspections of civilised (and hyper-civilised) man find plenty of outlet in his music (for instance, "A Mass of Life" and the operatic scenes, "Fennimore and Gerda", based on J. P. Jacobsen's novel, "Niels Lyhne"), yet it is 'obvious from the titles of many of his most arresting works that they grew out of rivers, mountains, the sea, sunsets, the "primitive" races and their basic emotions: "Appalachia" (an old name for the Mississippi river), "The Song of the High Hills", "Sea Drift", "A Song of Sunset", "Koanga" (a Negro opera), "Hassan", "A Dance Rhapsody", "Life's Dance", etc. [1]

Admittedly many other Nordic composers have based their compositions on similar themes, but the most successful amongst these (such as Schumann, Grieg and MacDowell) have expressed the urges in miniature rather than life-size. It seems as if Delius is the first composer to give us "nature music" on the grand scale of a Bach, a Wagner, a Richard Strauss; it is as if "nature music"—dwarfed or childishly undeveloped before—has grown to man's estate for the first time in the music of Frederick Delius.

He thus stands as the lone giant presiding over the musical expression of the major urge of the period that produced him— the "back to nature urge" that, in its various ramifications, has given us such very diverse manifestations as a world empire based on raw materials, nature cures, free love, touristism, jazz, athleticism and nudism.

We may speak of the music of the Australian aborigines (and similar primitive music) as the music of magic or superstition, we may select de Machaut (1300–1377), Dufay (1400–1474) and Chopin as composers pre-eminent in the expression of lovelornness; Palestrina, Byrd, Handel, Bach, César Franck may seem to us outstanding as religious composers; Haydn and Mozart we may classify as courtly composers (their music obviously growing out of court dances such as the minuet, gavotte, etc.);

[1] It is true that many of Delius's finest works are examples of "absolute music"—works whose titles (such as "Concerto", "Sonata", etc.) do not reveal their underlying emotional impulse. But the texture and mood of these conpositions is so similar to those of Delius's "nature music" works as to suggest a kindred source of inspiration.

Beethoven looms as the supreme revolutionary composer, and Wagner and Tchaikovsky bulk big as the interpreters of the "human" (passionate) emotions. In a like spirit of generalisation we may designate Delius as the first superlative genius amongst the "nature music" composers. As such he naturally excels in the musical depiction of those moods that invariably accompany the "nature" emotions: loneliness, wistfulness, frailness, dreaminess, turned-inwardness, vagueness, and a sense of distance.

From its claims to priority as the first full-size "nature music" Delius's muse draws great human, national, social and historical importance; not, however, that it needs this added interest, musically speaking, for its quality as "absolute music" is quite enough to stamp Delius as one of the transcending composer-geniuses of all time. Delius (like all the truly greatest composers) has that cumulative ability that enables him to fuse all sorts of contrasting musical elements in the melting-pot of his own originality, and just as Bach was able to create a definite musical entity out of a blend of Couperin, Palestrina, Buxtehude and Vivaldi, just as Wagner emerged as the most original known composer after swallowing (and digesting) the hitherto un-combined methods of Weber, Chopin, Italian Opera, Bach and Mediæval music, so did Delius's music grow strongly personal on a musical diet of Bach, Chopin, Grieg, Wagner, Negro-American folk music and Debussy. This is the nature of all originality: The ability to instinctively and effortlessly combine more elements than the average critic can trace to their sources. As Ruskin so truly said: "Originality is genuineness, not newness."

Delius's music, like all true music, makes its appeal largely by its "texture"—that is, by the charm of the actual sound, induced by the critical care with which the component notes of chords are distributed in the part-writing. But whereas fine composers of past periods had other avenues of appeal (in Bach's case the vitality of the part-writing, in Wagner's case the pithiness of his motives, dramatic contrasts, and so on) that vied with their "textural" attractions, Delius relies almost wholly on the beauty and touchingness of the part-distribution in his chords—since themes and their development, or contrapuntal complexities, arbitrary formal devices, or striking orchestral effects are things too artificial to appeal strongly to Delius's deeply emotional, straightforward musical nature. Thus his music is apt to seem monotonous to those whose ears expect the spiciness, skittishness and "effectiveness" of 18th and 19th century music, while it provides rare—almost un-rivalled—rapture for those who demand calm beauty, nobility, grandeur and depth of feeling in music and are weary of slighter offerings.

Both Delius's parents were German (from the province of Brunswick) and doubtless it is from his racial background that he draws his typically German ability to conceive music in grand and large dimensions. But he himself was born and brought up in Yorkshire (Bradford) and the mood of his music is typically English—strikingly akin to the nature moods in such English and American poets as Keats, Shelley, Tennyson, Swinburne, Walt Whitman.

The way Delius came to devote himself seriously to musical composition (after the age of twenty, by the way—a circum-stance almost unique in the lives of great composers) is typical of the colonial phase of life to which he belonged—that period in which the European races turned to the New World, or to some other part of the extra-European world, for their romance and adventure. The Delius family was a musical one; string quartets were heard weekly in the home and Delius's brothers and sisters could play by ear and improvise to the amazement of other Bradford-dwellers. Delius, too, studied the piano some-what and could play some Chopin and Bach before he, as a young man, went to Florida (U.S.A.) to manage his father's orange plantation there.

On the plantation he was so touched by the beauty of the untutored part-singing of the Negro labourers that he decided to become a composer and begged his father to allow him to study the art in Leipzig. When his business-minded father would not agree to this plea Delius got a job, somewhere in Virginia, as a singer in the local synagogue, increasing his earnings by giving piano lessons. His ability thus to self-support himself as a musician for six months so impressed his "hard-headed" father that the permission to study in Leipzig was then granted.

In Leipzig Delius met Grieg and came to worship Grieg's music. This is not so surprising, since the primitive, country-field note in Grieg's music was quite in keeping with the English colonising mood that informs Delius's own art. Thus, in Leipzig, the Norwegian musical influence was added to the Negro-American musical influence and blended with it. An amusing instance of this blend is seen in the chief theme (Delius's own) of the "Dance Rhapsody" (orchestra), which begins in a typically Norwegian folkscale (with a sharp 4th—D sharp in A major) and ends with a characteristic Negro-American cadence.

These influences (Grieg, Negro-American folk-music and early impressions of Bach and Chopin), plus the Wagnerism that any impressionable composer would pick up in a musical centre like Leipzig at that time, constitute the abiding ingredients of Delius's compositional style throughout his life.

I need not here say more of the nature of Delius's music or of the main events of his life, since such information can be culled from Philip Heseltine's matchless book on Delius (his life and work) published by John Lane in 1923, and from most representative books discussing modern music.

I will confine myself to such anecdotes as Delius told me with his own lips or to such happenings as I myself witnessed as his fond friend and worshipping fellow-composer. These sidelights I consider of some interest as showing the eternal balance preserved by a great genius between the higher and lower, the deeper and shallower, the ideal and practical sides of his nature.

In Delius's music all is loftiness, grandeur, rapture, harmoniousness, tenderness, exquisiteness, aloofness, purity, angelicness, wistfulness, calmness. But in daily companionship (at least with his friends) he was, in the main, delightfully saucy, argumentative and mischievous—quite an "enfant terrible". When alone with a friend he could suddenly reveal unsuspected depths of solicitude, affection, tenderness and helpfulness. But as a rule (and particularly when several people were present) he was alive with a Voltaire-like wit and thrust, eager to tease, and in all ways shrewdly self-protective. Such tactics reveal the need that a creative soul experiences to protect the sensitiveness, purity and freshness of its emotional life against the onslaught of a rough, only half-civilised, world.

The way that Delius got married is typical of his subconscious-moving, not-according-to-plan nature. His now wife (then Jelka Rosen—born in Serbia while her father was German Ambassador there) and her friend Ida Gerhardi (later a distinguished painter) were studying painting in Paris. They were living with Jelka's mother in a lovely old house, with a charming garden skirting the river Loing, at Grez—a rural village some miles from Paris, near Fontainebleau. At gatherings in Paris that included artists such as August Strindberg and Paul Gauguin the two young women met Delius (both thinking him very gifted and finding his smooth English looks and eccentric ways most attractive), and asked him to visit them and Madame Rosen in Grez, which he—seemingly quite casually—promised to do. But evidently the prospect of seeing the ladies in their countryfied home beside the old river struck a genuine note of joy in his subconscious self.

Just then he was leaving for America, there to try to find a vanished Negro sweetheart. Failing in his quest, he returned to France, but instead of seeking lodgings in Paris drove down to the Rosen home at Grez with all his belongings. Feeling happy and at home there he stayed on and on, never discussing his departure. He has "stayed on" there ever since. Jelka Rosen and Ida Gerhardi—both in love with him romantically and artistically—quarrelled violently over him, but later made the quarrel up and remained devoted life-long friends.

Eventually Fred and Jelka married, enjoying rare spiritual unity together. It was an unforgettable treat to see them listening to Delius's music at a concert—leaning slightly towards each other, aware of each other as they drank in the strains that were nirvana to them—for Delius was as much in love with his own music as the rest of us were. On such occasions it was evident that Delius desired only Jelka close to him; he wanted no other friends near.

Jelka Delius's sweet and clever nature comes out in her delicious paintings, which enjoyed her husband's warm admiration. "Doesn't Jelka paint charmingly?" he would say to me; "such truly feminine painting, so utterly unlike a man's art." Jelka Delius is also a skilful poetess, translating from English or Scandinavian into German the texts of many of her husband's songs and choral works.

Delius (unlike many intellectuals) was not mentally chilly toward, or critical of, womanliness, although he was acidly critical of normal manliness—its laws, its wars, its politics, its business, its all-round meanness. "A woman can never be quite as stupid as a man; for no woman is without some sensuality," he said to me around 1907 (a typical remark).

My first contact with Delius's music almost overwhelmed me, when (in 1905 or 1906) I saw the full score of his "Appalachia" lying on Robin Legge's (music critic of the London "Daily Telegraph") piano, in Chelsea, and started to read the first *a capella* outburst. I was amazed to find that anything so like my own chordal style existed. It struck my mother the same way: "What piece of yours is that?" she called from the next room, taking for granted it was mine, yet not able to recognise it.

Curiously enough, Richard Strauss seems to have sensed a similar likeness—but to his own music—when he first heard Delius, presented in Berlin by Beecham. "I never dreamt that anybody except myself was writing such good music," he exclaimed, characteristically.

Around 1908, Delius and Elgar joined forces in creating the League of British Composers—an organisation arranging performances of the works of the younger British composers. When the constitution of the League was drawn up Delius called upon both Sir Hubert Parry and Sir Charles Stanford, to ask if they would join. But neither of them would, shrewdly sensing that Elgar and Delius had created the League in order to break down the sway that they (Parry and Stanford—"the Old Guard") held on British musical life, at least in Festival circles. The first Festival of the League of British Composers was held at Liverpool in 1909 and Delius stipulated that some representative works of mine were to be given. He was a fierce champion of my music at that time and his advocacy of it was the more effective since he seemed cold to wellnigh all other British music. He would say to me: "You are the only composer over here (London) whose music I care for. But you must hear what you write.[2] It is no use just scribbling and scribbling on paper; you must hear how your orchestration actually sounds, otherwise you will never become a practical composer." Kind and sound advice, which I followed. So my compositional career owed as much to Frederick Delius as my pianistic career did to Edvard Grieg.

At about that time (1909–1910) a certain well-known society woman in London was pulling strings (at least, so she said) to get Thomas (now Sir Thomas) Beecham knighted, and she offered to do the like for Delius. "Keep your hands off me," he brusquely replied, "you can make a fool of Tommy if you like, but none of you are going to turn me into a Sir Frederick, that I can tell you!" On such occasions his Bradford, Yorkshire, dialect (always well in evidence) became stronger than ever.

Beecham was his good angel amongst conductors, performing him oftener and better than any other baton wielder. In those years the Delius scores (often rather misleadingly tempo-marked and carelessly edited) were a real puzzle to many conductors, yet Beecham (without even asking Delius for

[2] At that time I (then about 27) had resolved to avoid all public performances of my compositions until I was 40.

advice) always seemed to sense right speeds and interpretations intuitively. Those who worship Delius's genius (and the tenderness and sensitiveness of heart that alone could inspire such touching art) must give thanks to Beecham for all the artistic joy and fulfilment his Delius performances brought into the composer's life. So it was no wonder that he "stuck up" for Beecham (who had been mountaineering with him in Norway, performing, in Delius's opinion, great feats of pluck and endurance) when Ethel Smyth (now Dame Ethel Smyth), the stirring English composer, complained of Beecham's carelessness in producing new operas (he had done hers as well as Delius's):

Delius: "But you can't judge Tommy until you've seen him with his back against the wall."

E. Smyth: "But that is precisely the position I don't want any conductor to get into who produces an opera of mine."

Delius was consistently averse to all nationalism, all patriotism. All reference to his German forebears, to his English birth or to the English quality of his music brought the same reply: "I am a good European" (Nietzsche's words). No partisan could "get any change" out of Delius. When he was in Germany in 1923 he would start to delight his German hearers by criticising the behaviour of the erstwhile Allies, but just when their faces became suffused with pleasure at his remarks he would turn the fire of his criticism upon Germany ("You started the whole thing yourselves") to the great surprise and discomfiture of his listeners.

Six months before the outbreak of the Great War, Delius (with the foresight of several international artists) sensed its coming and transferred all the money he had invested in Europe into North and South American securities. Delius has always been a man of some means, though the end of the war saw him financially threatened—partly due to the fact that so many of his works had been published by German and Austrian publishers. On this occasion the English composer Balfour Gardiner (so often the fairy god-father of British music and the generous benefactor of British composers) came to the rescue with characteristic alacrity. Hearing that the Deliuses found it necessary to sell their lovely Grez home he bought it from them, in quite a businesslike way, and afterwards handed them a paper in which the place was deeded over to them for their lifetimes. Yet Delius had always (good-humouredly and uncensuringly, of course) called Gardiner "the most selfish man in the world";

showing that even the intuition of international composers may fail occasionally.

During the war he wrote "A Pagan Requiem", dedicated to all the young men of all countries that had died in the war, and with the voluminous manuscript of the full score of this composition strapped to his chest, underneath his clothes (in case of shipwreck), he, accompanied by his wife, crossed the submarine-threatened Channel from France to England.

Added to his Yorkshire accent were certain un-English words and phrases (quite unconscious, of course) that lent quaintness to his speech and were the result of so many years of residence in France, Germany and Scandinavia (Delius spent seventeen summers in Norway). One day when he was lamenting the backwardness of music in England he wound up with: "and it's all because of that old canal"—meaning that the English Channel produced insularity. In German and Scandinavian the words for "channel" and "canal" are identical.

In the first weeks of the war the German advance upon Paris threatened Grez and the Deliuses had to flee southward, enduring a long and trying journey in an open railway truck. These and other trials and nervous strains during the war are believed by many to have broken his health (never strong) and paved the way for his blindness and partial paralysis, which loomed up around 1922 (when Delius was about fifty-nine) and were established by 1924. That he was able to live for another ten years was clearly the result of the loving care and wise planning that his utterly devoted wife lavished upon him. Never was invalid better and more tenderly tended and catered for; physically by Jelka and by a succession of male German nurses; artistically by radio, readings aloud and by visits from musicians who played his music to him.

Delius in his invalid chair, emaciated but alert, was a vision of spiritual beauty. He never seemed unhappy or broken in spirit by his helplessness—though, perhaps only he and Jelka could really judge of that. He listened contentedly to book after book of Edgar Wallace, in German translations, read aloud to him by his German nurse, never correcting the latter when he repeatedly pronounced the author's name "Valla-kay"—an instance of Delius's almost Oriental passiveness and stoicism. Another instance of manly stoicism occurred when several of us were rowing him—blind and upright in his chair in the middle of the boat—along the romantically pretty stream that flows past his house. The oar of a passing skiff grazed his chest—not at all violently, but enough, one might think, to upset such a frail invalid. But all Delius said was: "What's that?" with gentle inquisitiveness.

The afore-mentioned German male nurses (one after the other) came to nurse him because they were members of a Protestant Christian brotherhood that laid the obligations of self-sacrificial service upon its members. Yet although he owed the boon of their service to their religious doctrines Delius never dreamed of refraining from spouting his usual atheistic tirades against Christianity in their presence. Delius strove manfully, by constant argument, to undermine their religious beliefs, and in the case of one succeeded, I believe.

This Brother voiced to me one day his surprise that Delius was so anti-Christian and asked me if I were religious. I told him I was not. "And yet you are what I would call a good man, and so is Mr. Delius," said the puzzled Brother. This Brother became deeply attached to Delius, and when, being removed to other service, he begged his Order to allow him to return to Delius and they refused, he killed himself.

Delius had the power to awaken quite unusual devotion in some natures—not that this seems surprising in one possessing so much greater depth of feeling, a brain so much clearer-seeing, and a moral (or shall we call it "immoral"?) courage so much more relentless than most men's. Around 1929 a young North-English musician, composer and organist, Eric Fenby by name, wrote to Delius, saying that he worshipped his music so greatly that he was willing to come to Grez and devote his life to him for several years—act as his musical amanuensis or in any other musical capacity desired. Delius accepted the young man's offer and Fenby was soon installed at Grez, completing Delius's unfinished works from Delius's dictating—an almost insuperable task that both of them accomplished with almost unbelievable concentration and application, giving the world of music a whole sheaf of significant Delius works which without Fenby would forever have remained unfinished, unrealised. The mode of procedure (as described to me) must be unique in musical composition:

Fenby: "What shall we do today?"

Delius: "Get that manuscript with 'Air and Dance' written above it and look up the end where there is a melody without accompaniment. (When MS is produced.) Now put chords to it like those at the end of the Prelude to 'Hassan'."

Fenby: "Something like this?"

Delius: "No, make them sound more hollow. Use more open fifths, like in the 3/2 section for extended strings somewhere near the beginning of 'The Song of the High Hills'. Yes, that's excellent, my lad." (Etc., etc.)

Some of these works, completed through Fenby's amanuensis-ship, were included in the six-day Delius Festival that Sir Thomas Beecham (using several choirs and orchestras) gave in London in 1929, with the invalid composer-genius present, to whom it must have seemed the crowning æsthetic event of his life.

Delius (as may be imagined from what I wrote above) was always a great champion of Grieg's music. A group of modern French composers were engaged in their favourite discussion: To what music is modern French music indebted? With the inevitable reply: To Rameau, Couperin, Lully and so on. At this point Delius chimed in: "Fiddle-sticks! Modern French music is simply Grieg, plus the 3rd act of 'Tristan'." To which Ravel replied: "C'est vrai, c'la. Nous sommes toujours injuste envers Grieg." ("That is true. We are always unjust to Grieg.")

Delius preferred Ravel's music to Debussy's—an unusual judgement. He detested Brahms and (as I have recorded in a former article) made great fun of the Mozart-cult. ("If a man tells me he likes Mozart I know in advance he's a bad musician.") Haydn and Beethoven he liked no better, and it was impossible to interest him in Richard Strauss or Stravinsky and other would-be moderns. Schönbergism he dubbed "the wrong note craze", and when a young Hungarian musician played some Hindemith to him Delius burst out with: "I only know one thing; that that composer has a vulgar soul (eine gemeine Seele)."

As far as I can remember he never varied in his admiration for Bach, Chopin, Wagner and Grieg; though even here it was difficult to foresee his changing moods. One year he would say, "Play me lots of Bach." When I would return next year with my trunk full of Bach he would exclaim: "You know Bach bores me. Can't you play me Chopin's F minor 'Ballade'—the best of the lot?"

In literature Delius and I got on as well as we did in music, for we had in common an almost boundless admiration for the fearlessness and straightness of Scandinavian thinking and its manifestation in books. I never heard Delius adversely criticise the Icelandic Sagas, or waver in his allegiance to the prose and poetry of J. P. Jacobsen and the Norwegian fairy stories collected by Asbjörnsen and Moe (these fairy-tales inspiring his orchestral piece "Eventyr"). He worshipped at the shrines of those two great seers, Walt Whitman and Nietzsche, basing his "Sea Drift" upon the former, his "A Mass of Life" upon the latter.

Delius was very open to influence. Immediately he met me and heard my music he adopted three of my ideas and procedures:

(1) After hearing my "Hillsongs" (I and II) he wrote his "The Song of the High Hills".

(2) After hearing my Passacaglia "Green Bushes" he wrote his "Brigg Fair" and "Dance Rhapsody" in somewhat similar passacaglia-like forms—as contrasted with the variation form he had used in "Appalachia".

(3) After hearing my "wordless syllables" in such numbers as my choral "Irish Tune from County Derry" he adopted that method (in "The Song of the High Hills", etc.) and abandoned the "la la" method employed by him in "Appalachia".

That he could so readily absorb the methods and attitudes of a man twenty years younger than himself proves the elasticity of his mind in middle age. The borrowings I am alluding to are perfectly compatible with intense originality; for it is a fact that anything Delius absorbed into his music became instantly and fully his own. Delius said to me more than once: "I am an affirmative nature (eine bejahende Natur")", and no truer words could be said of his whole personality.

He was in love with life itself, but not with men's views or interpretations of life. Thus he threw himself wholeheartedly into all life's joys (at least, those that pleased him) while he was entirely deaf to all moral superstitions and religions. I doubt if I have ever met a man so impervious to opinions, arguments, ethics, cant. He was unfailingly immoral (anti-moral rather than a-moral) in his judgements, his counsels, and I never on a single occasion heard him give vent to a goody-goody or play-safe viewpoint, or condone one. There are those who considered Delius's paralysis to be the aftermath of his wildness in younger life. If so, one can only say that he paid the price of his joy-worship unflinchingly and unregrettingly. He made fierce fun of my teetotalism and vegetarianism, saying to me: "Why don't you enjoy a nice mug of ale and a good beef steak? Why don't you enjoy yourself while you can?" When he heard that a fine 'cellist (devoted to Delius's music and giving

Delius great joy through his playing of it) was a Christian Scientist he did not attack him openly on that score, but always took care to let fall wounding remarks about the stupidity and gullibility of Christian Scientists.

Delius detested all "churchiness" in music and fell very foul of me for my use of harmonium and organ in my later orchestrations: "Percy, my lad, you'll spoil all your music with that horrible treacly droning sound that comes out of that cathedral over there" (he was living opposite the Frankfurt Cathedral at the time).

When I urged reforms in the make-up of the orchestra, saying that it lacked a proper balance of tone, he would reply: "You people want to reform the orchestra because you don't know how to write for it as it is. I find the orchestra sounds just as I want it to." When I argued against the "sauve qui peut" methods of 19th century life and spoke in favour of co-operative and other strictly organised group movements, he would come back with: "Percy, you have always been an individualist in everything I have known about you." In short, it was impossible to catch him with any isms, any claims, any "movements", any artificial plans. He would not endure a yoke; if he attacked the arguments, the beliefs, the ethics of others with such mischievous glee, it was, maybe, because he felt all moral enslavement to be degrading. His was a balanced, elastic soul, responding to all natural appeals, but with no tendency to limit himself to any doctrine, no leaning to excess or fanaticism in any particular direction. Perhaps that is the secret of the wonderful beauty and sensitiveness of his music— that it arose out of a free soul not enslaved and hardened by habits, beliefs, excesses, exaggerations.

("The Australian Musical News", July 1934.)

Jelka Delius photographed in the garden at Grez in July 1932.

Jelka Delius   by Heinrich Simon

A few months ago the public learnt of the tragic death of Jelka Delius, wife of the composer. People had naturally heard of her before, and some years ago, at the time of the Delius Festival, when Delius, blind and paralysed, was brought over to his native country, she had been spoken of as his devoted companion, as his loving nurse during the dark days of his life, and her devotion had been praised. At her burial, when she was laid to rest beside her beloved husband, no music resounded, no words were spoken to her memory, for his funeral had been too near (only a few days earlier) and she had always kept quietly in the background. As an old friend I feel that this silence must, for once, be broken.

At Delius's funeral Sir Thomas Beecham said that his mortal remains lay in the grave, but that the immortality of the man—his work—lives, and will always live. This is a big way of remembering a great man, because the work of a man is always greater than himself. But for those of us who not only love the work but also knew the man, the memory of his personality is precious too, and we cannot get away from the life of the man who created the work.

The life of Frederick Delius had been linked with that of Jelka, his wife, ever since he settled down in a small village, not very far from Paris, on the river Loing, in 1897. Before that she had been living in Paris, partly with her mother, and partly with a girl friend who, like herself, was studying art in the Latin Quarter, where she had met Delius a few years previously. She was at that time a highly gifted young artist, though she was considered modern, and was influenced, as were most good artists of the day, by the Impressionist school, and by Monet, Seurat, and artists who employed the same technique—Pointilism. She came of a rather conventional family, though they were all people of culture and artistic instincts. On her mother's side she was related to the Moscheles family, who could count among their members a noted musician and painter (the well-known composer and friend of Mendelssohn was her grandfather), and through a brother's marriage she was connected with the family of Charles Dickens.

She must have been a charming, though rather shy, girl. In later days she used to relate how, until the actual moment of her engagement, she could not believe that this good-looking young Englishman, adored, as she knew, by a crowd of beautiful Society women, should be interested in her. Delius must have been exceedingly attractive at that time, and indeed, in his latter years, when blind and paralysed, he was still so. He was so natural, so devoid of prejudice, so absolutely independent, and at the same time so cultured, refined and noble in his attitude towards life and men. Soon after his meeting with Jelka Rosen he went back to Florida to settle up his affairs. After a very short time he must have realised that she was the ideal companion for him, for almost immediately on his return he sought her out in her new home at Grez, which in the meantime she and her mother had bought—and there he settled down to work for the rest of his life.

Very often some instinct tells a man of this kind what is best. It is not selfishness in the ordinary sense; it is an economy of nature, which seeks to get the utmost out of what it meets with. Creative genius must be selfish. Delius was no exception and in that sense was an egoist. He must surely have felt that this woman would become his best and most devoted friend and yet would not lose her own personality—a thought abhorrent to Delius, who hated colourless people and loved the beauty and variety of life. He was a good traveller and liked reading new books and meeting new friends. In his time he had loved all the sensations that life could offer. But he always came back to this lovely place on the river, to this old-fashioned garden with its tall old trees, riot of flowers, and the sound of church-bells in the air. Jelka was the guardian of this garden. The idea that a genius can work and create under whatever circumstances he may live is nonsense. What possibilities are often lost because a man has not the chance of perfect environment in which to write, paint, or compose what comes to him as a revelation! I am absolutely sure—and he himself knew it too—that without Jelka Delius would never have accomplished his work in the way he did.

Her sacrifice was great. She was a genuine artist. Anyone who knows something of pictures and art and has seen some of her work—the little she managed to get through by the side of this man to whom she had devoted practically every hour of her life—will realise how great the sacrifice was. Throughout his life Delius was deeply interested in art. In his younger days he even preferred to have painters and writers rather than musicians as friends. Can we ascribe this to the influence of Jelka? One can never distinguish between cause and effect in personal relationships. Earlier works of Delius such as "Irmelin" and "Margot la Rouge", which have never been printed, do not show the definite facility for sound-painting which appears so strikingly in later works. It is quite possible that through living with an artist of the talent and taste of Jelka Delius developed his inborn sense of colour.

When the Deliuses settled in Grez, the place had not yet been "discovered" by the Paris painters. With her charming sense of humour Jelka used to tell stories of how some ecclesiastical neighbour was shocked at seeing her beautiful young female models walking up and down in the garden as though in Paradise. She was a splendid story-teller. Listening to her telling the life-stories of the people of the village with her talent for vivid portraiture, you would think that you were hearing a tale by Maupassant. I visited her at Grez at the beginning of this year, six months after her husband's death. Still devoted to his memory to the exclusion of all else, she read to me some of her reminiscences. There are only a few chapters, but they ought to be published as a document which vividly portrays the charm of her personality. Only one who has from the very beginning closely watched her struggle against her husband's disease, the unceasing efforts to find the right doctor, the best cure, and later on the suitable nurse for the difficult patient, can estimate the moral strength and human greatness necessary to endure all this. She lived through all her struggles with the same encouraging enthusiasm, with the same hopeful smile, when circumstances led to disappointment, never losing sight of her friends and their troubles, in spite of her own difficulties.

Some may argue that by being so lovingly spoiled by her and kept so far away from all the difficulties with which most other creative artists have to contend before the hand of fate fell upon him, Delius may have become, in a way, too happy, too remote from the tragedies of life. And as this tragic side of life is such a very real one, it may be held that her great love and devotion to a certain extent impeded a development which he might have acquired through darker and sadder experience. I do not agree with this view. I think he was born to listen to the harmony of nature and sounds around him, to all the beauty which nature and life could give, so that he could reproduce them in his work. Through Jelka he fulfilled his mission, and because of her he was able to fulfil it. It was fate which helped him to find this wonderful companion, who was so strong in her devotion that, as a dying invalid, she could hardly be prevented from leaving her bed of sickness because she felt that she must be present at the funeral of the man who had meant the whole world to her throughout her life. Strength through devotion has become a rare quality in our time. It is good to know that it still exists.

("The Monthly Musical Record", December 1935.)

Memories of Delius
by Cecil Gray

My first acquaintance with the music of Delius dates back to
1912, when I heard what was announced as the first performance of a new work entitled *In a Summer Garden*, given by the
Scottish Orchestra in Edinburgh under a Polish conductor
named Emil Mlynarski. I was considerably mystified, and in
retrospect I am not at all surprised, having since heard many
mystifying performances of the music of Delius under conductors and with orchestras much better qualified to interpret
it. Nevertheless, enough of the composer's mentality filtered
through what must undoubtedly have been an abominable performance to give me the sense of contact with something rare
and unusual.

My next experience of his art was a performance of *Sea Drift*,
given by Sir Thomas Beecham, which must have taken place in
1915 or 1916, in Queen's Hall, London. On this occasion any
doubts or uncertainties I may have entertained concerning *In a
Summer Garden* were completely dispelled. I was profoundly
moved by the experience, and when, shortly later, under
circumstances I have described elsewhere[1] I came by chance to
know Philip Heseltine, who was then Delius's *aide-de-camp* and
standard-bearer, I became one of the most devoted adherents
to his cause. At the same time, I was never such a wholehearted
worshipper at the shrine as Philip was. His excessive reliance on
cloying and over-luscious harmonic mannerisms, particularly
his fondness for interminable series of chromatically descending
sevenths, which he had learnt and taken over from Grieg, together with his complete formal invertebracy, especially in
works written on a large scale, repelled me as much as the
quality of latent feeling and emotion attracted me.

I only came to know Delius personally in the last year of the
war (1918), when he visited England; but from then onwards
until his death we were in close contact whenever he was in

---

[1] *Peter Warlock*. (Jonathan Cape 1934)

England or I in France, and on several occasions I stayed with him and his wife, Jelka, at his house in Grez-sur-Loing, near Fontainebleau.

Even at the time when I most admired his work I cannot honestly say that I enjoyed these visits, and I always used to heave a sigh of relief on my departure. There was something indescribably sinister about the household—and I am by no means the only one to have felt it—even before the onset of the terrible illness from which he increasingly suffered for so many years, and eventually died. Mr. Eric Fenby[2] has already described these latter years at length, and so vividly that I am glad to be absolved, on the plea of redundance, from any necessity for traversing the same ground again. I can only say that I am amazed at Mr. Fenby's fortitude in enduring, for several years, experiences that nearly drove me insane after only a few days.

Delius, it must be frankly admitted, was not a lovable man at the best of times, and his character was not of the kind that improves or mellows with illness and the passing of the years. Heroic courage and endurance in the face of his afflictions he certainly displayed, but once that has been said there is nothing else left to say in his favour as a human being. Always a pitiless egotist, interested in no person but himself, in nothing on earth but music, but ultimately in no other music than his own, except that of Chopin and Grieg, and that only because he had taken so much from them: he became, in the terrible last years, an absolute tyrant, dominating the entire lives of those who surrounded him and draining their vitality like a vampire. These may seem strong words, and too melodramatic, but no one who came within that orbit, I am sure, will question their truth.

Nothing about Delius was more extraordinary than the contrast between his art and his personality; the former characterized chiefly by an almost overpowering sweetness, gentleness and tenderness: the latter by hardness, cruelty and callousness. It is interesting to compare him in this respect with Béla Bartók who, as I have said already, was the absolute antithesis of Delius in every respect. One thing, and one only, they possessed in common: a complete devotion to art, and an equally complete indifference to any art other than their own. But while Delius in his work chiefly aimed at, and achieved, a sense of pity and tenderness, the perfect expression of the Virgilian *lacrimae rerum*, and was in life, in his relationships with fellow-mortals

[2] *Delius as I Knew Him.* (Bell 1936, Quality Press 1948, Icon Books 1966).

cold, hard and ruthless; Bartók, on the contrary, displayed in his art, especially in his middle period, an almost sadistic violence and brutality, but as a man was kindly, shy, diffident, gentle and wholly lovable.

This paradoxical dichotomy is less uncommon than might be supposed; in fact, it may even be the rule rather than the exception. The artist whose life and work are all of a piece is a rare phenomenon: more often than not it will be found that in his work he aspires towards his opposite.

"When I think of any great poetical writer of the past," (says Yeats), "I comprehend, if I know the lineaments of his life, that the work is the man's flight from his entire horoscope, his blind struggle in the network of the stars."

Yeats himself, so he sometimes said, would sooner have been a man of action than a poet. Similarly, General Wolfe would rather have written Gray's *Elegy* than won great battles. The over-sexed Tolstoy continually preached asceticism; the under-sexed D. H. Lawrence was obsessed by the sexual act almost to the exclusion of everything else in human life. Nietzsche, who continually exhorted his disciples to be hard, strong and callous, was himself the mildest and gentlest of mortals, incapable of hurting a fly; and it was this inner contradiction which ultimately destroyed him. It is, in fact, recorded that one fateful day in Turin, after having penned a masterly chapter of his *Will to Power*, decrying the Christian virtues of meekness, gentleness and pity, and glorifying the pagan virtues of pride, strength and ruthlessness, Nietzsche went out into the street and saw there an Italian cab-driver unmercifully beating his horse; whereupon the eloquent apostle of the manly pagan virtues burst into tears, threw his arms around the neck of the astonished and, no doubt, slightly embarrassed quadruped, kissed it on the nose, and was then led quietly away to the lunatic asylum from which he never again emerged except to be taken to another kindred establishment.

This brings us back to Delius, whose most ambitious work is undoubtedly the *Mass of Life*, from the *Also sprach Zarathustra* of Nietzsche. But such is the strange complexity of the nature of the heart of man, that although Delius in his personal life was a very much better Nietzschean than Nietzsche himself, and consistently behaved in the manner approved of by the master, the music of the *Mass of Life* frequently belies the intention of glorifying the pagan values and breathes a spirit of tender melancholy and wistful resignation which are exceedingly difficult to reconcile with the ideal expressed in Nietzsche's famous injunction: "Be hard, my brethren!" Sadness, in fact, keeps breaking in, and the pages in which it does so are generally more convincing than the triumphant hymns in praise of the joys of life.

This curious and inexplicable contradiction is characteristic of everything about Delius. A violent, bigoted, doctrinaire atheist, he spent his last years surrounded and cosseted by representatives of every variety of Christian faith, from Roman Catholic to Moravian Brother, to say nothing of the occasional intrusion of a Buddhist mystic or a theosophist; he professed to despise England and everything English, and lived his entire life abroad; yet, in the last days of his life it was his expressed desire to be laid to rest in an English churchyard. This is, to say the least, disconcerting. If there had been a dramatic last-minute deathbed conversion to the faith against which he had rebelled all his life, *that* one could have understood.

But there was nothing of the kind. Up to the end he remained an unrepentant old pagan. Why this Christian burial in England ? Why this combination in the end, of the two things he had always disdained above everything else ? Perhaps, after all, the explanation is simpler than it might appear to be. The quintessential spirit of his best work has always seemed to me to be fundamentally Christian, and essentially English. As I have written elsewhere:[3]

> "How magically do the first few pages of *Brigg Fair* evoke the atmosphere of an early summer morning in the English countryside, with its suggestion of a faint mist veiling the horizon, and the fragrant scent of the dawn in the air! What art could be more fitly described as 'simple, sensuous, and passionate ?' . . . It is as well to bear in mind that this very sweetness and sensuousness is perhaps the most noteworthy characteristic of English art . . . It is the very quintessence of the English spirit."

So, also, is his characteristic indifference to problems of formal construction. I can imagine how the old man would have writhed if I had told him to his face that he was at heart a Christian and an Englishman—I would never have had the courage! But I believe it is the ultimate truth, none the less, and

[3] *A Survey of Contemporary Music*, Oxford University Press, 1924

that his last expressed wish clearly shows it. Yet in the end one has to come back again to the question: which is the fundamental Delius—the ruthless egotist that he was in his life, or the tender, wistful idealist that he was in his best work? In short, is Yeats right when he suggests that in his art man aspires towards his opposite? And if so, which is the intrinsic, ultimate reality—the man or the work?

So far as I am personally concerned, I have already indicated the presence of a very decided dichotomy in my nature which corresponds in a sense with that postulated by Yeats: represented by the composer and the critic, the musician and the writer. But without entering again into the question as to whether I am both, alternatively one or other, or neither, I am conscious of being completely consistent within the terms of each separate aspect of my duality. In neither the music nor the words I write am I "in flight from my entire horoscope." As a critic, it is true that I am attracted to my opposite, as I have already abundantly shown, but the kind of prose I write is by no means that which I most admire, or would choose to write if I had any choice in the matter. And so in music, as I have said, my critical admiration for the work of others has never enabled me to assimilate anything from them, however much I have wished to or tried. I cannot escape from my horoscope, in fact, with the best will in the world. The network of the stars holds me as a spider's web holds a fly. I am chained to my affinities like a prisoner to the walls of his cell. If I had my will and my way, I would write prose like Walter Savage Landor, but I know I cannot; and I would infinitely prefer to write music like that of van Dieren, or Bartók, or Sibelius, if only I could, rather than that which I do.—Not Delius, observe. I would not choose to write like Delius; perhaps because he is a partial affinity, too close in some respects, too far apart in others.

I have already spoken of his lack of formal sense, and his complete indifference to such considerations, while for me form is the primary consideration in a work of art. Again, I always find myself irresistibly drawn to contrapuntal writing, whereas Delius is the most homophonic of composers—the fugue in the *Mass of Life* is unique in his work, and a dismal failure at that. For me, melody is the most important element in the musical synthesis; for Delius it was harmony. But there is one striking and curious affinity between us, namely, a common pre-dilection for similar melodic formulas—curious, because this element, so far as I am concerned, derives unmistakably from

Hebridean folk-song, which I came to know before I ever heard a note of Delius, and which Delius never knew at all. There is, for example, a melodic progression in the *finale* of his music to *Hassan* which is almost note for note identical with one of the themes in my *Deirdre*, yet there can be no question of direct influence one way or the other, since my melody existed on paper long before Delius wrote his incidental music to Flecker's play, and he did not see my opera until after he had completed his score.

I can only ascribe this coincidence—and there are others like it—to a common experience: that which is known to mystics as "the state of illumination", a kind of ecstatic revelation which may only last for a split second of time, but which he who has known it spends the rest of his life trying to recapture. It is not necessarily an attribute of great art. Some of the greatest have never experienced it, while many lesser talents have, and some with no talent at all; but those who have experienced it can always recognize the presence of the peculiar quality which appertains to it. The music of Delius is an example, and I was immediately aware of it in the first work of his I heard, in spite of an imperfect performance. I knew, too, the exact moment at which that experience must have occurred in Delius's life, and when I asked him if it were so and if I were right, he was surprised and admitted that I was. The occasion was one summer night, when he was sitting out on the verandah of his house in his orange grove in Florida, and the sound came to him from the near distance of the voices of the negroes in the plantation, singing in chorus. It is the rapture of this moment that Delius is perpetually seeking to communicate in all his most characteristic work.

Nothing Delius ever wrote is a flawless masterpiece. He lives, and will continue to live, by virtue of exquisite passages of almost unendurable sweetness and poignancy, in which he succeeds in recapturing that moment of ecstasy experienced in his youth. Those to whom such moments have never occurred will probably find nothing in Delius. Those to whom they have, will forgive him much for his manifold imperfections, of which no one is more acutely conscious than I, in spite of his intimate, personal appeal to me.

It must have been the recognition of this deep fundamental understanding between us that impelled his wife, Jelka, after his death, to approach me with a view to inducing me to write the "official biography" of the master: a suggestion to which I reluctantly acquiesced out of a sense of duty (for I did not at all relish the task), but only on condition that I should be allowed an absolutely free hand to write as I thought and felt, without concealment of any facts or adverse critical judgments. I insisted on an absolute *carte blanche*, in fact, to which she gave her consent. Nothing came of the project, however, as the result of a letter which I received from her, dated 14th December, 1934.

Grez-sur-Loing.

MY DEAR GRAY,

Yesterday I had a letter from Beecham. He proposes to write the biography himself; in fact he says that most of it is already written in a number of essays on the Delius works, and he wants to do the remaining portions with the aid of a young writer under his leadership. This rôle you could, of course, never accept, and needs a willing collaborator under Beecham's orders. You will, I hope, understand that I cannot do otherwise than accept Beecham's proposal.

I never expected this, as he has already such multiple activities, but of course he holds all the threads of the Delius in his hands and it is natural for him to wish to be associated with him also in a literary way.

Yours ever affectionately,
JELKA DELIUS.

Jelka died shortly after writing me the letter quoted above, worn out by the strain and stress of the many years of utter devotion which she had dedicated to the art in which she believed so completely—for I am more than inclined to think that it was the art rather than the man that she was in love with. It would have been surprising were it otherwise, for, as I have already indicated, Delius was a singularly unlovable man, and life with him must have been a purgatory at the best of times, until it became a hell at the worst.

I doubt, in fact, whether there was ever any real, deep, human relationship between these two strange people. Jelka herself was an artist *manquée*, a painter of appalling pictures in which the predominating colour key was a sickly pink, and which hung in scores on the walls of the house at Grez, contributing in no small degree to its depressing atmosphere. She had entirely given up her own art on uniting her life with that of Delius, and sought to realize herself through him and his art—chiefly his art, in which she felt herself fulfilled. He, on his side, received in return the care and attention which he needed in order to achieve his work.

I am confirmed in the belief that such was the basis of their relationship by the fact that he was always insisting that there could be no other possible form of marriage for an artist. The speech recorded by Mr. Eric Fenby[4] was one which he had already made to Philip Heseltine and to me, and no doubt to many others. Its burden was indeed an obsession with him. I quote from Mr. Fenby's version:

> "No artist should ever marry . . . Amuse yourself with as many women as you like, but for the sake of your art never marry one. It's fatal. And if you ever do have to marry, marry a girl who is more in love with your art than with you."

I think Jelka would have subscribed to that dictum and supported it with a statement of her own complementary belief, namely, that a woman should not marry a man for love of him, but for the work of which he was potentially capable, or for children. They despised love, in fact; and I even sometimes think that Jelka hated Delius the man as much as she worshipped the artist. She had every reason. His selfishness and callousness towards her, in spite of his complete and utter dependence on her for everything, was sometimes horrifying to witness. Yet I only once remember her uttering a single word of complaint, reproach, or resentment against his behaviour during these last terrible years when, in reply to some particularly unkind and unjust remark on his part she said sadly, with beautiful dignity: "I sometimes wonder, Fred, whether you ever realize how unkind you are to me, and how deeply you wound me. If you did, I cannot believe you could do it." But it had no more effect on him than on a stone. He merely rolled his head slowly from side to side, with a sardonic sneer on his tightly pursed lips. Whatever his sufferings—and no doubt they were great—I felt at the time, and still feel, that no human being has the right to inflict such unmerited torment on another one, so utterly devoted as she was. With all my admiration for his art I find it difficult to forgive Delius for such inhumanity. And when one tries to reconcile this trait with the gentleness and tenderness of his best music, one has to confess oneself baffled. Never has there been a stranger or more violent dichotomy.

At the same time, it must always be borne in mind that in

4 Op. cit.

herself ultimately she was nothing, possessing only, in superlative degree, the great feminine capacity of self-sacrifice and
dedication to an ideal embodied in one person; and that through
him she achieved a fulfilment which she would otherwise never
have known. She suffered greatly, but with an ecstatic pain,
like that of the early Christian martyrs—no woman who has
ever lived has had such a highly developed capacity for self-
immolation as Jelka Delius—and it may well be that in the
balance, when all things are weighed, she accomplished her
destiny. She believed implicitly that Delius was the greatest
composer of all time, and if she had doubted it for a single
moment she could never have endured what she did. Ironically
enough, it was the fact that she understood so little of music
that enabled her to cherish this fond delusion. In the end she
reaped the reward of her long martyrdom and devotion. She
lived to experience the triumphant apotheosis of the art of
Delius in the great festival devoted to his work which was given
by Sir Thomas Beecham in 1929; and she was fortunate in not
living long enough to witness the inevitable automatic reaction
against it, or to suffer even for a moment the slightest doubt in
the reality of her faith and vision. For that reason she may
surely be accounted to have had a happy life, and even to have
achieved the summit of earthly bliss; but what she had to
endure in order to achieve this ultimate felicity seemed, to the
eyes of the objective beholder, and even to that of the subjective
sympathizer and admirer of the art of Delius, as I then was, and
with qualifications still am, wholly incommensurate with the
reward. But of that no one can judge save the person concerned.

So far as his views on the married state in connexion with
artists is concerned, I must admit that I believe him to be right.
In other words, there may be many happy exceptions, but as a
rule marriage is fatal to artists unless they have already achieved
material success or have independent means. I have seen too
many promising artists wrecked on the shoals of matrimony to
be able to doubt it.

I have already said that Frederick Delius, considered simply
as a human being, was one of the strangest and most inexplicable who has ever lived; and that as an artist also he was
singular, unique, unclassifiable. Not the least strange thing
about his art is the flagrant contradiction that exists between his
early and mature work. With all its beauty there is in the latter
an unmistakably morbid quality—and I use the adjective both
in its original Latin signification of "diseased" and in its Italian

143

derivative meaning of "over-softness"—which stands in striking contrast to the more virile, energetic, exuberant quality of the former, as exemplified particularly in the Piano Concerto, *Paris*, and other works of the same period. But the contrast is not merely one of thought and feeling, but also of technical mastery. The early works referred to are in many ways much more accomplished than the later ones; so much so, in fact, that the orchestral virtuosity of *Paris* and the pianistic brilliance of the Concerto have, to many admirers, only appeared explicable as the outcome of a collaboration on the part of some hitherto unidentified partner or "ghost".

The suggested explanation is plausible, but I think unsound. Apart from the fact that there is not a shred of material evidence in support of it, I am convinced that the clue to the problem is to be found in the affliction from which Delius suffered, the cause of his blindness, paralysis, and death, and to which it is now possible to refer without giving offence to any living person namely, syphilis. It is to this source that I attribute the lack of formal balance and critical sense, the technical instability and cloying chromaticism, the phenomenal egocentricity amounting almost to *folie de grandeur* which characterize his later years. It is significant in this connexion to note that his friend, Paul Gauguin, the painter, whose art is so closely akin, in both qualities and defects, to his own, also suffered from the same malady. Note, moreover, the same striking contrast between the early, virile work of Gauguin in his Breton period and the nostalgic, opulent art of his latter years in the South Seas. The equation is precisely the same in both cases, and I cannot believe that it is a mere coincidence.

I conclude these recollections and observations concerning Delius with an extract from a letter which he wrote me concerning my *Survey of Contemporary Music*; not so much on account of its initial testimonial, which was no doubt prompted to a great extent, if not entirely, by the glowing eulogy of his own work which is contained in my book, as because it sums up in a few words his whole simple æsthetic creed.

MY DEAR GRAY,

Many thanks for your book, which you so kindly sent me. I have just finished it and have read it with the keenest interest. I am full of admiration for the sincerity, the breadth and fearlessness of your outlook. As a survey of contemporary music it stands alone. I will not mention your style and erudition, which are of course amazing.

In my opinion there is no music without emotion; it is the first and last essential of beautiful music and intellectuality must only play a secondary rôle. Hence all these researches of quarter tones and atonality will and can lead nowhere. Ugly sounds are not music, nor have they anything to do with music. I have not heard *Pierrot Lunaire* but what I have heard of Schönberg was either weak Brahms or weak Wagner, or very academically constructed ugly sounds. A monstrous orchestra does not make the *Gurrelieder* either strong or original. Musical theorists have as yet never been able to write beautiful music—whether they are called Busoni or Schönberg. The real musical genius writes for no other purpose but to express his own soul, and in so doing finds life's greatest satisfaction and joy.

Despite the naïvety of expression, I do not think that Delius was fundamentally wrong in his definition of music. Where he was utterly and preposterously wrong was in denying validity to any and every other kind of emotion than his own. To be unable to find anything in Schönberg or Busoni but perverse intellectualism is wildly absurd. The violent, Strindbergian emotionalism of Schönberg is the first and most important thing about him; the deep feeling of Busoni, though much more subtle and complex, is no less real and fundamental . . .

("Musical Chairs", Home and Van Thal, 1948.)

Delius in America   by William Randel

Frederick Delius twice visited the United States. The first visit, of about twenty-six months, was of great significance to his eventual career as a composer: he was in Florida from March 1884 until September 1885, and then in Virginia until the May (or June) of 1886. The second visit, in 1897, was very brief, for specific business purposes.

Like Elgar, Delius was largely self-made as a composer. His one extended period of formal instruction, under the master teachers at Leipzig where he went in the fall of 1886, was disappointing. He may have been exaggerating when he remarked that the only teaching of any real value to him was the instruction in counterpoint given by Thomas Ward, a former Brooklyn organist who had moved to Florida for his health. If true, this can hardly be counted among his debts to America; somebody else, in Norway, in France, in England, might have taught him counterpoint; it was mere chance that he met Ward in Jacksonville. But in no other country he visited could Delius have been exposed to the lush semi-tropical sights and sounds of Solano Grove, or to the Afro-American melodies he heard there and in Virginia, which were so remote from European tradition and so unmistakable in his music—in the *Florida Suite*, for example, or *Koanga*, or *Appalachia*. The American influence on his music does not stand alone, but it is close to being central and in any event, for such a musical individualist as Delius, outweighs in significance a few lessons in counterpoint.

Delius first crossed the Atlantic aboard the *Gallia*, a Cunarder leaving Liverpool on 2nd March, 1884, and docking at New York on the fifteenth or sixteenth, after a stormy passage. Nobody on the passenger list was important enough to interest the reporters; the only individual mentioned in the press was the barkeeper, George Paynter, for whom this was his five-hundredth crossing.[1] In New York at the time, southbound

[1] "Marine Intelligence", New York *Times*, March 3, 17, 1884; "City and Suburban News", March 16, 1884.

travellers had their choice of three competing coastal lines—
Mallory, Clyde's, and the Ocean Steamship Company; depending on which of these Delius chose, he would have landed either
at Fernandina, on the coast northeast of Jacksonville, or at
Jacksonville itself, some dozen miles up the bar-plagued St.
Johns River,[2] one of the few major rivers in the United States
flowing north. The final forty miles by water, up the St. Johns
to Picolata, would have been on one or another of the numerous
packets. From the Picolata landing Delius had to go about five
miles, by wagon on a primitive road or by a small boat, to
Solano Grove. The entire trip from England, if he did not
linger in New York or Jacksonville, must have been a matter
of at least eighteen days.

Solano Grove and its environs were hardly as isolated in the
1880's as Sir Thomas Beecham and other Delius biographers
seem to have supposed.[3] True, the cottage Delius occupied
was on its own ample tract, but that area of Florida was already
well developed, and he had neighbours easily accessible by
boat, many of them, incidentally, recent transplants from
England. Jacksonville was close enough, and riverboats numerous enough and with regular schedules, to make going there an
easy trip; and Tacoi, a river community just beyond Picolata,
was connected by rail with St. Augustine on the Atlantic coast.[4]
Indeed, for his first arrival Delius could have landed there
instead of at Jacksonville and reached Solano overland, by railroad to Tacoi, and then by wagon.

Solano Grove was a property of about a hundred acres,
quite flat, on the east bank of the St. Johns River, which at that
part of its course is four miles wide, a virtual lake. The name
derived from Matthew Solana, a member of the Secession
Commission just prior to the Civil War,[5] who bought the tract
from the state for fifty cents an acre. In the years following
there were numerous changes in ownership, with some portions

[2] James Wood Davidson, *The Florida of To-day; a Guide for Tourists
and Settlers* (New York, 1889), pp. 72–73.
[3] Sir Thomas Beecham, *Frederick Delius* (London, 1959). Clare
Delius, *Memories of My Brother* (London, 1935).
[4] George W. Pettengill, Jr., *The Story of the Florida Railroads,
1834–1903* (Boston, 1952). An advertisement in the *Florida Times
Union* (Jacksonville) for October 14, 1883, suggests taking the river
and rail route to St. Augustine. "No dust! Well Ballasted! Smooth
Track!" Trains left Tacoi at noon and 3:45 P.M.; the one-way fare was
88¢, the round trip $1.50.
[5] Caroline Mays Brevard, *A History of Florida* . . . (Deland, Fla.,
1924), Vol. II, Appendix 5.

being sold off, and a considerable fluctuation in price. In 1880, when the buyer was Guy R. Pride of Honeoye Falls, New York, the cost was $1,500, and it was $6,500 when Pride sold it to Julius Delius on 13th August, 1884.[6] This was not, however, an instance of gouging a trans-Atlantic purchaser, for Pride had improved the property and had built a substantial cottage "in Yankee style", facing the river and about fifty feet from its bank. A centred front door opened to a hall off which were four rooms, each with windows on two walls and a fireplace; the walls were plastered. Two chimneys served the four fireplaces. Above was an unfinished attic. There was no cellar; the house stood on posts about two feet above the ground, open underneath for welcome ventilation—in this Pride followed the Southern style rather than the Northern. Verandahs in front and back were shaded by the pitched cottage roof, broken only by a low gable over the front door. The kitchen was a separate structure connected with the house by an open-roofed passage,[7] a common plan in the South. The term "shack" or "shanty" applied to this house by authors of books on Delius is absurdly inappropriate for the house when Fritz lived there. Later, after years of standing vacant, it lost its white paint and acquired the run-down look and shabbiness of any abandoned building. Fritz, with his characteristic Yorkshire flair for straight-faced deception (he once told an interviewer that he had been born of poor but honest parents), had apparently used the word "shanty" in a letter to his sister Clare, who later used it in her biography of him. True, the rooms were small in comparison with the family house, almost a mansion, in Bradford, but they were ample even when Delius's Bradford neighbour Charles Douglas was there, or when Thomas Ward came from Jacksonville for a visit, or when Delius's brother Ernst showed up unexpectedly.

As spring gave way to summer, Fritz must have suffered, as any north European would, from the intense inland heat. The river, and the breeze sweeping across it, would have some-

---

[6] Abstract of title. Copies of titles and deeds are in the Delius Collection, Haydon Burns Library, Jacksonville, Florida. Julius Delius first had an option to purchase.

[7] The house can be seen today on the campus of Jacksonville University where it was moved and completely restored in the 1960's. The description of the original house was given to me orally by Harvey Pride, the builder's son, on February 1, 1962, at the formal dedication of the restored cottage. The kitchen wing was not moved to Jacksonville.

what tempered the humidity; but even more welcome was the dense shade of the great live oaks, with wide-spreading horizontal limbs festooned with Spanish moss. If Fritz was indolent, indolence was a way of life in the Florida summer before air-conditioning. With no experience or instruction in citrus cultivation, with his mind preoccupied by thoughts of music, and with his senses deluged with strange new impressions, it is easy to understand why Fritz did not turn oranges to profit as his money-minded father apparently expected him to do without delay.

A few of the orange trees, gnarled with age but still producing fruit (not salable but edible), survive of the grove set out by one of Fritz's predecessors at Solano Grove. Today, that part of Florida is somewhat north of the commercial citrus belt; the risk of winter frost is too great to warrant large-scale citriculture. In the 1870's, however, and until 1886, when a severe winter killed many of the groves and ruined their owners, oranges were a rapidly growing crop in all that northeastern part of Florida. The most famous grove was probably Harriet Beecher Stowe's at Mandarin, about twenty miles north of Solano; and Duval County, surrounding Jacksonville, once ranked sixth among Florida's counties in the annual harvest.[8] A book issued in 1883, *Practical Orange Culture*, gave all the details prospective growers could want and, though it did not help young Delius, it may have contributed to the record set on 15th December, 1884, when nearly eight thousand boxes, averaging 130 oranges to the box, were delivered at Jacksonville warehouses; the packet *Chattahoochee* unloaded 3,190 of the boxes, the largest single cargo recorded up to that time.[9] Delius arrived, it is evident, at the very peak of citrus production.

Like many another developing region, north Florida had its active promoters encouraging settlers. The English migrants so numerous along the St. Johns above Jacksonville had responded, unquestionably, to an effective promotional campaign. The Land Mortgage Bank of Florida, Limited, maintained a London office in Whitehall and branches in several other English cities including Bradford. It is reasonable to conjecture that either Julius Delius visited the Bradford office and con-

[8] Pleasant Daniel Gold, *History of Duval County, including Early History of East Florida* (St. Augustine, 1929); Morita M. Clark, "The Development of the Citrus Industry in Florida before 1895", unpublished M.A. thesis, Florida State University, 1947.
[9] *Florida Times Union*, December 16, 1884.

ceived the notion of sending his wayward son to grow oranges in Florida, or that Fritz himself saw it as a way to escape the hated family wool business and suggested the idea to his father.

Statistics in books and pamphlets about Florida that were being widely circulated in Great Britain in the early 1880's were no doubt reassuring to the practical wool merchant. Jacksonville was growing fast: its population increased from 6,912 in 1870 to about 14,500 in 1883–1884; but an annual influx of winter visitors—estimated at 49,000 in 1883–1884, 60,000 in 1884–1885, and 65,000 in 1885–1886[10]—stimulated business of every sort but particularly the tourist trade. In those days only a few daring vacationists went further south; Jacksonville was enjoying its heyday as "Winter City in Summerland". The St. James, the National, the Duval, the Everett and the Carleton were all substantial and justifiably popular hotels. When the St. James was built in 1869 it was dubbed "the Fifth Avenue Hotel of Florida"; in 1883 it boasted the first electric lights anywhere in the state—eight in the lobby and eight outside. The Sunnyside and the Grand View followed suit in January 1884. By 1885 a second generator was built in Jacksonville to supply the lighting for bazaars, curio-shops, and stores along Bay Street, and the next year a third generator was extending current to private homes and more of the hotels. Streets were of sand, seventy to eighty feet wide, bordered by walks of bricks or planks and lighted by gas until conversion to electricity began in 1885. The greatest attraction was the abundance of live oaks with their far-spreading branches and dense shade. Horsecar lines connected the railroad depots and made a circuit past the chief hotels and fine mansions. Drinking water was abundant and of excellent quality. The St. Johns River, which made Jacksonville the major port of a vast trade region, was pleasing to look at and, conversely, the view of the thriving city from the numerous sight-seeing steamboats was exciting. Visitors may not have been greatly interested in the five lumbermills and the two brickyards that were kept busy by the expanding construction, or the fourteen cigar factories, or the wholesale food distributors, but for business-man Julius Delius, reading the statistics of commercial growth, they were tangible proof of solidity. This was an Eden he could appreciate, with a productive capacity of its own and a

[10] T. Frederick Davis, *History of Jacksonville, Florida and Vicinity, 1513 to 1924* (Jacksonville, 1925).

promise of wealth for men willing to work—as he must have hoped that Fritz would be inspired to do. The large number of English families who had settled in the city and region was one further source of reassurance; this was no frontier outpost peopled by ruffians.[11]

What Julius overlooked, if he actually weighed the probabilities from the facts and figures available, was that Jacksonville, during the winter season at least, was a veritable hive of culture —a role encouraged by the thousands of refugees from colder climes. American communities had much more live theatre and music in the late nineteenth century than after the advent of movies and radio, but Jacksonville, from the evidence, had a disproportionate share. From December to March, for every year-round resident there were three or four visitors, demanding entertainment and able to pay for it. Shortly before Delius arrived, the Park Opera House, seating 1,200, opened on Washington's Birthday with a performance of *Faust* starring Minnie Hauck. During the tourist season not a week passed without a stage production of some sort, put on by touring professional troupes or stars, or by local dramatic clubs or church groups.

Even more distracting, for a youth as enamoured of music as Fritz Delius, was the rich musical life of Jacksonville. At several of the hotels the Negro waiters doubled as singers, with daily vocal concerts for patrons and passers-by; if Delius paused only long enough to eat one meal in the city before going on to Solano Grove, he may well have had his introduction to Negro spirituals and folk songs. Then, aboard the riverboat for the final leg of his journey, it is quite probable that he heard more vocalising; for ship owners encouraged the deckhands to sing as they worked, or between their watches. Delius never forgot the singing as he heard it, day or night, carried sweet and clear across the water to his verandah at Solano Grove, whenever a steamship passed; it is hard to imagine conditions less conducive to cultivating oranges—or more conducive to composing.

The water-borne singing was a constant reminder that in Jacksonville, a bare three hours away, were several music stores, frequent concerts, numerous professional musicians, most of them European, and youngsters eager for instruction. "Professor" George Frisch, a graduate of the Royal Institute of

[11] Information about Jacksonville in the 1880's is found in Davis, Gold, and in the files of the *Florida Times Union* (Jacksonville). Promotional literature includes George M. Barbour, *Florida for Tourists, Invalids and Settlers* . . . (New York, 1882).

Saxony, advertised for piano and organ pupils; his contact point was Clark's Music Store on Bay Street. Victor E. Metzger, "Pianist, from Leipzig Conservatory", sought pupils in all grades, and another teacher offered "Music Lessons given in Exchange for Dressmaking". Baratta's Band was available "for all occasions".[12] Mr. Campbell of Campbell's Music Store told a reporter in March 1884 that he had recently sold eight pianos in a single day, and forty organs in a month—nineteen of them to Negroes. He handled Bay State and Mason & Hamlin organs, Chickering, Arion, Mathusek, and Grovesteen & Fuller pianos. The "coloured trade", he said, bought more guitars than banjos, and four organs for every piano.[13] The same newspaper quoted Mr. Campbell on 23rd November as saying he had ordered a ton of sheet music from the North, all of which he expected to sell before the season was over. In April, Merriday & Paine opened their new music rooms, "unsurpassed in beauty, convenience and extent by any music store south of Baltimore", and promised to sell musical instruments without the intermediate profits hitherto charged by Savannah dealers.[14]

The Hebrew Temple, dedicated in 1882 by Rabbi Marx Moses, was a centre of music and lectures for the city. Rabbi Moses spent June and July of 1884 in Europe. In an interview on his return he spoke of a visit to Leipzig, "the home of music, you know". Well known as a lecturer, Dr. Moses also gave voice lessons and encouraged the young musicians of the city by having musical programmes at the Temple. In July 1885 he moved to Omaha, Nebraska; his final sermon on 10th July drew a large attendance about equally divided between Jews or Gentiles.[15]

There were many music teachers in Jacksonville. On 22nd May, 1884, an advertisement appeared in the special notices of the *Florida Times Union*: "Teacher of Music—William Jahn, late pupil of Conservatory of Music at Leipsic, Germany . . . desires pupils on piano . . . Merryday and Paine's music store."

A few weeks later a recently arrived violinist sought pupils, jointly with a language teacher: "F. Delius Teacher of the

[12] Advertisements in the *Florida Times Union*, October 20, 1883, April 4, 1884, March 11, 1884, January 27, 1884. Grier Moffat Williams, "A History of Music in Jacksonville, Florida, from 1822 to 1922", unpublished doctoral dissertation, Florida State University, 1961, has furnished leads.

[13] *Florida Times Union*, March 5, 1884.

[14] *Florida Times Union*, April 29, 1884.

[15] *Florida Times Union*, August 22, 1884, and July 11, 1885.

Violin, Stephen G. Sessar Teacher of Foreign Languages, Bingham House, cor. Julia and Forsyth Sts., Jacksonville, Fla." This advertisement first appeared in the *Florida Times Union* on 9th July, 1884, and ran through to the issue of 16th August.

Whether or not Delius had many pupils in response to this announcement, he did enter into the musical life of the city, on 20th November taking part in an impromptu soirée at the St. James House. Some thirty people were present, including Rabbi Moses. A man named Strini planned the programme and sang in three duets from well-known operas; and "Mr. Fritz Delius" played two violin selections: Raff's "Cavatina" and Schumann's "Romanza". The climax of the evening was "The Soldier's Farewell" sung by a male quartet, Messrs. Burbridge, Delius, Paine, and Strini.[16]

On Christmas Eve 1884, it is possible that Delius sang in the choir or the mixed quartet, "under the animated touch of the organist, Mr. Ward", at the midnight mass in the Church of the Immaculate Conception.[17] The name of Thomas F. Ward crops up often in Jacksonville news items. In addition to being organist at the Catholic church, he participated in various benefits and musicales, sometimes as piano soloist, sometimes as accompanist; and he organised a singing class at the Cathedral in St. Augustine.[18] In an advertisement in the *Florida Times Union* for 4th and 5th February, 1885, he offered piano lessons —$1.00 for one lesson a week, $1.75 for two. Whether Delius and Ward met at one of the music stores, or were introduced by Edward Suskind, a Stuttgart native who had prospered in lumber in Jacksonville and subsequently became a patron of the arts,[19] the two became and remained close friends. After Delius left America and was studying at Leipzig, Ward sent him an inscribed copy of Byron's poems.[20] The instruction in counterpoint that Ward, eight years older than Delius and much more experienced, was able to provide was important at just that point in Delius's career.

[16] *Florida Times Union* and *Florida Daily Times*, November 21, 1884.
[17] *Florida Times Union*, December 25, 1884.
[18] St. Augustine *Chronicle*, April 7, 1887.
[19] "Death Claims Edw. Suskind, Pioneer Here", *Florida Times Union*, January 13, 1931. The obituary contains this statement: "It was Edward Suskind who befriended Fritz Delius . . . finding him a teacher, the organist of one of Jacksonville's churches."
[20] "New and Complete Edition", Philadelphia: Porter and Coates, no date. Presented in 1962 by Eric Fenby to the Delius Association of Florida and deposited in the Jacksonville University Library.

In view of his commitments in Jacksonville it seems doubtful that Ward made any long visit to Solano Grove. A manuscript notebook owned by Delius and dated 1884, with exercises in counterpoint, preserves the record of their relationship; its date suggests that Delius met and began studying with Ward quite early in his Florida visit. Delius owned at the time an English translation of Berlioz's *A Treatise upon Modern Instrumentation and Orchestration* (second edition, 1858) and a Bach *Organchoralbuch*.[21] If Ward persuaded Fritz to buy these volumes, he was of greater service in helping him buy a grand piano and in overseeing its delivery. In 1961 the actual piano was located in Daytona Beach, with the attached notation: "F. Delius, Solano Grove after awaiting instructions from Thos. Ward."[22]

Ward was far from being the only musician in Jacksonville who knew and helped Delius. William Jahn, formerly of Leipzig, not only advertised for pupils but shared with Delius the hope of winning fame as a composer. His "Moonlight Dream Waltzes", copyrighted in 1892, bears a notice of "Zum Carnival Polka" by Delius, dated the same year and dedicated to Jahn. Both were published in Jacksonville by A. B. Campbell.[23] That Ward and Jahn both kept in touch with Delius after he left Jacksonville is evidence of one of the most credible truisms about Delius, that he had a genius for forming and maintaining firm friendships. These friends in Jacksonville confirmed what Delius no doubt already knew, that Leipzig was *the* place to go for an aspiring musician.

Other musical friends of Delius in Florida included members of the Mordt family. In the 1880's Mr. and Mrs. Mordt with their nine children left Oslo and settled in the United States. According to family legend the five youngest children, all girls, studied at the conservatory in Cincinnati. One of the girls, Dagny, after gaining momentary fame in operatic roles in Norway married Halfdan Rolland, a singer and violinist, and moved to Jacksonville, followed by several other members of the family including her sister Jutta. By 1884 Jutta was married

---

[21] Notebook and books given by Eric Fenby to the Delius Association of Florida and now in Jacksonville University Library.

[22] Charles Hoffman, "He Set Florida to Music", *All Florida and TV Magazine*, November 4, 1962, p. 3. The piano is now in the Delius house at Jacksonville University.

[23] The copyright copy of "Zum Carnival" in the Library of Congress is dated January 20, 1892.

to Lieutenant Charles Edward Bell of the Royal Navy and was living on the St. Johns near Picolata.[24] For as long, and as often, as Delius was at Solano Grove, the Bells were his closest neighbours. Evidence of a subsequent friendship in the 1890's in London and Paris, after Jutta had left her husband, suggest that in Florida she and Delius found a common bond in music. It is no strain on the imagination to suppose a mutual attraction, even if its effect was limited at the time to Jutta's encouragement of the dream of becoming a composer.

A young Bradford neighbour, Charles Douglas, was with Delius at Solano Grove for some of the time, until an estrangement developed between them. [25] They shared the many pleasures of the region, some of them hardly imaginable in Bradford. Delius never forgot them, and they may reasonably be thought of as objects of the nostalgia that imbues much of his music. Even allowing for his Yorkshire habit of legpulling, the adventures he reported to his sister Clare, which she conscientiously included in her biography of him, were the sort that any lively young visitor would have engaged in—shooting ducks, for example, and hunting alligators by night. Solano Grove, even in its present abandoned condition, retains traces of the romantic majesty which, in its prime, could hardly fail to make a strong and durable impression on Delius—the river like a lake in its breadth, the live oaks with their pendant Spanish moss, the strange calls of indigenous birds, the sometimes eerie night cries of panthers and lesser beasts, the mysteries of impenetrable hammocks, the Southern moon, the deep contrasts of sun and shadow by day, and music carried far across the water when a riverboat passed. How could a son of grimy Bradford fail to appreciate such sensations? Three hours away, moreover, was a city as rich in music as any its size. What a combination for a youth whose mercantile father hoped to wean away from profitless dreams!

[24] Family memorabilia of the Mordts made accessible by Mrs. John R. Bennett of Jacksonville. Jutta's name is sometimes given in the family clippings as Hutta, indicating the Norwegian pronunciation. The assumption that Bell and Jutta went out from England as bride and groom seems improbable since their marriage is not recorded in Somerset House. No doubt they met and were married in Florida. I have not been able to find out what happened to Lt. Bell after they moved back to England sometime after the "Big Freeze" of 1886.

[25] Charles Douglas, who died in 1960 at the age of ninety-four, remained silent on the matter, according to a letter to me from his nephew, Mr. F. G. Blagbrough, September 13, 1963.

But something made Fritz quite willing to leave what may have seemed an earthly paradise. Somehow he learned of an opening in Danville, Virginia, and used most of his cash to go there, [26] arriving early in the fall of 1885. When we recall that he abandoned an attractive cottage with a new piano inside and an exciting vista outside, we may well wonder about the reason. It would not have been mere wanderlust. Perhaps it was the rupture of his friendship with Douglas, never fully explained. Likeliest of all was a determination to make his own way, and to free himself from the constant pall of his father's financial tyranny.

In Danville his first mentor was J. F. Rueckert, who had no store but enterprisingly advertised pianos and organs for sale "at bottom cash Factory prices", at the same time soliciting work as piano tuner and repairman "capable of attending to every department personally. He is not connected nor interested in any measure with any other house in Danville, therefore persons should send him a postal card or call at his residence on Patton street, second door west of courthouse." In the same issue of the Danville *Daily Register*, 3rd October, 1885, the following notice appeared:

Fritz Delius will begin at once giving instruction in Piano Violin Theory and Composition. He will give lessons at the residence of the pupils. Terms reasonable. Apply at the residence of Mr. J. F. Rueckert, or by postal card, care P. O. Box 454, Danville, Va.

Three days later the newspaper again carried this notice, together with another musical item, in the column "In a Nut Shell", which promoted Delius to professor: "Prof. Fritz Delius assisted by the interesting Rueckert Quartette and vocal talent, expect to give some classical concerts during the winter which will be free to all students in music in our midst. They will not only be very enjoyable but all very instructive to those attending them."[27] For a recent newcomer to Danville, Fritz was making rapid headway.

Delius was soon on good terms with Robert Phifer, professor of music at the Roanoke Female College (now Averett College).

---

[26] A conjectural advertisement for the Danville opening, in a Jacksonville paper, has not been located despite an assiduous search.

[27] Although there is no file of the Danville *Daily Register* the issues of October 3 and 6, 1885, are in the Duke University Library. The advertisement has the small notation "Se-29-f" at the end, indicating that it began September 29.

A graduate of the Leipzig Conservatory, Phifer had been a prime mover of musical activities of all sorts in Danville ever since his arrival in 1878; he was continually organising classes and concerts not only at the college but in local churches.[28]

Danville was quite a change from Florida. Located in a hilly section of Virginia that William Byrd, over a century earlier, called "the land of Eden", it offered excellent walking, a form of recreation that Delius always enjoyed as a boy on the moors surrounding Bradford and, one summer and another in later years, on the lofty fells of Norway. Founded in 1793 and thus much older than Jacksonville, Danville sloped down to a bend in the River Dan; with its emphasis on manufacturing it was a "New South" town, but in its gridiron street layout and central square it was also a "Main Street" town, like thousands of others in the South and the Midwest. The 1880 census reported a population of 7,526 (3,129 white, 4,397 coloured). In 1881 construction began on both a new federal building (courthouse and post office) and a cotton mill that was to become the heart of the now famous Dan River Mills. Tobacco was easily the dominant industry, however, when Delius was there; thirty-odd factories turning out plug and twist tobacco, a hundred other firms devoted to handling, reprising, and shipping assorted tobacco products, and several warehouse and brokerage companies collectively made Danville the nation's leading market for bright-leaf tobacco. There were newspapers—daily, weekly and semi-weekly; private schools and female colleges; a Young Men's Debating Society; two music groups—the Gottschalk and the Beethoven Musical Associations; and James Fischer's Jewelry and Musical House, which boasted of being the largest music store in the South. There was not the rapid growth one was quickly aware of in Jacksonville, or the large annual influx of winter visitors to encourage or demand entertainment; local pride centred, instead, on Danville's place in history as the last capital of the Confederacy.[29]

Years later, pride shifted to the remarkable career of a local girl, one of "the Langhorne beauties", who, as Lady Astor, became the first woman member of Parliament.[30] Delius could

---

[28] Phifer Papers (Scrapbook, clippings, programmes), in the Southern Historical Collection of the University of North Carolina Library.

[29] Edward Pollock, *Illustrated Sketch-Book of Danville, Virginia: Its Manufactures and Commerce* (Danville, 1885).

[30] *Virginia: A Guide to the Old Dominion*, compiled by Writers' Program of The Work Projects Administration (New York, 1940), pp. 597-599.

have known her, but she was only seven when he lived in Danville and there was no dearth of somewhat older charmers to catch his roving eye. A handsome English violinist would be a cynosure at any girls' college and, if we can credit the memories of various elderly ladies who were in their late teens in the 1880's, Delius met charm with charm. His centre of interest was probably Viginia Ann Watkins. She wore his ring, but she was not engaged to him, she later insisted, because there were two other boys she wanted to date. When Delius left she gave back the ring; the next year he sent her his photograph from Leipzig, which, for some reason, she tore in half.

Delius frequently attended soirées at the Phifer home on Jefferson Avenue, taking part in group singing and enjoying the collation of sherry and cake served at the sideboard. Mrs. Phifer said that he used to come to their house and "engage with my husband on harmonic progressions which defied all rules of theory". One of his pupils was the Phifers' son Robert; other pupils were daughters of the landed gentry in the area. He also taught French and German on demand. Mrs. Phifer, as Isabelle McGehee, had been brought up at "Burleigh", the McGehee plantation at Semora, across the state line in North Carolina, about twenty miles from Danville. Whether or not Delius was ever there, "Burleigh" was like other plantations where he gave lessons, with a large main house, separate kitchen with huge fireplaces at each end, carriage house and other buildings nearby. One of the large downstairs rooms was a music room.[31]

Delius himself lived at Mrs. Richardson's in North Danville

[31] Material about Virginia Ann (Watkins) Hunt and other items concerning Delius in Danville are found in an article by Gerard Tetley, "Fritz Delius in Virginia", Richmond *Times-Dispatch Magazine*, November 27, 1949, p. 8. The copy at Averett College has pencilled comments. Another article on Delius by Tetley was in the same newspaper May 16, 1948. Later he contributed "Delius in Danville", to *Virginia Cavalcade*, IX, no. 1 (1959), 16–20. The late Mr. Tetley, a Yorkshireman who became editor of the Danville *Bee*, did considerable amateur sleuthing on this period in Delius's life, and I am indebted to him for information in letters to me during 1962 and 1963. However, Mr. Tetley died without learning of the newspaper items at Duke or the Phifer Papers at North Carolina. When I visited "Burleigh" in December 1962, the music room still had a Chickering piano, a music stand, metronome, large piles of sheet music and scores, and assorted concert programmes. Some of Mrs. Phifer's reminiscences at the age of ninety-one were reported in an article by Paul Ader, in the Durham *Herald Sun*, March 23, 1941.

where another young man named Hoppe also stayed. They had two upstairs rooms and their meals were sent up. On 5th March, 1886, Delius was on the programme of a Roanoke Female College Concert: "Concerto for Violin. Op. 64. Mendelssohn. Allegro molto vivace. (Last movement.) Mr. Fritz Delius." The *Danville Register* the next day reported the event and said that "in addition to the good music, there was a fine display of drawings and paintings from the art department".[32]

On his frequent walks, Delius would stop to listen to the Negro hands singing in the tobacco stemmeries; sometimes as many as three hundred workers would be singing in one room. The management encouraged the selection of one man or woman to "line out" a spiritual or song, for a "singing bunch" did better work. One tune Delius had heard earlier in Florida he heard again in Danville; it is still sometimes used as a hymn tune in Negro churches. Delius adopted it for the theme and variations of *Appalachia*. He acknowledged his debt to Danville by sending Professor Phifer a score of *Appalachia* inscribed 25th January, 1910.

By June 1886 the college year was over and Delius was packing to leave for Leipzig. He could not find his copy of Cherubini's book on orchestration and asked one of his young lady students, Joan Armistead, if he had left it at her home. She thought not but much later found it and wrote asking if he still wanted it.[33] He obviously was popular in Danville, and kept up a correspondence with friends there, but study at Leipzig was his goal; the decision had probably been made even before he left Florida. Danville was only a stop en route, to earn his fare to Germany, but if while there he picked up the theme for *Appalachia*, it was a stop well worth making.

[32] Programme and newspaper clipping in Phifer Papers, University of North Carolina.

[33] An invitation to the Roanoke Female College commencement programme exercises, in the Phifer Papers, gives the dates as May 30–June 2. Mrs. S. W. Venable (Joan Armistead) wrote Delius July 4, 1909, and September 25, 1909, after seeing an article about him in *Etude*. She referred to his stay in Danville, and his leaving there for "Leipsic", and asked if he still wanted his book, which she had. These letters are the property of the Delius Trust. Mr. Phifer also kept in touch with Delius; letters from him dated July 27, 1894 and February 16, 1910, are in the Delius Papers of the Delius Trust in London. I am especially indebted to the late Mr. Philip Emanuel, former co-trustee of the Delius Trust, for the privilege of examining the Delius Papers.

He sailed from New York on the *Aurania* in June[34] and, after a brief visit with his family in Bradford, by August he was in Leipzig. The musicians he met there were probably of more value to him than the classes he attended. Most important was the interest that Edvard Grieg took in him, for it was Grieg who persuaded Julius Delius, at a London meeting in April 1888, to allow Fritz to continue his musical vocation. By the summer of 1888 Fritz was living in Paris where his uncle Theodor, a dilettante who had sold out his interest in the family wool business years earlier, helped him in many ways. Delius loved Paris, and worked hard at composing, but by 1896 he was increasingly uneasy about his financial status. His Uncle Theodor, generous and amiable for so many years, was beginning to share his brother's impatience: when was Fritz going to earn something from his music? From Bradford, meanwhile, came rumours of mismanagement and declining family income, hints that Julius might have to reduce or stop altogether the monthly remittance, and renewed suggestions that Fritz leave Paris for America, where money could be earned as a music teacher, in Danville or some other city, and where Solano Grove awaited only determined working to produce substantial income. Fritz could hardly share his father's faith in his managerial competence, but he did think of several possibilities for Solano Grove.

Neither Julius nor Theodor knew of of another reason, the most important, for the second American visit. An American impresario, Victor Thrane (1868–1936), had become acquainted with Delius, perhaps on one of his European trips in search of new talent for American concert tours, and was sufficiently pleased with Delius's music to think it might appeal to American audiences. Surviving letters indicate a warm friendship—the kind Delius usually formed with acquaintances in the world of music.[35]

Over Christmas dinner in 1896 in Paris, Delius and his

[34] Peter Warlock, *Frederick Delius* (London, 1952), p. 45, names the ship. The Cunard liner *Aurania* sailed from New York Saturday, June 12, 1886, and arrived at Queenstown June 20th at 4 A.M. on her way to Liverpool (New York *Times*, June 13, 21, 1886).

[35] Thrane was a music impresario from 1893 until 1900; later he was in the lumber business in Michigan. Short notices about Thrane are in the *Musical Courier*, May 30 and June 13, 1900, and obituary notices in *Musical Courier*, December 26, 1936 and *Musical America*, December 25, 1936. Letters from Thrane to Delius dated 1897 and 1898 are in the Delius Papers.

violinist friend Halfdan Jebe from Norway discussed the final details of the trip. With them was Jelka Rosen, a young artist who was one of the group Delius saw frequently at Mère Charlotte's crèmerie in the rue de la Chaumière. Jelka sat listening with growing self-pity; once again she was to be left out of Delius's life.[36] She was well aware that Fritz knew a good many women, some of whom she had every reason to dislike. The leading candidate for her disapproval must surely have been Princesse de Cystria, who made up in assiduous pursuit of Delius what she lacked in middle-class morality. It was Jutta Bell, Fritz's neighbour in Florida, who had introduced him to Marie-Léonie, Princesse de Cystria.[37] Jutta and her children were living in Paris in 1894, while Jutta studied voice with the famed Mme. Marchesi, teacher of Calvé and Melba. Jutta (who soon opened a school of elocution in London, as Mme. Bell-Ranske) and Delius had kept in touch through letters, and while she was in Paris Delius continued to consult her; he seemed especially to value her opinion in literary matters.

About the middle of January 1897 Delius and Jebe boarded a steamship for New York. When it was several hundred miles out, life was given a startling light opera twist when the Princesse de Cystria suddenly appeared. They could hardly be rid of her so they treated it as a lark. In New York, where Thrane served as host, it was great fun apparently to pass off Jebe as Cyril Gray and the girl as a Russian princess; but it posed certain problems for Thrane who wrote Delius later that he did not think his family had really been satisfied as to who they were.[38]

From New York the threesome proceeded to Danville, where they consented to give a concert on Saturday, 30th January. The newspaper report next morning could hardly be improved upon:

[36] From Jelka's notes written for Beecham, excerpted in Sir Thomas Beecham, *Frederick Delius* (London, 1959), pp. 85–86.

[37] According to the *Almanach de Gotha* (1927), Princesse de Cystria was Marie-Léonie, daughter of Hippolyte Mortier, Marquis de Trevisse, who died in 1892, and Louise-Jeanne-Gabrielle de Belleyme, who died in 1923. Born in Paris, February 8, 1866, Marie-Léonie was married in Paris April 26, 1888, to Rodolphe de Faucigny-Lucinge et Coligny, Prince de Cystria, who was born May 2, 1864, and died at Basse-Terre, Guadeloupe, November 15, 1907. An affidavit with the Jutta Bell letters in the Haydon Burns Library states that it was Jutta Bell who introduced Delius to the Princesse de Cystria in Paris.

[38] Letter from Thrane to Delius, August 17, 1897, property of Delius Trust.

THE DELIUS CONCERT

A most delightful concert took place at the Danville College for Young Ladies last evening. From an artistic point of view there was little indeed to be desired, but the attendance was not such as the merit of the entertainment demanded. Madame Donodossola gave delightful rendition to several choice selections, and was heartily encored. Mr. Lemmanoff, by his brilliant technique, charmed his audience in his violin numbers. Mr. Delius was very happy in his accompaniments, and his old friends in the city were pleased to hear the evidence of his talent as a composer in the composition of his which Madame Donodossola so faithfully rendered. . .

Perhaps may be mentioned especially the aria by Handel, with violin obligato. This piece was so beautifully given by the artists that it was repeated at the request of the entire audience.[39]

Delius and his friends spent an evening at the Phifers. One of the Phifer girls thought "the Russian woman" had a magnificent voice, but the thing that impressed her most was what big feet she had![40]

Whether Delius and Company prolonged their hoax with an appearance in Jacksonville is doubtful; one or another of the local newspapers would have reported it, as they reported every musical event, however minor, in that culturally oriented city, even at this time when the major subject of local interest was the activity of the Cuban junta, which based its gun-smuggling enterprise in Jacksonville.[41] The lack of news items suggests that the Princesse had by that time gone her separate way. If she was still with Delius, a concert would have been almost unavoidable, as a means of explaining her presence.

With funds as limited as they presumably were, Delius would have been likely to spend most of the time at Solano Grove rather than in a hotel in Jacksonville. Thrane wrote in February expressing a wish that he could join them at the Grove for a

[39] "The Delius Concert", Danville *Register*, January 31, 1897. This is one of the few extant issues of the paper (Duke University Library).

[40] Robert Phifer to Delius, February 16, 1910, property of Delius Trust. In the letter Phifer mentions the 1897 visit. Willa (Phifer) Giles later reminisced to Mr. Tetley about Delius's return visit.

[41] This was the period of Stephen Crane's extended visit to Jacksonville, when he was writing "The Open Boat"; it is inviting to imagine that Crane and Delius met, perhaps at Cora Taylor's fascinating Hotel de Dreme.

rest.[42] Delius himself must have been happy to return to Solano Grove. Elbert Anderson, the Negro caretaker, was expecting him, and Delius knew he must make some arrangement with Anderson about the property. The list of things in the house which Elbert had sent in December did not include the piano,[43] but whether at the Grove or in Jacksonville Fritz spent much of his time composing a piano concerto.

As for the orange grove, it was not profitable. In 1886, the year a great freeze wiped out most of the citrus groves in the northern half of Florida, people began growing tobacco in the shade of their orange groves, and within a decade tobacco-growing reached boom proportions. The depression of 1893 was a temporary setback, but the introduction of Sumatra seed, smuggled out of the East Indies, and the adoption of cheesecloth for more uniform shade, so improved the product that by 1895 demand far exceeded the supply, and it was predicted that Polk County, Florida, would soon replace Cuba as the major source of cigar wrappers. Shade tobacco was on everybody's tongue,[44] as citrus had been earlier and as real estate would be shortly after the turn of the century; it is easy to picture Delius seeking to lease Solano Grove for its production.

Being a cigar smoker Delius had a special interest in tobacco. While at Solano he wrote George A. W. Wendell of Quincy, a north-central Florida town in what has since become a major producing area of shade (or cigar leaf) tobacco. Wendell sent Delius a receipt, dated 19th April, 1897, for 500 cigars; the cost, including shipping to England, was $9,75—less than two cents each. But, in August, Wendell had to write that the steamship company would not accept the package; a British law forbade shipment of less than fifty pounds of tobacco to England. Delius must have written to ask what had happened, and also to ask about larger shipments; Wendell said he would find out the delivery costs to England and Norway for lots of 10,000. He added that his own tobacco had done very well; he had four

---

[42] Thrane to Delius, February 24, 1897, property of Delius Trust.

[43] Anderson to Delius, December 16, 1896, property of Delius Trust.

[44] Items in the *Florida Times Union* on tobacco are numerous during this period. A thorough study is Joseph M. Leon, "The Cigar Industry and Cigar Leaf Tobacco in Florida during the Nineteenth Century," unpublished M.A. thesis, Florida State University, 1962.

barns full, curing, and he predicted a vast extension of tobacco-growing all over Florida.[45]

While he was in Florida, Delius had no difficulty in drawing up a one-year contract with D. and H. C. Brannen to grow tobacco at Solano Grove, but it was not exactly favourable. He agreed to provide not only the house and land but the costs of tobacco planting up to $1,050.[46] If the Brannens had honoured the contract, he might have turned a decent profit; but they soon backed out. Anderson wrote that they came but he was not there and he never saw them. In January 1898 Delius signed a new lease with Robert Starke of Detmold, Germany. By August, however, Starke had not arrived, to the disgust of the caretaker, who expressed the wish that somebody would take the property over, for he was tired of working for nothing.[47]

Delius had stayed on in Florida during the spring of 1897 sketching out sections for the piano concerto. Things were looking up. Solano was to become a tobacco plantation. Victor Thrane in New York had a number of Fritz's songs and was hoping to get some prominent singers to try them. He was in touch with other artists too and wanted Delius to send more of his work. The concerto was taking form.

That summer when Fritz returned to France he had the satisfaction of believing that Solano Grove, after years of neglect, would finally become productive and profitable. The hope came to nothing, all too soon; it was easy to write lease contracts but impossible to collect if the lessors never stayed on the property. The second (and last) American visit was unsuccessful financially, whatever its pleasures for Delius. He never saw Solano Grove again.

Solano might have acquired a far broader fame if the writer D. H. Lawrence had been able to establish there the ideal intellectual community he conjured up in his imagination early in World War I. Learning about the Grove from Delius's young friend Philip Heseltine, and supposing it was available for such a purpose, Lawrence began in the fall of 1915 to urge various friends—among others Katherine Mansfield, Michael Arlen, Aldous Huxley—to join him there. "Let us all live

[45] Wendell receipt and letter from Wendell to Delius, August 31, 1897, property of Delius Trust.

[46] Copy of contract on backs of two letters dated February 24 and 26, 1897, property of Delius Trust.

[47] Anderson to Delius, September 9, 1898, and the lease signed "in Januar", property of Delius Trust.

together and create a new world . . . here all is destruction and dying and corruption". [48] Aldous Huxley testified how magnetic Lawrence could be, virtually compelling a positive response even when ordinary caution dictated a negative one. Although Huxley never met Delius he knew of Lawrence's dream of using the orange grove for the new Pantisocracy.[49] But Lawrence's mental picture of the "forsaken estate" did not square with the realistic details that Delius, approached for information, could easily supply; the cottage was hardly big enough for a communal experiment, the land was not suitable, and far from being inexpensive, Florida was no place to live without ample resources.[50]

Solano Grove passed through many hands. Finally in 1947 the two acres holding the river front and the house (by that time totally dilapidated) were purchased by a patron of Delius and his music, Mrs. Henry L. Richmond of Jacksonville. The house was later moved to the campus of Jacksonville University, while at Solano only matted grass, scattered rubble, a few stunted orange trees, and the magnificent sweep of the St. Johns reward pilgrims who find the original site. The enduring memorials to Fritz Delius's two visits to America are the tone poem *Appalachia* and the *Florida Suite* by Frederick Delius, the name he used after his marriage to Jelka Rosen in 1903.

("The Virginia Magazine of History and Biography", July, 1971.)

[48] Lawrence to Katherine Mansfield, December 20, 1915, in *The Letters of D. H. Lawrence*, ed. Aldous Huxley (New York, 1932), p. 301.

[49] Letter to me from Aldous Huxley, July 13, 1963.

[50] Letter from Delius to Heseltine, November 24, 1915, quoted in "Additions, Annotations, Comments", by Hubert Foss, Peter Warlock, *Frederick Delius* (London, 1952), p. 147.

Bay Street, Jacksonville, in the 1870s. In the street were a number of music stores and it was in one of them, Merriday & Paine's, that Delius is said to have met Thomas Ward.

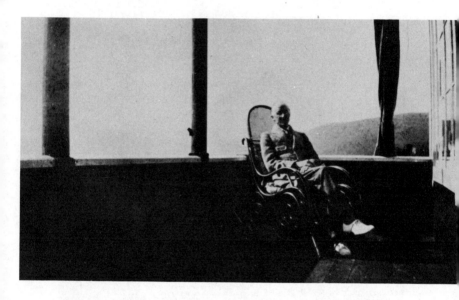

Delius sitting on the verandah of his house at Høifagerli, Norway, on his last visit in the Summer of 1923.

Frederick Delius and Norway by Rachel Lowe

Originally published as Frederick Delius and Norway *by Rachel Lowe-Dugmore in* Studies in Music *Number 6, 1972, pp. 27–41, University of Western Australia Press, Nedlands, Western Australia, this article now includes subsequent corrigenda and addenda from* Studies in Music *Number 7, 1973 and further additions and is reprinted by permission of Professor Frank Callaway and the Editorial Board of* Studies in Music.

The Delius family in England was typical of the German families who invaded the Yorkshire woollen industry in the middle of the nineteenth century. Frederick Delius, or Fritz as he was called until 1903, was the second of three sons who were expected to carry on the business and provide handsome dowries for their nine sisters. Ernst, the eldest son, had quarrelled with his father and had gone to New Zealand. In an effort to encourage his second son to take his place, Julius Delius in 1882[1] sent Frederick to Europe to represent the firm for a few months. Already a passionate lover of walking over the Yorkshire moors, Frederick was immediately attracted to the mountains of Scandinavia. After a short stay in Norrköping, Sweden, he despatched some business in Stockholm and Christiania as quickly as possible and then made his way to the mountains, until the autumn and the wrath of Julius brought him home.

In 1883 Frederick eagerly accepted another business trip to Norway, and became sufficiently well acquainted with the spoken language to be able to understand the plays of Ibsen and Bjørnson, although he does not seem to have made the acquaintance of the artistic world of Christiania at this time, nor to have travelled further north than Hardanger.

Despite the superficial character of these two visits to Norway,

[1] See Sir Thomas Beecham, *Frederick Delius* (London, 1959), p. 20, but note that Peter Warlock, *Frederick Delius* (London, 1952), places this first Scandinavian visit a year earlier.

they were important for his future development as they were the start of a love affair with the country, the people and the spirit of Norway which lasted throughout his life. He even went so far as to consider living at least half of each year in Norway,[2] and shortly after the 1914–18 war built a summer home for himself at Lesjaskog, Gudbrandsdal and called it "Hoifagerli".

Although the Delius home had been musical and Frederick had heard great artists such as Joachim and Piatti play there, it was not the prevailing taste for the Viennese Classics which had aroused his musical sensitivity but the harmonies and rhythms of Chopin and Grieg, the choice of local musicians. As he described it later in a letter to Nina Grieg, "a curtain went up".[3] Despite a subsequent devotion to Wagner and an interest in Richard Strauss, one self-made task soon after settling down to a life of music in Paris in 1888, was to orchestrate that first Grieg experience, the "Wedding Procession" from Opus 19.[4] It was not very thoroughly done, and remains in pencil manuscript, but the gesture was made.

The year 1884 brought Delius an abrupt change of scene from the uplands of Yorkshire and Scandinavia to the work of an orange farmer on the banks of the St. Johns River, in the woods and swamps of Florida. This was not a wise investment on the part of Julius Delius, either as a business venture or as an effort to divert Frederick from a musical career.

From his own telling, in a now famous passage, Delius experienced there that state of contemplation of which poets are more apt to speak than musicians, but which is at the heart of all true art. This, he said, he learnt from "sitting and gazing at nature",[5] and, on the basis of the Jacksonville archives, one feels tempted to add "when his very full social life and strenuous music lessons with Thomas Ward allowed". But there is nothing phoney about this claim to have experienced contemplation and his insistence on the importance of it in the life of the artist. When Zarathustra in *A Mass of Life* sings "Now is the World made perfect", it is the voice of experience and every note rings true to it.

[2] Delius to Grieg, 19 October 1888. Unless otherwise specified, copies of the letters referred to are in the Delius Trust Archive, London.

[3] Delius to Nina Grieg, 26 May 1890.

[4] Delius Trust Music Archive. Vol. 3 ff 69–78, the title page is dated "(le 2 Dec^ber 1889)".

[5] Eric Fenby, *Delius as I Knew Him* (London, 1966), p. 164.

Critics have deduced that the point of entry into this moment of rapture was the sound of voices in close harmony heard over the water. Perhaps he had already heard such singing in Norway and experienced intimations of such a mood; but, from this time onwards, he was to try continually to translate this experience into musical terms, to hold it motionless in an essentially moving medium. This was to dictate his methods of harmonic counterpoint, his chorale-like uses of voices a capella for the peak points of emotion, his use of instruments as voices, his use of wordless voices as instruments. Florida was the necessary catalyst for his imagination and his will.

Delius's Florida notebook shows how hard he found it to write textbook exercises. An average school child could do better, but every so often, there are snatches of free composition in which are shown hints of the future, a definite predilection for Norwegian rhythms and Grieg-like experiments with secondary sevenths and chromatic discords. Two extant manuscript songs from 1885 are "Two Brown Eyes"[6] with words by Hans Andersen, and "Over the Mountains High",[7] to Bjørnson's words in English translation. The latter has an undistinguished vocal line supported by broken chords, but is noteworthy for a two-bar wordless refrain.

Local Jacksonville historians have suggested that the wife of Delius's neighbour in Florida, Jutta Mordt Bell, was a relation of Nina Grieg and that it was she who urged Delius to meet Grieg; but a letter written by Delius to Mrs. Bell, when later she was living in England, would seem to indicate that she did not know Grieg. It reads as though she had needed Delius's help to effect an introduction after a London concert and had been shy to use it. Undoubtedly, though, Mrs. Bell encouraged Delius to take advantage of Ernst's arrival to leave the farm for a post as a music teacher in Danville, Virginia, and this, in turn, contributed to Julius Delius's decision to allow his son to have eighteen months at the Leipzig Conservatoire.

At Leipzig Delius found among the maturer students the composers Sinding and Halvorsen. Sinding and Delius became great friends and one wonders whether the help and influence of Sinding have not been under-estimated. Sixty-one letters have survived from Sinding to Delius between 1888 and 1905. They correct some entries in Grove's *Dictionary* (1954 Edition)

[6] Moldenhauer Archive, North Western University, Evanston, Illinois, U.S.A.

[7] Delius Trust Music Archive, Vol. 36 f 12.

concerning Sinding's movements during those years and they show that it was Sinding, along with Grieg, who first introduced Delius to the Jotunheim mountains in 1889.

During the summer vacation in 1887 Delius re-visited Norway for the first time since 1883 and stayed in the region of the Sognfjord. Among the Delius papers housed at the Grainger Museum, Melbourne, is a small red notebook begun before leaving America for Leipzig, and carried by Delius on this solitary tour and also on subsequent Norway holidays of 1889 and 1891 mentioned in this article. On the 1887 tour, Delius avoided Bergen, and began by walking in the Hardanger region, where he was unexpectedly invited to join a village wedding party and where he also experienced a climb which reads like a verbal draft for *The Song of the High Hills*. Thence he worked his way northwards, over the Hardanger Vidde to the Sognfjord, completing his holiday by boat to Molde and train through Romsdal to Christiania.[8] He began a notebook of musical ideas and tried his hand at taking down folk-songs in the field. This grey clothbound manuscript book[9] was carried by Delius on mountain holidays for many years. His enthusiasm for fieldwork waned almost as soon as it began, but, in the great *Song of the High Hills* (1911), for which first sketches appear in this book, one of the three main themes is in the Lydian mode, despite the predominantly pentatonic nature of the others. The Florida experience had confirmed in him a liking for tunes of a pentatonic type, with the characteristic gap of a minor third, and it is this, rather than any liking for the study of national characteristics that gives his music the ability to sound essentially "southern" in *Appalachia*, Norwegian in *Song of the High Hills* or *Fennimore and Gerda*, and oriental when the pentatone is judiciously flavoured with chromaticism as in *Hassan*. This tonal characteristic together with his preference for the melismatic way of developing a theme is what caused Sir George Dyson to write: "It is sometimes hard to tell where folk-song ends and Delius begins".[10] It also explains why, when Grainger presented Delius with Grieg's setting of "In Ola Dal"[11] and his own setting of *Brigg Fair*, they inspired Delius to write two perfect works, *On Hearing the First Cuckoo in Spring* and *Brigg Fair: An English Rhapsody*.

[8] Grainger Museum, Melbourne, Victoria, Australia.
[9] Delius Trust Music Archive Vol. 38.
[10] *The New Music* (London, 1924), p. 146.
[11] Peters Edition No. 2860. Norske Folkeviser Opus 66, no. 14 "I Ola-dalom, i Ola-kjønn".

Delius's second Christmas in Leipzig was to bring the friend-ship of Edvard and Nina Grieg,[12] who were there for the first performance of Grieg's Violin Sonata in C minor on 10th December, with Adolf Brodsky as violinist and Grieg at the piano. The Griegs stayed on until April, when Delius left the Conservatoire and Grieg made his first concert tour in Britain. A year later, looking back on New Year's Eve 1887/88, Delius wrote to Grieg: "a whole year has passed since we were together in my place on the 4th floor of the Harkort Strasse & drank Benedictine punch & the ringing of the bells came in at the window as we all clinked glasses . . ." Grieg, for his part, in a letter to Beyer, March 1888, said "When I think . . . of how lucky I have been in my associates this winter . . . I can say with good reason that my journey was worth while, and that is saying something".[13]

A performance of Grieg's Quartet and two hearings of the Piano Concerto, the first in London with Grieg at the piano, continued to inspire Delius in 1888. Delius's own Piano Con-certo, dated 1897, owes much to Grieg, although it is not in the same category as a work of art.

The Norwegian violinist Halfdan Jebe, whose acquaintance Delius made a few years later in Paris and with whom he revisited Florida in 1897 while he was writing the concerto, had different views about the validity of national music such as Grieg's. Writing to Delius in 1905 he says in a characteristic-ally irreverent way: "it would be more logical and modest to avoid one's own merely incidental name on so-called 'national works' and quite simply say for instance, Piano Concerto (A minor) by Norway".

There is no doubt that Delius's love of a party made him many of his Scandinavian friends. Grieg's Christmas Eve party in Leipzig, 1887, is described by Peter Warlock as having been given for Delius, Sinding and Halvorsen. Each composer was to bring a composition for the others to criticise, but, he ends,

---

[12] A second notebook at the Grainger Museum is in the handwriting of Jelka Delius and contains Delius's dictated memoirs concerning the composer Grieg. These prove conclusively that Delius's first meeting with Grieg took place in Leipzig in the autumn of 1887 and not in Norway previously as has often been stated. It confirms the evidence of the letters concerning the 1888 meeting with Julius Delius in London, but states categorically that Grieg "persuaded" Julius Delius to allow his son's plans to proceed.

[13] Quoted in David Monrad-Johansen, *Edvard Grieg* (New York, 1945), p. 282.

"good cheer and general festivity prevented this project".[14] Delius played his little *Sleigh Ride* for piano which, posthumously edited and recorded in orchestral version by Sir Thomas Beecham, is now a firm concert favourite with children.[15]

Just before leaving the Conservatoire, Grieg wrote a letter to Delius, which has been quoted in full by Sir Thomas Beecham in his biography of Delius.[16] Although the two composers, using German as their means of communication, did not use the familiar style of address until after the autumn of 1889, this letter is unusually formal considering the close circle they had moved in together in Leipzig. This suggests that it was written as a testimonial and as a little ammunition for Delius in his struggle with his father. The letter urges Delius not to accept "a position of merely outward significance", but to devote himself fully to his art while he is young. He stresses the necessity of choosing the right country and surroundings in which to work, and it reads like the famous letter Grieg had himself received as a young man from Ibsen: "No dear Grieg, your future is something more and better than a post as conductor of an orchestra . . ." Grieg's belief that Delius will develop as a composer "in the grand manner", suggests his approval of the scores of the symphonic poem *Hiawatha*, still in manuscript, and *Florida*, the orchestral suite which was edited and posthumously published by Sir Thomas Beecham.

The letters which passed between the Griegs and Delius form the chief source of information about the younger composer's apprentice years after leaving the Conservatoire. Thirty-seven have survived from Delius to the Griegs and seventy-one from the Griegs to Delius. The majority are dated between the years 1888 and 1894, although the friendship continued until the death first of Edvard in 1907 and then of Nina in 1935.

Grieg's part in persuading Julius Delius to allow his son to live and work as a composer in Paris has been variously told, but the evidence of the letters is quite simple. Julius and Fritz attended Grieg's concert in the St. James's Hall in London and then entertained him to supper at the Hotel Metropole. Delius's letter inviting Grieg shows that he was, in fact, already en route for Paris to stay with his Uncle Theodor. Julius cut his son's

---

[14] Peter Warlock (pseud. for Philip Heseltine), *Frederick Delius*, ed. Hubert Foss (London, 1952), p. 46.

[15] Grainger Museum. See footnote 12.

[16] *Op. cit.* p. 39.

allowance in half when he decided to live in Paris, but we do not know whether things would have been more drastic without Grieg's evident approval of Fritz. [See footnote 12 p. 171.]

On arrival in Paris, Delius immediately blossomed. "Even the streets enjoy life", he wrote to Grieg. But it was left to Sinding to pour a little cold water on his enthusiasm. Sinding was still in Leipzig, working at his studies with the aid of a state grant, and producing his Quintet and his Piano Concerto. He wrote: "I can quite understand your sympathy for the French men and women, you old Joseph. I dare say you were in your element. With regard to music, however, may it not actually be better here? It was, after all, mostly German music in this murderous programme which you sent me . . ."

Sinding's letters are a splendid foil to the quiet wisdom of Grieg's. He is up one minute and down the next according to the state of his purse and his heart. At the same time he often gives good advice as, for instance, when Delius sent him a little string quartet with much incorrect stopping in the parts, and later, again, concerning opera production and publishing. Unfortunately, Sinding destroyed all Delius's letters.

Delius's Paris circle seems to have been small for the first two years. His chief companion was Arve Arvesen the violinist from Hamar, who died in Bergen, where he was in charge of the Academy of Music, as recently as 1951. The painters Eyolf Soot and Gudmund Stenersen were both studying in Paris at this time and visited Delius in his little house in Ville d'Avray and later in Croissy. He was also very friendly with Bergliot Bjørnson, daughter of the patriot poet, who was studying with Marchesi. It was through her invitation that he stayed with the Bjørnsons at Aulestad in the summer of 1891, the year before Bergliot married Sigurd Ibsen, the politician son of Henrik.

Between 1888 and 1892 Delius sent Edvard and Nina Grieg a number of songs to vet. Several remained in manuscript, as for instance, *Skogen gir susende langsom besked* (Bjørnson) and there may have been more songs sent to Troldhaugen than are now extant. Twelve of these songs saw publication in 1892 by Augener as *Five Songs from the Norwegian* and *Seven Songs from the Norwegian*, along with *Three Songs* (Shelley). Correspondence with Augener in 1894–98 shows that in 1895 Delius recalled the plates and the copyright of the *Seven Songs* and the *Shelley Songs* which were transferred to Concorde Concert Control in 1899, thence to Tischer and Jagenberg in 1910, who later transferred them to Oxford University Press along with other works. The *Five Songs* remain with Augener. The whole transaction suggests that the 1892 publication was at Delius's expense.[17]

Several of these songs used words already set by Grieg, who was not the least upset by this borrowing, but was a little alarmed about tendencies in the music. In a now famous passage he said to Delius that he was afraid of the combination of a Norwegian melody and a Wagnerian treatment of the voice, but he particularly liked the cadence in Delius's setting of Kjerulf's "Longing":[18]

On further thought he added that he was compelled to admit that the songs had "such fine feeling" which was "the main thing". "Fine feeling" was a phrase Delius was to use a great deal in later life when asked for criticism and advice by younger composers.

As time went on Nina Grieg complained that Delius's songs had become too erotic for her to sing, but she remained particularly fond of his setting of "Margaret's Lullaby" from Ibsen's *Pretenders*. Grieg had originally set it for Nina to sing to their baby daughter who had died in infancy. That they could still appreciate Delius's music speaks volumes for their friendship and for the discretion of his setting, which in a sense complements that of Grieg, as it is a little mood picture where Grieg's is a simple hymn.

A rejected version appears in the notebook begun in 1887.

[17] Dr. Lionel Carley has now ascertained that in 1896 Delius published "5 Chansons, musique de Fritz Delius" under the imprint of L. Grus Fils in Paris. The first three had been previously published by Augener:

    1. Berceuse (Cradle Song—Ibsen—1889).
    2. La Ballade du musicien (The Minstrel—Ibsen—1890) [transposed into baritone—contralto key].
    3. Chant Indien (Indian Love Song—Shelley—1891) [transposed into baritone—contralto key].
    4. Plus vite, mon cheval (Emanuel Geibel).
    5. Il pleure dans mon coeur (Verlaine—1895).
[18] Grieg to Delius, 23 September 1888.

Headed " 'Cradle Song' (little Haakon) August 5th", it bears
no year date. The published version dedicated to Nina Grieg
is dated 1889. This first draft, which might have belonged either
to the 1887 Sognfjord trip or the Jotunheim holiday with Grieg
in August 1889, is now conclusively dated 1889 also. The
itinerary recorded by Delius in the red notebook housed at the
Grainger Museum, Melbourne, shows that he sailed from
Christiania (Oslo) on the first stage of his return journey to
Leipzig on 30th July, 1887.

The letters of 1891, the year before the publication of these
songs, show that Nina visited Fredricksvaern on the South
coast of Norway at some point while Delius was there during
that Autumn. Fredricksvaern was a fashionable resort for
sailing enthusiasts and artists, notably the marine painter
Hjalmar Johnsen whose circle of friends and visitors included
the Griegs and the family of the Prime Minister, Otto Blehr.
Nina's singing of Delius's songs may well have contributed
both to his decision to publish (the Griegs were personal
friends of the Augeners) and also to the first performance of a
work of his in public, on 10th October, 1891, in Christiania.

The first evidence of this performance came to light in 1964.
The first clue appeared in Grieg's letter dated 22nd December,
1890: "I would love to hear your overture 'Paa Vidderne'."
Up to this point *Paa Vidderne* has referred to the melodrama
setting of Ibsen's poem which Delius finished in the autumn of
1888 and of which he never spoke again once Grieg had seen it
and returned it with due criticism.

Two more clues appeared in the archives: the first a letter
from Iver Holter, the conductor and founder of the Christiania
Music Society, apologising for not being able to include the
overture in the 1890–91 season in Christiania, and ending,
"Can I now retain the score and the parts until the autumn?
I shall then arrange for them to be performed".[19] The second
clue came in a letter from Delius to Grieg dated 16th July,
1891, at Fredricksvaern: "I am staying fairly long in Norway
this year in order to hear my overture which Holter is going to
perform".

At this point Gunnar Rugstad of the Institute of Musicology
in Oslo undertook a search of the Institute's collection of
programmes on my behalf and found as the last item of the
programme for the Christiania Musical Society on 10th Octo-

---

[19] Holter to Delius, 19 March 1891.

ber, 1891: *"Fritz Delius: 'Paa Vidderne' Concertouverture for stort orkester (Iste Gang) Manuskript"*.

The physical evidence of the manuscript full score in Delius's holograph indicates that it is substantially as originally written with some revision in the direction of condensation, presumably made for the later Monte Carlo performance. Delius's dates on his works are somewhat erratic, sometimes representing his starting point and sometimes the finishing point, more often the latter. As coming from 1892 it had puzzled biographers, including Beecham, by its forcefulness and lack of the charm and serenity characteristic of the early works. Seen from the standpoint of 1890 it represents the end of the first phase of Delius's efforts to find himself both as artist and man. Musically speaking this phase had begun with his attempt at setting *Paa Vidderne* as a melodrama and now ended appropriately with the overture of the same name.

This obsession with Ibsen's long and youthful poem is understandable, for its pure aestheticism and creed of art for art's sake had exactly mirrored Delius's own feelings on arriving in Paris in 1888. Hence the melodrama had been the serious work of that year. But all the time he was reading voraciously: Ibsen first and foremost, especially *Brand* with its "all or nothing" theme, Tolstoy's works, current talking points such as Max Nordau's pamphlets,[20] Wagner's letters and libretti, and the more popular elements of the German philosophical climate. He improved his orchestral technique by re-scoring *Florida* and felt that here and in the smaller pieces of 1889 he had really mastered the orchestra at last, even though from our vantage point it is hard to see any inkling of the mastery evinced from 1898 onwards.

His eagerly anticipated tour with Grieg and Sinding in the Jotunheim mountains (Grieg's "Holiest of Holies") in 1889, was the highlight of that year. The 1887 sketchbook went with him and there is an unusually decisive full score sketch of the opening of the *Paa Vidderne* Overture in A minor (modal). The decision to recast it in E minor, to omit the introductory chords and to make the striding tune pause in the second bar on the dominant, rescued it from a tea shop type of banality into which Delius's tunes could so often, but just never do, fall. This prompts the conjecture that this may have been the hut

---

[20] Delius to Grieg, undated letter [February 1889]. The Nordau work mentioned was "Die conventionellen Lügen der Kulturmenschheit" of 1883.

FINAL VERSION —"PAA VIDDERNE" OVERTURE — OPENING THEME

Upper strings divisi and tremolo E minor chord

Sketch book version headed ' "Leirings Hutte"—Jotunheim—Norge, August 1889

in which Delius read the works of Nietzsche for the first time.

The mood of exaltation produced by the Jotunheim lasted well into the next year. On 1st April, 1890 he wrote to Grieg: "I have at last arranged my life according to my own nature and truth... World Joy instead of World Woe (Welt Schmertz)...."

The little orchestral tone poem entitled *Summer Evening*, edited and posthumously published by Beecham, is a product of this golden mood.

During the summer, instead of going to Norway, he joined Sinding and Johan Selmer in Leipzig for rehearsals of his works by student orchestras. Selmer inadvertently poached on some of Delius's rehearsal time, and incurred the wrath of his impatient friend. Fortunately the difference was patched up and Selmer was to become a valuable advocate of Delius in Norway.

After attending the Wagner season in Leipzig, Delius retreated to the seaside to work. There, full of Wagnerian vigour and determination yet dreaming nostalgically of the Jotunheim, he wrote the overture which is a sturdy, ternary piece of autobiography *not* unaffected by Richard Strauss. As motto he appended the last verse of the poem in German translation:

Nun bin ich gestählt, ich folg' dem Gebot:
Ich soll auf der Höhe wandern!
Mein leben im Thal—für immer tot—
Hier oben Gott und ein Morgenrot—
Dort unten tappen die andern!

The question inevitably arises as to why Delius never told Heseltine of this early Christiania performance. Perhaps he had just lost interest in this unlikely offspring or perhaps Heseltine took Isidore de Lara's word that in 1893 at Monte Carlo, he was instrumental in obtaining the first performance ever of a Delius work, the overture *Sur les Cimes*.[21] Concerning the Monte Carlo performance of the overture *Sur les Cimes* (Paa Vidderne) always hitherto listed as 1893, Dr. Lionel Carley, the present archivist to the Delius Trust in London, has found conclusive evidence that the correct date is 1894. It should be noted that, while claiming he was instrumental in obtaining this performance for Delius at Monte Carlo, Isidore de Lara in his memoirs *Many Tales of Many Cities* does not give a date.

Certainly this work has been subject to some curious misstatements. In the 1946 Beecham festival of Delius it was performed and the programme gave the title as *Under the Pines*, presumably a telephonist's misconstruction of *Sur les Cimes*, and yet another first performance was claimed!

Delius abandoned the overture, but the opening theme appears in the *Song of the High Hills* (1911)[22] where, transfigured and set for wordless tenor voices in the Lydian mode, it weaves a gentle countertheme of climbing upwards towards the mystic a capella voices of the hills themselves.

PAA VIDDERNE

SONG OF THE HIGH HILLS

Very early in his Paris years Delius was introduced to the household of William Molard, an amateur composer, writer of articles on music, maker of translations and libretti, professional civil servant at the ministry of agriculture, and great

[21] For a full discussion of the evidence of the score itself see Rachel Lowe, "Delius's First Performance", *Musical Times*, March 1965, pp. 190–2; also *idem*, "The Delius Trust Manuscripts", *Brio*, vol. 5, no. 1, Spring 1968, and corrigenda, *ibid.* vol. 5, no. 2.

[22] In the interim it had become a Delius personal *leit-motif* with the possible added psychological connotation of human desire—one example occurring in the "Maud" Song Cycle of 1891 and another being the principal theme of the third movement, Allegro con moto, of the 1892 Sonata in B for violin and pianoforte.

friend of Gauguin, Strindberg and Edvard Munch. Molard was married to Ida Ericson, the Swedish sculptress, and their apartment was home from home for all Scandinavians in Paris. From letters and diaries of the group, in which the name of Delius crops up quite frequently, we can piece together this brilliant household picture.

In addition to the artists, we can imagine Gunnar Heiberg from time to time arriving on duty for the Journal *Verdens Gang* with a script to read to the assembled company, or Johan Selmer, on his way south for his health cure, showing Delius his latest work, perhaps *The Spirit of the North* or his *Funeral March* discussed with Delius in an exchange of letters. Jappe Nilssen, too busy to send more than a postcard to announce his arrival, chiding all artists yet much respected for the great critic he was; Hjalmar Johnsen's brother bringing news of life in Fredricksvaern, and then at the turn of the century Christian and Oda Krohg with their son Per, Alfred Hauge and Ludwig Karsten.

All these artists loved the countryside of the Ile de France as much as they enjoyed their Bohemian existence in Paris, and through them Delius met his future wife, the painter Jelka Rosen. From 1897 onwards he lived more and more at her house in Grez-sur-Loing. When they were married in 1903 he made Grez his permanent home until his death in 1934, although from time to time he rented a studio in Paris, especially, it would seem from correspondence, when Edvard Munch was working in Paris.

I am indebted to John Boulton-Smith for pointing out a glimpse of Delius as he was seen from story memories of Molard's step-daughter, Judith Ericson. She had a young girl's passion for Gauguin, and, describing his vivid personality she says "beside him everyone paled, even Delius". She also notes that of this circle Delius was the only "rich" one. This impression of riches was unfortunate, for it was far from true, but it seems to have been an impression which Delius frequently made, perhaps because of the ease with which he also fitted into a certain aristocratic circle of the time, perhaps because he was a rich man's son. Fortunately, to correct the picture we have Jelka Rosen's own account given to Sir Thomas Beecham and short pen pictures of Delius's hard work and frugal living from the memoirs of the composer Isidore de Lara, entitled *Many Tales of Many Cities*.

Despite his small allowance, Delius, through extreme self-discipline, managed to visit Norway at least in alternate years.

There, when he was not walking in the Jotunheim, he stayed with the Griegs, Sinding, Bjørnson, and Mr. and Mrs. Otto Blehr. (Otto Blehr was Prime Minister from 1891–93).

Delius's letters to Mrs. Blehr were received in the Delius Archive in 1964 after enquiries made through the Royal Norwegian Embassy in London were received by her son Sigurd Blehr. The source of the search was a single letter, undated, signed "Randi", monogrammed "RB", written from Holmenkollen on a Saturday at nine o'clock in the evening, to Delius "down there" presumably in Oslo, and mentioning the words "Paa Vidderne". In view of the tightly knit artistic and political circle of the day in Norway, it seemed that this letter, overlooked by previous handlers of the archive, might be from a person of some consequence and that the "B" might just possibly stand for "Blehr". The resulting letters helped to round out the story between 1892 and 1896.

From the Blehr letters we learn that the only Norwegian artist in Paris with whom Delius had no sympathy of feeling was Frits Thaulow. Although Grieg sent messages to Jonas Lie via Delius, there seems to have been no great friendship there either. Sir Thomas Beecham mentions a walking tour in Norway with Knut Hamsun, but I have found no documentary evidence as yet.

In 1892 Sinding stayed with Delius in Paris and in the following year introduced the poet Vilhelm Krag to him. In 1896 Edvard Munch, writing home to Norway, says that he is with Delius and Krag nearly every day. One gets the impression that, having steadily widened his circle of friends in Paris between 1890 and 1896, Delius then deliberately began to narrow it down.

Despite the multiple claims of friendship between 1890 and 1896, Delius had worked very hard to produce an operatic trilogy of Wagnerian dimensions. He evidently regarded his little Nordic fairy tale opera to his own libretto, *Irmelin* (1891–92), as a proving ground, for he made no effort to publish or produce it, but went straight on to bigger things.

The plans for the trilogy were discussed at length with Mrs. Bell, who had left Florida, and, as Mrs. Bell-Ranske, had resumed her career as a writer and speech coach. She borrowed Delius's flat in the Rue Ducouëdic in 1894 while he was following the Wagner season in Bayreuth, and it would seem from extant correspondence that she wrote the first draft of the libretto for *The Magic Fountain*. This opera, based on the story of Ponce de Leon and his discovery of Florida, was to "en-shrine" the Indian peoples of America. The libretto was eventually re-written by Delius, and no sooner was the work finished than he was discussing the second opera *Koanga* which was to "enshrine" the Africans of America. The libretto of this was finally entrusted to C. F. Keary, and Delius re-worked the score of the first two acts while staying in Norway in the Valdres district in 1896 just prior to a second quick visit to his farm in Florida. The third act was written on his return, at Grez-sur-Loing, where Jelka Rosen had settled during his absence.

"For me", Delius said at this time, "dramatic art is almost taking the place of religion. People are sick of being preached to. But by being played to they may be worked upon. . . . I want to tread in Wagner's footsteps".[23] Some jottings in short score have survived to show that he made a careful analysis of *Meistersinger* at one time and it is possible that there were similar analyses of other Wagnerian works which have not survived. Fortunately for us, these early operas did not lead Delius into Wagner's dreamworld of gods and heroes, but into the inner dreams of ordinary Swiss peasants in *A Village Romeo and Juliet* (1900–01), and the Scandinavian middle class *Fennimore and Gerda* (1908–10).

The bridge from Wagnerian ambition to his own way in opera was one of necessity provided by the realist dramatist Gunnar Heiberg, who required some incidental music for his play *Folkeraadet* (The People's Parliament), which opened in Christiania in October 1897. This satire on Norwegian parliamentary government and the political tension existing at that time between Norway and Sweden seems an unlikely work to inspire Delius, but the politics of Scandinavia were of great interest to him throughout the period 1891–97. In 1892 when the Norwegian consular question had flared up, he had written most anxiously to Sinding for information, but Sinding had been deep in his work. So Delius had turned, appropriately, to Mrs. Blehr, and in the course of the resulting correspondence had elaborated his current theory that humanity is divided into three groups: "The All or Nothing People", the "Something People" and the "Nothing People". He might almost have been writing the plot for *Folkeraadet* if we substitute the

[23] Delius to Bell, 29 May 1894 (Bell–Ranske papers, Jacksonville, Fla.).

parliamentarians for his "Something People", Delius's "real egoists" who wish only for their own comfort, the Boots of the Hotel for the "Nothing People", who yet sometimes arrive at the solution by instinct, as when Boots blows up the bridge to drown the enemy, while the Poet who stakes all on speaking the truth to the nation is the true leader, the "All or Nothing Person".

A students' riot on the first night of the play was the result of Heiberg's heavy satire and Delius's use of the Norwegian National Anthem *Ja Vi Elsker* in the minor key as a Chopinesque funeral march for the Parliamentarians in the fourth act. It is clear from the notices in the newspaper *Verdens Gang* that the full import of the music had escaped the audience. With the exception of the appearances of the poet and Ella the music is almost entirely based on the National Anthem. Even the opening, after the chord of C major tutti and forte, is an excellent example. The cellos introduce a quaver theme, to be imitated in fugato style. Suggesting the pawky entrance of the Parliamentarians, it is the National Anthem's opening phrase in diminution.

Several printed versions of this incident, including that in Grove (5th Edition, 1954), say that a student shot at Delius. Marginalia from Jelka Delius to Eric Fenby[24] at Delius's dictation, giving information to be passed on to Gerald Abraham in answer to a query from him dated 28th November, 1932, states categorically: "Nobody shot at Delius". She goes on to explain that a blank shot was fired at the conductor.[25]

Three articles in the liberal newspaper *Verdens Gang* are especially noteworthy: the first, dated 23rd October, 1897, is a profile interview with Delius by Krohg, who was at that time writing a great deal about art and allied topics; the second, dated the same day, is a statement that Delius had asked the management to withdraw his music; and the third, dated 28th October, 1897, is an editorial by Christen Collin, decrying the use of the National Anthem in this way, and expressing his amazement at the tactlessness both of this English composer

[24] Delius Trust, Fenby Accession F103.
[25] This letter is corroborated by the profile interview, conducted by the journalist and painter Christian Krohg after the first performance, which indicates that Per Winge was conducting, although Beecham, and recently Fenby, have said that Delius conducted the first performance. See *Frederick Delius 1862–1934. A Catalogue of the Music Archive of the Delius Trust, London* by Rachel Lowe (Delius Trust 1974) Appendix V pp. 172–174. Translation by L. Carley.

and the way in which Norwegian composers, notably Johan Selmer, had allowed him a second hearing. After Collin's condemnation the music was withdrawn, but received another hearing as *Norwegian Suite* at the 1899 concert in London under the baton of the German conductor, Alfred Hertz, and again years later by Sir Thomas Beecham. The score is physically interesting because of these conductors' markings.

A month after this stormy scene in Oslo another overture inspired by Norway, *Over the Hills and Far Away*, was performed at Elberfeld by Dr. Hans Haym. There are still traces of direct homage to Grieg, but this is the first work in which we feel that we have the authentic Delius from first to last without any editorial assistance. In this sense it is correct to say that 1897 is the end of the apprentice period. It is also the beginning of a German interest in his work which was to continue until the Nazi era, interrupted only by the First World War.

The year 1897 also saw the completion of the *Seven Danish Songs*, 1898 produced the *Mitternachtslied* from Nietzsche's *Zarathustra*, September 1898 to February 1899 saw the composition of the first version of *Life's Dance* (*La Ronde se Déroule*) based on Helge Rode's poem of that name, and the tone poem *Paris* was completed in 1899. The sudden accession of power is uncanny, but is to some extent paralleled and explained by the change in his literary allegiance and a shifting of emphasis within his circle of friendship. Instead of Ibsen and Bjørnson, he now finds closer affinity with the poems of the Danish Jacobsen and the philosophy of Nietzsche. Jelka Rosen's influence is clear here and significantly coincides with a deepening friendship also with Edvard Munch, Norway's great expressionist painter.

There is no written evidence of close friendship until 1896 but as Delius knew their mutual friend, Helge Rode, as early as 1889 or 1890, it is possible they had met earlier. From 1899 onwards forty-seven letters and five draft letters remain to show a relationship of mutual reliance and respect rare between artists in different media. On the basis of this correspondence, which gives the impression of many unrecorded meetings and many more lost letters, John Boulton-Smith, writing for *Kunst og Kultur* and *Apollo*,[26] has constructed a year by year account of the friendship until the third decade of the twentieth century when Delius's illness and Munch's own maladies made its continuance difficult.

[26] John Boulton-Smith, "Portrait of a Friendship", *Apollo*, 1966, pp. 38–47.

Munch, writing in 1929, recalls one meeting thus: "Do you remember how we . . . you, Helge Rode and I spoke in Aasgaard-strand over 30 years ago about things to come . . ." This meeting was probably that arranged in 1899[27] to discuss an evening of Jacobsen's poems, with Munch's etchings and Delius's music. That Rode was there is appropriate considering the pre-occupation of all three at that time with the Nietzschean theme of *Life's Dance*. The evening never took place, as far as we know, but it is impossible to appreciate fully the development of Delius's works from the first version of *Life's Dance*, 1899 to the final published version of 1912 without some understanding also of the work of Munch.

Throughout these years, 1899 to 1912, there is a steady progress away from pure impression. Like the poet Wordsworth, Delius is at his most approachable when portraying natural scenery, as in *Summer Night on the River* or the opening of *In a Summer Garden*, but we are missing a greater portion of his work if we neglect the fact that nature is more frequently seen as symbolic of the poet's state of mind in relation not only to nature, but human nature. *Sea Drift* with Whitman's words and *Songs of Sunset* with the poetry of Dowson are major landmarks on this road. The process is accelerated in the opera *Fennimore and Gerda*, after the novel *Niels Lyhne* by Jacobsen, and completed in *An Arabesk*,[28] 1911, to the poem of Jacobsen, after which Delius found himself able to complete the third and final version of *Life's Dance*, 1912. Of this he wrote to Mr. Tischer, the publisher: "I think the *Dance of Life* [*Life's Dance*] is my best orchestral work. I have had it in my file for some years for the ending did not please me very much but at last I have found what I was looking for and it is now complete".[29]

This spiritual progress is confirmed in a letter from Jelka Delius to Eric Fenby on 27th October, 1933, in which she says: "it is no good mentioning the Danish author [Rode] [for the purpose of analytical notes] as Fred's piece has quite detached itself from it . . ." She adds: "He [Delius] just said this: 'I wanted to depict the Turbulence, the joy, energy, great striving of youth—all to end at last in the inevitable death'."

[27] Munch to Delius, 24 June 1899.
[28] This is Delius's own spelling in the English title at the head of his manuscript (B.M. loan 54/3 from the archive of Universal Edition [Alfred A. Kalmus Ltd]).
[29] Delius to Dr. Tischer, 20 March 1912.

The relationship of the 1912 version of *Life's Dance* to that of 1898 is much the same as the relationship of Munch's murals in the University of Oslo aula to his earlier *Life Frieze*. Of this relationship Munch writes in 1918: "The actual mood that pervades the various panels of the frieze is a direct result of the conflict of the 1880's constituting a reaction to the prevalent realism of that period. . . . The Life Frieze is the individual man's sorrows and joys seen at close quarters—the University decorations are the great eternal forces".[30]

Technically, the period from 1899 to 1912 is marked by an increasing richness in texture culminating in an almost excessive use of chromaticism both in melody as well as in harmony and the creation of what Warlock aptly defined as a uniquely personal counterpoint of chords rather than of moving melodic lines. The setting of *An Arabesk* for baritone solo, mixed chorus and orchestra mirrors in music the sinister forces of nature symbolised by the demonic aspect of the god Pan, the destruction of summer by winter, of life and love by mutability and madness. A short work of great concentration, it inevitably takes Delius into a post-impressionist world. He never repeated the experience and it is significant that in the period of his life after 1912 he turned increasingly to the problems of absolute form in sonata and concerto and, in such impressionistic works as *On Hearing the First Cuckoo in Spring*, *Eventyr* and *North Country Sketches*, returned to a simpler viewpoint in mood and texture.[31]

The concertos and sonatas of this later period were, for long, dismissed as outside the proper province of this composer. Only in this last decade have they begun to be valued as an essential part of Delius's output, and as possessing their own individual principles of cohesion, seen to be not the formless outpourings of a declining mind, but the inevitable climax of a life work.

This is not really surprising if we look back at the great *Song of the High Hills*, that piece of Norwegian impressionism which was in gestation from 1897 to 1911. More than any of the other tone poems it approximates to a symphony. The construction is pyramidal, evolving from the opening chords

[30] Quoted in Johan H. Langaard and Reidar Revold, *Edvard Munch fra år til år* (Oslo, 1961), p. 84.

[31] This does not mean that the orchestral forces employed are any less in number and kind unless Delius is deliberately writing for small orchestra.

through a series of themes treated melismatically, each in turn gathered up in the wordless singing of the choir a capella before the inevitable descent from the "Great Solitude", "the vast wide distances", is made by the unwinding of those themes until the chordal matrix of the whole matter is reached again.

Dying in 1907, Grieg never saw the works which fully justified his early belief that Delius would develop as a composer in the grand manner. Many forces contributed to that development, but none was more enduring and productive than Norway.

ACKNOWLEDGEMENTS

The thoughts expressed in this paper first took shape as a lecture to the Anglo-Norse Society, London, given at the headquarters of the Arts Council of Great Britain on Norway's National Day, 1965. To all who assisted me then and in my subsequent researches I am most grateful. I am especially indebted to: the Delius Trustees, London; the Grieg Trustees, Bergen; the Trustees of the Grainger Museum, University of Melbourne, Australia; the librarian of the Royal Norwegian University Library, Oslo; the Director of the Munch Museum, Oslo; Mr. Gunnar Rugstad and the Institute of Musicology in Oslo; Mr. John Boulton-Smith; Mr. Sigurd Blehr, Mr. Hans Heiberg and Mr. Per Krohg of Oslo; the legal heirs of the composers Sinding and Holter and of the violinist Arvesen; the librarian and staff of the Jacksonville University Library, Fla., and Mr. Geoffrey Driggers of the Jacksonville Library now the Haydon Burns Library; the late Mr. Hugh Alderman of Jacksonville; Mr. James Alldridge and Mr. Per Thorstad, translators to the Delius Trust during my time as archivist 1964–1966; Mr. Alan Denson, the previous archivist, 1962–1963; my successor, Dr. Lionel Carley, the present archivist to the Delius Trust; and to Mr. Robert Threlfall, musical adviser to the Delius Trust. Thanks are also due to Augener/Galliard Ltd for permission to quote from *Longing* by Delius, and to Alfred A. Kalmus Ltd for permission to quote from *The Song of the High Hills* by Delius.

("Studies in Music", 1972.)

Hans Haym: Delius's Prophet and Pioneer
by Lionel Carley

We know a great deal about Sir Thomas Beecham's work on behalf of Delius. Indeed, it might even be said that we know too much, in the sense that this extraordinary collaboration has largely overshadowed an earlier partnership which was perhaps equally remarkable and scarcely less significant. Hans Haym, Musical Director in Elberfeld, took up an almost completely unknown Delius ten years before Beecham heard a note of the composer's music, paving the way from his performance of "Over the hills and far away" in 1897 to Delius's widespread acceptance in Germany as a first-ranking contemporary composer within a very few years. It was under his direction that "Paris", "Das Nachtlied Zarathustras",[1] the piano concerto, "Appalachia" and the complete "Mass of Life" were first given in that country, and it was chiefly due to his own enthusiastic proselytising that we may ascribe many other early performances in German towns and cities of these and other works. It was above all to Haym that Delius owed the considerable reputation which he enjoyed in Germany by 1907, when Wood and Beecham were turning their attention to his music in England. How strange that this unique music, with all its complex beauties, should have come to first flower in Elberfeld. And how easy it has perhaps been to forget that it was in fact in this grimy industrial town to the south of the Ruhr that a performing tradition for Delius's music was first established.

First, a word about Elberfeld. In name, at least, it all but disappeared from the map of Germany in 1930. In 1929 the town had been merged for administrative purposes with the smaller adjoining town of Barmen, a number of neighbouring villages had been thrown in, and the resultant agglomeration had become known at Barmen-Elberfeld. A year later the name was

---

[1] Although this was the title by which the work was generally known in Germany, Delius's unpublished manuscript bears the title "Mitternachtslied Zarathustras". To complicate matters it has also been performed as "Das trunkene Lied".

187

again changed, this time to Wuppertal, with Elberfeld becoming a district within a city whose population has grown today to close on half a million. At the turn of the century it was a plain but prosperous industrial town which, taken together with Barmen, stretched for some nine attenuated miles along the banks of the river Wupper in the north-east of the Rhine Province. The town centre was a hotchpotch of mills, factories and dye-works—ugly but substantial visual evidence of Elberfeld's undoubted prosperity. The surrounding country-side was green and pleasant, but the wooded hills which rose quite steeply from the valley were a factor in maintaining an atmosphere over the town which was as heavily polluted by smoke as was the river by the industrial filth that was discharged into it. This was a period, however, when many of the town's older, insanitary buildings were being swept away and replaced by new constructions more conducive to its civic pride and comparative wealth: a town hall, a theatre, fine shops and business premises—and a spectacular monorail railway suspended over the bed of the river.

With a population at this time of about 150,000, Elberfeld was perfectly capable of sustaining a reasonable number of educational, artistic and philanthropic institutions, civic or otherwise, and like many German towns of comparable size and status it boasted choral and orchestral societies which enjoyed the support of a wealthy and numerous middle-class. Handel and Haydn oratorios had been the staple fare during the early years of the Choral Society (the Elberfelder Gesangverein), which had been founded in 1811 as the Elberfelder Singschule. Its first Director was Johannes Schornstein. The Concert Society, or Elberfelder Concertgesellchaft, was founded in 1861; subscription concerts were soon started and the town's musical activities expanded.

Hans Haym was appointed Musical Director in 1890, but a word should first of all be said about his predecessor Julius Buths, who will be mentioned again in these pages. Buths had himself succeeded the Choral Society's second director, Hermann Schornstein. As a young man he had founded a choral society in Breslau and gained some knowledge there of the administrative aspects of musical affairs. He conducted a particularly good performance of "The Seasons" in that town in April 1879; this was noted by the management of the Elberfeld Concert Society, who duly offered him the Elberfeld post which had recently fallen vacant. Not only a skilled orchestral and choral conductor, but a virtuoso pianist and harpsichordist, Buths stayed for eleven seasons and then moved on to nearby Düsseldorf when the musical directorship there was offered to him. Elberfeld was sad to see him go but he handed over to his successor an adventurous and thriving musical organisation.

Hans Haym was born in Halle on 29th November 1860 (he was, therefore, a little more than a year older than Delius). As a student he had read philosophy and classical philology in Jena and Tübingen and had earned himself the degree of Ph.D. with a dissertation entitled "On the Recognition of Reality". He then reverted to his first love and studied composition, the piano, organ and singing at Munich. There followed a period of teaching in Giessen until, in the middle of 1890, he was offered and accepted the Elberfeld post that Buths was relinquishing. He was then twenty-nine. This earnest, likeable young man soon established a happy and lasting relationship both with the town and with his performers. He continued Buths's policy of blending the old with the new, and although for the most part he had to defer to the conservative tastes around him he was as generous as he could be in introducing the works of younger composers. His first Strauss, for example, was an early performance of "Till Eulenspiegel" in 1895, only a few weeks after the work had been given for the first time, and his first Delius, as we have seen, was "Over the hills and far away", which he gave under its German title "Über die Berge in die Ferne" on 13th November 1897.

This was the first time, so far as we know, that Delius's music was publicly performed in Germany. It was Ida Gerhardi, a mutual friend, of Haym and Delius, who had effected the introduction of this new music to Haym. Ida was a painter, like her close friend Delius's future wife Jelka Rosen, and her family home was not very far away from Elberfeld. By the time of that first performance of "Over the hills" she, Delius and Jelka were all settled at the latter's recently-purchased house in the village of Grez-sur-Loing, near Fontainebleau. Delius himself had been on an autumn trip to Norway, where he had heard his incidental music to Gunnar Heiberg's play "Folkeraadet" performed for the first time. He broke his homeward journey in order to attend the performance of "Over the hills". What he heard must have left him reasonably satisfied, at least with the conductor's interpretation of his music, and this was the beginning of a close and fruitful, not to say historic, collaboration that was broken only by the outbreak of the First World War.

A short review of "Over the hills" appeared in the columns of Elberfeld's daily newspaper, the *Täglicher Anzeiger*, on 16th November:

> In contrast to the Brahms, the rendering of the first item in the programme, the new fantasy overture by Fritz Delius, which the orchestra read from manuscript, did not come up to expectations. The opening evoked interest and tension, and the work is certainly rich in original ideas and pretty melodies and is in many places brilliantly and skilfully scored. But it did not hang together logically, and generally lacked a clear train of thought. Furthermore, the colours were often laid on too crudely.

Not, by any means, an unfair or unfriendly criticism of an immature work, particularly as the critic went on to end his review by asserting that the young composer was "very talented", and that there would undoubtedly be greater things to come from him. There is little evidence to suggest that at the time and in itself this particular performance had wide repercussions. The continuing struggle that Haym was to have over a period of years to get Delius's works into his programmes suggests that the musical public at large in Elberfeld, together with a majority of the Concert Society's committee, remained on the whole indifferent. I do not think therefore that this performance triggered off any notably hostile critical reaction, as has sometimes been maintained. Elberfeld's strong reaction was not really to set in until the autumn of 1904, when it clearly began to be felt in local circles that Haym was pressing the composer's claims too far, and that for some tastes too much Delius was being played.

It would appear that no orchestral work, at least, by Delius was played in Elberfeld for another four years, and it is not until December 1901 that we find Haym writing to Delius: "Paris will be done!" (Paris wird gemacht!)—the words which open a correspondence comprising some fifty-five letters and postcards written to Delius by Haym which have come down to us. Delius's own letters to Haym have apparently not survived. The first performance of "Paris", a work composed in 1899 and dedicated to Haym, took place in Elberfeld on 14th December and brought forth some acid critical comment from the *Täglicher Anzeiger*, with flippant reference being made to the composer putting his audience on an omnibus and shuttling them from

Hans Haym (1860–1921).

Hans Haym and Delius discussing the score of "A Mass Of Life" in Haym's music-room at Elberfield on 12th December 1909.

one Parisian night-spot to another: "But he doesn't let us hear the tuneful gypsy melodies in the boulevard cafés, always just cymbals and tambourine and mostly from two cabarets at the same time at that". (When Busoni gave the work in Berlin almost a year later a comment on the same level compared the music to the next-morning feelings induced by a "night out".) At least, though, the two Delius performances that Haym had now given had raised a sufficient amount of interest in Elberfeld's musical establishment for the composer's works now to be given more often in the town.

The next landmark came towards the end of 1902 with a performance of a setting of Nietzsche, "Das Nachtlied Zarathustras". This choral and orchestral work had been composed in 1898—a year during which Delius also made four song-settings of Nietzsche—and it had first been performed at that notable concert of his works which was arranged by the composer in London in May 1899. (It was not until 1907 that another Delius performance was to be given in an English concert hall.) The piece was later incorporated in "A Mass of Life", of which it now forms the magnificent last movement, except for the final peroration. In that initial London performance the *Morning Post* had discerned a composer who was "deeply impressive and original" and who "does not shrink from employing the strangest and most perilous harmonic progressions".

Buths had seen the score of the "Nachtlied" at about the same time as Haym. He was not quite so enthusiastic about the work, feeling that it showed signs of immaturity, but his interest was sufficiently aroused to have a copy made of the score and to signal this fact to Delius. Three years later he took up the work again and re-reading it found much more to please him, declaring his intention to perform it when an opportunity arose. Buths, wrote Haym to Delius in July 1904, "has become converted to Zarathustra". Haym's enthusiasm for the "Nachtlied" was immediate and is reflected in a passage he wrote a few years later describing the final section of the "Mass": "The solemn grandeur . . . that holds the hearer spellbound from the first note to the last, is probably unparalleled in modern musical literature except for analogous parts of 'Parsifal'." In December 1902 Max Schillings, a conductor-composer with a considerable reputation which was to be consolidated at Bayreuth, told Delius that he found the "Nachtlied" "very interesting and full of genuine feeling" (Delius had

191

sent the score to him) and that he would recommend it for performance at the next *Tonkünstlerfest*. His words carried weight and it was given in Basel on 12th June 1903 under Hermann Suter and with the composer present. Suter, too, later asserted that Delius's "Zarathustra-music" had moved him deeply. Haym was unable to go to Basel but sent a congratulatory note to Delius on his success there and took the opportunity to remind his friend always to send him anything new that he wrote. That the performance was indeed successful is best evidenced from a letter Delius sent to Grieg shortly afterwards: "I think I have even managed a publisher thereby!"

The spring and summer of 1903 saw Haym studying "Lebenstanz", the piano concerto, "Appalachia" and "Paris". He spent a great deal of time on the concerto particularly and visited Buths in Düsseldorf where they played through the work on two pianos. "We consider", he told Delius,

that you still betray your descent from Grieg quite noticeably in the concerto, although only in occasional turns of harmony. The main thing is that out of the whole speaks an original spirit. Everyone must come from somewhere, after all, but whereas most people keep to well-worn paths, you are a pathfinder, and to be allowed to follow you—thanks to our prophetic little lady friend—is an experience which gives me great joy.

Only a few days later Buths and Haym played their two-piano versions of "Paris" and "Lebenstanz", both twice through, to a few specially-invited visitors at Haym's home. "Lebenstanz", wrote Haym,

is a splendid composition. Perhaps not as significant as Paris, but much more readily insinuating, much that is quite wonderful and ravishing, and in any case in the orchestral score a great step forward, it must sound magnificent.

The German boom is in fact getting under way, as Delius reports to Grieg in the autumn:

I'm writing exclusively orchestral music—every year I have three or four performances in Germany—Buths in Düsseldorf & Dr. Haym in Elberfeld produce my latest scores every year—Buths has arranged "Paris" the Song of a Great City—a symphonic work of mine for two pianos & Dr. Haym has done similarly for "Lebenstanz". I shall try to send you these arrangements when an opportunity occurs.

He adds: "*My* Mitternachtslied I don't need to tell you has absolutely no relationship whatever with Strauss's "Zarathustra" which I consider a complete failure".

A little earlier in the summer Delius had invited Haym and his wife Cornelia to spend a holiday in Grez. Although tempting, the invitation had to be declined; the Hayms could not afford a holiday that year. Haym was never a rich man, living comfortably but carefully. He had, after all, five children to provide for and conscientiously wanted the best for them. Similarly, in mitigation of what he felt was his Concert Society's reluctance to put on Delius's works, it must be said that budgetary limitations applied as much to musical activities in Elberfeld as elsewhere, and "popular" works had inevitably to take pride of place in the calendar. Indeed, recurring deficits were now a commonplace for the Society, and the reason, according to one contemporary chronicler, was that the Society was motivated by purely artistic intentions rather than commercial ones. Be that as it may, it was because of the comparatively poor financial situation that projected performances of such works as the piano concerto and "Lebenstanz" had to be postponed—to Haym's great sadness, as he was particularly anxious to undertake them. On the other hand he himself decided at the end of the year voluntarily to postpone "Appalachia", for the reason that he had had insufficient time to study it in detail and had no intention of performing the work without knowing it thoroughly.

It was an attitude he generally adopted toward each of the Delius works that he took up: weeks, if not months, of painstaking reading, playing, rehearsing were an almost imperative requirement before he allowed himself the luxury of a public performance. This aspect of his musicianship is best revealed in 1909, when a semi-public rehearsal which he gave of several sections of the "Mass" formed a prelude to its German première over five months later. The time he spent would arguably have been shorter had not some of the scores, initially in manuscript, to be copied from Delius's hand, which was not easy to read when conducting, and the orchestral and choral parts had in their turn to be written out. All this, too, cost money, and in November 1904, for example, we find Haym having to tell Delius that he hoped to recoup some of the costs of lithographing the choral parts of "Appalachia" from the Düsseldorf organisers of the following year's *Musikfest*—providing the work was accepted for performance there. Otherwise he would have to ask Delius for the money.

So it was that by the end of 1903 it had become clear to

Delius that Hans Haym and Julius Buths held the keys to his success in Germany. Due primarily to Haym's influence, a stage-work of his had been accepted for performance at the Stadttheater. On 28th December he wrote to Grieg: "My opera 'Koanga' is being rehearsed in Elberfeld", and within a month he and Jelka were settled in the town at the Hotel Bristol, to help with preparations for this first-ever production, due to open in the following March.[2] The Intendant at the Elberfeld Theatre was Hans Gregor; Fritz Cassirer was musical director and Jacques Goldberg stage director. "Koanga" was well staged and notably well received, with the composer, Cassirer and Goldberg, decked in flowers and laurel wreaths, taking repeated curtain calls at the end of the first performance. Delius himself had already been called to the stage by an enthusiastic audience on the conclusion of the second act. If for them the opera had been a triumph, the Deliuses were none the less happy finally to return—although this was probably not until April—to their home, with its spring blossoms and idyllic atmosphere. Elberfeld had been a rude contrast to Grez, Jelka finding it a "dismal town, full of black smoke, modern industry, machines, rich and ugly people".[3]

It is not clear whether Haym went to any of the "Koanga" performances—possibly not, because it was about this time that he fell ill, with the result that he spent some two months from the end of April convalescing in the Tirol. His first task on settling down in the mountains was to finish an analysis of "Paris" which he had recently begun. This he quickly completed and sent to Delius by the beginning of May:

It is awfully difficult, if not impossible, to do this sort of thing, and if you feel that I have written nonsense, please excuse this on the grounds of it being a thankless task to dissect a living artistic creation, to peel away the vigorous

---

[2] It is interesting to note that although the New York impresario Victor Thrane, a friend of Delius, had asked the composer to send the score of "Koanga" to New York as early as 1898, the American première of this work had to wait until December 1970, when a highly successful production was mounted in Washington. It was seen in London in 1972 and recorded a year later.

[3] See L. Carley, "Jelka Rosen Delius: artist, admirer and friend of Rodin. The correspondence 1900–1914", *Nottingham French Studies*, May and October 1970, p. 95. Jelka tells Rodin of the preparations for "Koanga" in a letter dated 27 February 1904.

flesh & display the bare bones. What a barbaric thing to be expected to do!

Barbaric? Perhaps—and yet Haym was later to undertake a similar study of the "Mass"; and even now he acknowledged that his task had given him a deeper insight into "Paris" itself—given the opportunity to perform it again he would do it "much better than before". Fortunately the opportunity was to occur quite soon.

Haym in convalescence was not content just to sit in the sunshine. Although confessing that he enjoyed "a primitive existence like this in the country . . . the only real one you know", he told Delius soon after the analysis had been despatched: "I still have one link with civilisation in my work on your 'Appalachia', to which a few morning hours are devoted each day". He projected performances, notably of "Appalachia" and the piano concerto, for the 1904–5 season. He asked Delius to send on to Elberfeld the score and some choral parts of one of the Dance Songs already composed for the "Mass". This, which he lightly referred to as "Zarathustra II", he intended to rehearse following his expected return home at the end of June. However, back in harness, he soon discovered that there would be no room in the concert calendar for this particular item and gave up the idea of rehearsing it, during the summer months at least. Initially, anyway, it was not to his taste; he found it quite different from Delius's other works and was at a loss as to how to approach it. Buths, too, had been nonplussed. There were things in it that delighted him, but its "harmonic style"? its practicability? He had sent it on to Haym. By now (i.e. late in July) Haym was aware that Delius was at work on the "Mass" itself and was anxious to be the first to see it on completion.

In spite of some opposition Haym pushed through no fewer than four Delius works for performance in Elberfeld in October 1904. "Appalachia" was given on the 15th, and the piano concerto, "Lebenstanz" and "Paris" on the 24th. Buths was to play the concerto and in August played through both this and "Appalachia" with Haym on two pianos: "He has a splendid command of it", wrote Haym, "& will play it magnificently . . . we admire & love your truly original genius!" Delius made arrangements to travel to Elberfeld again for the performances, Haym asking him to send in advance some biographical details and notes on the works for publicity purposes.

Following "Appalachia", in itself another first-ever performance for Elberfeld, the "Delius Evening" on the 24th was anticipated with more than usual interest, since antagonisms had now come out into the open: indeed it seems that a state of war between the pro- and anti-Delian factions was now a fact of the town's musical life. Presumably many of those who disliked this new music particularly intensely simply stayed away, but a sufficient number were there to ensure that lively, not to say heated, discussions could be overheard in the corridors of the concert hall that evening. Snatches of conversation were reported in the local newspaper. So-and-so did not know the first thing about art, declared one member of the audience. "Ravishing", "enchanting", enthused others. Many sat on the sidelines, prudently declining to pass judgement on something they felt they could not understand. It would be safe to say that the majority of the audience did not "understand" Delius's musical offerings that evening and were more at home with the more traditional items in the programme—a Bach aria, an Adagio and Allegro by Corelli and the "Marriage of Figaro" overture. Jelka Delius had earlier told Rodin of her amusement at seeing Delius "frighten the worthy Germans with his ultra-modern ideas", and it is indeed clear that the citizens of Elber-feld considered her husband's music to be pretty revolutionary. The critic of the *Täglicher Anzeiger* sided with the majority. After the "oppressive weight of this modern music" he had found the Bach aria a breath of fresh air; the "old school" was so much more readily comprehensible, whereas the new was too far removed from the natural feelings of most people. He conceded however that it was worth listening carefully to Delius's music and found the third movement of the concerto *überoriginell* (the work was receiving its first performance, in its original three-movement form). Buths had made a good job of the demanding solo role, playing from memory, but the orchestra had been rather shaky. It had fortunately given a more assured and confident account of the other two Delius works.

But there was now no doubt about it—Haym had gone too far. Delius was well enough aware of the adverse reactions to his music in Elberfeld for us to assume that it was no great surprise to him when Cassirer wrote to him in the following March: "Dr. Haym has been fiercely attacked at a meeting of the Town Council, on account of—Delius! One councillor recommended his dismissal". Gregor, who was in Paris at about the same time (March 1905) wrote to tell Delius that he was on his way back to Elberfeld, and he too hinted at troubles in the town's musical affairs: "Our beautiful town of Elberfeld, how I adore it (!), especially this winter when I have difficulties there such as you would not believe". In fact Gregor was probably glad that he could see an end to his responsibilities there, as his plans for founding a comic opera in Berlin were, by the time he wrote these lines, well advanced; indeed, less than two years later he was to present "A Village Romeo and Juliet" in that city, in its first-ever production.

What Haym did not realise, as 1904 drew to a close, was that he was not, it seems, to have an opportunity to conduct a major work of Delius in Elberfeld for another five years. His opponents had won the day. However, the correspondence between the two men continued unabated, and a letter which Haym sent to his friend (on 18th November 1904) gives a good idea of the sort of effort that he was putting in outside the bounds of the concert hall on Delius's behalf:

Send Seadrift to Buths. Should I not send the Danish songs to Wood right away? Just the full score or the parts as well? I can't find piano reduction of "Sommer in Gurre" [Summer Landscape] otherwise everything is there. I'll write to Mottl about Appalachia. If he sends it back, I'll try the Leipzig publishers. Suter asks for scores. I could send him the old Paris score. And why not Lebenstanz too?!— Hausegger will probably be writing about the Paris parts, I have them at home now. In return he must send me the piano reduction. The 2nd of Appal. has turned up at Tillmann's. A pity that I haven't read the Zarathustra text of your "Mass of Life". Not too polemical, I hope?! The enclosed critique of Busoni will interest you.

This was the first time that Haym, in writing at least, had referred to the "Mass" by name, and Delius kept him informed of his progress on the work. Haym reminded him to write "philanthropically" for chorus—"not like in the 'Tanzlied'!" It was not until November 1905 that he was able to tell Delius: "I'm enormously pleased to hear that the Mass of Life is finished. I am of course extremely curious & would like to do the piano reduction if it can wait till the New Year". He had, however, to wait until the following February before the score was in his hands, and it may be reasonable to assume that Fritz Cassirer, who had collaborated with Delius in the selection of the text, had had first sight of the finished work. No record apparently exists of Haym's initial reaction, but by March we find him thinking of putting together for performance a number of movements: "The 1st Movement with the Introduction would have to be included. The Tanzlied with the 'double fugue' as well. And then 'O Mensch, gieb Acht', which is surely the hit of the whole work? I am also considering the cradling barque piece."

Whether this idea of performing something like half of the "Mass" was prompted by the fear that a continuingly indifferent or even hostile management would be unlikely to agree to a whole evening being devoted to Delius, or whether Haym himself at this stage doubted his own or his performing forces' ability to undertake this unexpectedly vast work, is something we do not know. He had, however, already grasped one important fact about the work which has sometimes eluded later critics: "As far as I can see, the connection between the individual movements is not so important as to prevent one from making such a selection". He was to make the point again later in his published commentary on the "Mass": "No attempt is made to weld these fragments into a whole, either by the insertion of narrative or by any other device." Sections of "Zarathustra", he declared, had been chosen and used as subject-matter for a number of "evocative musical pictures". "The grouping of the various numbers has been dictated by purely aesthetic considerations of contrast and cumulative effect." In other words his fears about the "polemics" of the work had proved groundless and he had realised, as we do now, that musically at least Delius had been essentially attracted by the evocative and often intensely beautiful prose-poetry of Nietzsche: the underlying philosophy was fully accepted—indeed taken for granted. "Zarathustra" in any other language[4] or from any other pen than Nietzsche's would not have inspired the "Mass", and later performances of the work in English have demonstrated just what can be lost in translation of its many verbal felicities.

One may guess that Delius was none too happy with the idea of his new work being performed in this fragmented state, but whether he agreed or not with Haym's suggestion was, in the end, of no more than academic importance. The Elberfeld management had acceded often enough to Haym's represent-

[4] "Fred's idiom is English, his language is English", wrote Jelka Delius to Philip Heseltine in June 1929. "Apart from the exceptionally beautiful Zarathustra, German poetry has never appealed to him, as you know." (J. M. Backhouse: "Delius Letters", British Museum Quarterly", xxx [1965]).

ations, but now they had had enough, and within a week he had to tell Delius that this scheme had fallen completely through: "Delius = red rag! Why not offer it to Suter in Basel?"

Although not actually performing any Delius in 1905, Haym attended at Whitsun the famous Lower Rhine Music Festival, held that year at Düsseldorf. A high point of the Festival was Buths's performance of "Appalachia", which served to establish that work in German critical esteem. Probably, too, he was at Essen the following year to hear the first performance of "Sea Drift". The young Carl Schuricht was certainly there and straightway fell in love with the work, of which he was later to become a noted exponent. He repeatedly asked Delius for the score, his letters to the composer showing quite clearly that he considered "Sea Drift" to be a masterpiece. 1906 saw Haym taking a holiday, for once away from his family, in France and at last staying with the Deliuses at Grez. This was in April. Before returning to Elberfeld he spent a few days in Paris, seeing as much as he could of the city's theatrical and artistic life in the short time he had at his disposal. He was disappointed at not having been able to find the pictures Jelka was exhibiting at the Salon des Indépendants, but was hardly to know at the time that she had been indexed in the catalogue under her professional name, Jelka-Rosen.

Another landmark in Delius's musical career was the first production, in February 1907, of his opera "A Village Romeo and Juliet", with Cassirer conducting. Haym was desperately disappointed at being unable to go to Berlin for the occasion. He had a heavy programme of concerts and rehearsals, and had also somehow to be in Strasbourg at the beginning of March, as he was among the contenders for the post of Director of the Conservatory there: "Who knows, perhaps Strasbourg will take the place of Elberfeld for your music in the future." This was not however to be, and Haym returned home empty-handed and disappointed. Soon, too, it became clear that Delius's prospects for 1907–8 in Elberfeld were no more promising than they had been for the preceding two seasons. "Shall we ever see one another again?" wrote Haym to Jelka in May 1907. "If I remain here I still plan to get the Tonkünstler-versammlung held here one day. This would possibly be the only hope of ever performing a work by D. in Elberfeld again! Just now I'm feeling rather sad."

In March 1908 Delius was able to tell his friend that his works were gaining ground in England. Haym was particularly interested to hear that the "Mass" was to be performed in London: "I'm very sad that I couldn't have been the first to perform it, but I just haven't been able to overcome all the difficulties here." He referred ironically to the fact that a markedly inferior attempt to set Nietzsche to music had been published immediately in Germany. This was Karl Bleyle's recent "Lernt lachen", for soloists, chorus and orchestra. "If only I could perform your Mass!" lamented Haym. "Or at least have it at home! '

The truth of the matter was that the score of the "Mass" had by now gone the rounds of a number of conductors on the Continent without success. Suter, in Basel, had had the manuscript after Haym, but found the demands it made on his choral forces to be too great. He felt that "Sea-Drift" would be an easier work for him to take on, and any hopes that Delius cherished of a Basel performance of the larger work during the 1906–7 season remained unfulfilled. In November 1906 it was in Max Schillings's hands: "I stand in awe before your gigantic score, whose secrets do not reveal themselves at first glance." He planned a performance in Dresden in 1907, but by February of that year the project had foundered, once again on the apparently insuperable difficulty of getting a choir which would be able to tackle the work successfully. For precisely the same reason he thought it unlikely that he would be able to effect a performance of the work in Munich. Fritz Cassirer had had ideas for performing the "Mass" ever since its completion. He had at one time suggested to Delius that he (Cassirer) should conduct it some time during the autumn or winter of 1906–7 in Berlin. Later we find him proposing to perform the work in that same city the following season. He also had his eye on London, hoping to be able to give two concerts of English music there in November 1907, one of them possibly to include the "Mass". But again there was the realisation that it might be difficult to find a large enough choir at comparatively short notice. He soon had to drop the idea of a second concert and settled for "Appalachia" to share the billing on 22nd November with Strauss's Dance from "Salome". Beecham, who had never heard a note of Delius before, was in the audience.

Not until April 1908 did Delius learn that a performance in Germany of his "Mass" was virtually assured, and even then it must have caused him considerable disappointment to hear that it was not to be given in its entirety. Schillings had after all succeeded in getting it accepted at Munich for a performance at the *Tonkünstlerfest* on 4th June. The conductor was to be Ludwig Hess, who himself suggested giving the second part of the work. This alone would involve a tremendous amount of work, whereas the whole of the "Mass" would have needed months of rehearsal—especially for the choir: "You know yourself", wrote Schillings, "how enormous are the difficulties for a choir which is not composed of professional musicians." Hess had become conductor of the Konzertgesellschaft in Munich only the previous year at the age of thirty. He found himself particularly attracted to the "Mass" for the qualities of power and vitality that he discerned in it. But as he prepared the work he encountered a number of obstacles, chief among which was the comparative illegibility of Delius's conducting manuscript, and he asked the composer to send a more easily readable copy. He proposed to interpolate the second movement, "Erhebt eure Herzen", in order to provide a contrast to the predominantly slow tempi of the rest of Part II. And he made a limited number of cuts in the (second?) "Tanzlied" when he found it was impossible for him to get a good choral response.

About a month before the performance was due to take place Delius wrote to Cassirer. An analysis was required for the programme. On 6th May Cassirer sent a terse reply:

As "Zarathustra" is absolutely not composed *thematically*, a *brief* analysis is impossible. I would send a few biographical particulars and merely mention that your artistic aim is the rendering of the *Zarathustra mood*, and nothing more. Any analysis would here be nonsense. I personally could not sign myself as author of the text, nor is this necessary; these analyses of "music" are the height of platitude, don't have anything to do with them. So, a short biographical note with the comment: the pure and simple rendering of the *mood* of the Zarathustra poem has been my aim. A thematic analysis is superfluous. Basta.

It was important for Delius (and indeed for Haym) that the performance of this larger part of the "Mass" should be a successful one, and in the event it was. Hess himself felt afterwards that at a number of points the performance had been uneven, but was pleased that it had generally made a deep and convincing impression on those who had heard it. It had certainly impressed him: "I think of you and your beautifully original work often and with pleasure", he was later to write to Delius. The composer himself was exultant, and dashed off a postcard to his friend Granville Bantock: "the 'Mass' was a great success" and the chorus was "splendid". He followed this with a letter: "My 'Mass' made an enormous impression—in fact much more than I ever expected—the Chorus was superb and the Tanzlied went splendidly."

Haym's hopes were re-awakened. Plans for the 1908-9 season in Elberfeld were perhaps too far advanced by now for room to be made for the "Mass". But by the following March he was proposing that the Concert Society should put it on during the 1909-10 season. He was able to point to the success of the work in its shortened form in Munich, and he probably referred to Beecham's forthcoming performance in London of the work in its entirety. Initially it seemed that like Hess in Munich he was going to be restricted to half an evening, but on 2nd April 1909, triumphant, he wrote to Delius: "Yesterday evening the concert management decided to perform your *Mass of Life in its entirety* on the 11th December!" He was overjoyed. At last he was to perform some new Delius in Elberfeld, and "enormous effort" would go into it. He suggested soloists. The event must be well publicised. "Are you just a little bit pleased?" His delight must have been tempered with a feeling of relief, as it was apparent that the decision had been a close-run thing: "Hartmann the bookseller turned the scales with an enthusiastic vote for your work. If you know him, you could send him a special thank-you."

Haym decided to come to London for Beecham's performance in June. His fares would be paid by the management of the Concert Society and he would stay at the home of an English friend in Stoke Newington. He intended to be in London in time for the final rehearsal, which he proposed to attend with Delius. In the meantime he started to rehearse the "Mädchentanzlied"—"quite the most perverse, difficult piece of the whole". In the event he found Beecham wanting. It was over three years earlier that Haym had first immersed himself in a study of the work, and apart from the composer it is almost inconceivable that anyone else could have had a deeper knowledge and appreciation of it. Nor could any other conductor claim twelve years' experience and absorption of Delius's unique musical idiom. So that although the London performance was notably well received by the English critics, it made a poor impression on Haym:

Dear friend,

Having safely returned home again, I plunged immediately

again into the labyrinth of your Zarathustra score and am delighted anew by the wealth of fine things that are contained in it, which by no means all saw the light of day at the performance. The work needs, after all, more rehearsal and a loving attention to detail. As I already told you, I believe that many passages where you have simply written a *p* or *pp* would gain by more precise indication, emphasis on particular voices etc.

Admittedly, I also have my own buts now! Of secondary importance and simple for you to alter is the passage with the impossible German declamation, piano reduction p.194: "da auch aller Lärm eurer Herzen". These two bars are quite clearly composed for the *English* words.[5]

P.86 is also easy to alter. The words "Ja aber du weisst es auch" are really meaningless as they stand. In Nietzsche the sentence breaks off & is followed by: "Und ich sagte ihr etwas ins Ohr", etc. And then it goes on: "Du *weisst* das, O Zarathustra?", etc. I would cut out the words altogether.[6]

The beginning of II, 5 presents a similar difficulty. The words: "Gottes Weh ist tiefer du wunderliche Welt" can easily be understood in Nietzsche in connection with the previous passage, but here, torn from this context, no one can make head or tail of it I'm afraid.

Not that there's anything to be done about it now. A curious indication of how much above all you always remain the musician, instrumental musician. Which is shown, moreover, in the whole treatment of the solo singing voices.

My worst heresy of all: it seems to be impossible for me to get on terms with the "Tanzlied der Mädchen"! You must be prepared for me to omit it. I don't like the first chorus very much either, but I will do my utmost with it. In London it was an empty noise. Finally I don't agree with the ending of the whole either. I feel that it is a great pity you do not end on the wonderfully solemn mood of "O Mensch gib Acht", but instead dissipate it in the *fortissimo* roar of the tutti. Is that necessary? Could you possibly decide to scrap this ending and—as was the case with the fragment that I once performed here—send the audience away with the eternity-*pianissimo* of a midnight sparkling with stars. This *ff* ending is really

[5] There is, to my knowledge, no evidence to suggest that Delius had an English text of the "Mass" before him when composing the work.

[6] These words were in fact omitted in the later Universal Edition vocal score.

not at all like you, for the little *pp* tail which you have tacked on can't put it right again.

Are you angry? I hope not, since you know well how I mean it. I'm enormously happy working on this and only hope that our abilities will somehow be equal to the difficult task. I'll send the score shortly. I have marked in red pencil a few more uncorrected errors. Best wishes to you both from

Yours
Haym.

E. 18.VI.09

Haym pressed on with rehearsals. In writing again to Delius he did not mention Beecham by name, but he made it clear that it was not his intention to fall into the same errors that he imputed to the English conductor: "I am becoming more and more aware just *how* unsatisfying & coarse the London performance was." It was clear that he felt that Beecham, no less than Hess, had failed to master the difficulties posed by the second "Tanzlied"; no real idea of how it should sound had been conveyed. And still later we find him dismissing the ending of the work in its London performance as a "noisy hullabaloo".

He soon found time to invite members of his concert management to his home, playing the "Mass" through to them. Whether the fact that he plied them liberally with "strawberry punch" helped in any way to convince them of the qualities of the work is perhaps better left unconsidered. But at least at the end of the exercise one beaming member declared that he had thought it was going to be worse. In July he had the orchestra play it right through for the first time and also, rehearsing with his women's chorus, found himself growing reconciled to the second "Tanzlied". He no longer wished to leave it out and looked forward to hearing how it could be made to sound when properly prepared. He was aware that its tempi would have to be taken flexibly and that many of the finely-wrought details in the score would be obscured if the movement were to be taken too fast. His thoughts turned to December: "It will be the most noteworthy concert this winter in the whole of Germany, critics of all the big newspapers should be here, not to mention musicians."

On the last day of July Haym rehearsed the work for two hours before an invited audience of about 100. He had a baritone soloist, small chorus and orchestra and performed a number of sections, reading out the text of each beforehand. He also gave an introductory talk on Nietzsche: "i.e. a tightrope dance, where I tried not to tread on the moral or religious corns of anyone. Nietzsche in usum Delphi! Pitiful performance. But what can you do—". He was delighted with what the exercise told him, even without three of the solo voices. These, he acknowledged, would have to be "höhere Menschen" to cope with their parts, which demanded "more than mere singing". The main problem would be finding a baritone who could successfully portray Zarathustra. Charles Clark, who had sung in London, had agreed to come to Elberfeld, but Haym doubted if he had sufficient command of German, suggesting further-more that Delius might consider adapting the part for a bass-baritone, such as von Kraus or Messchaert. The "ominous" second "Tanzlied" remained a worry. At the rehearsal the small chorus of women's voices and the orchestra seemed to be waging an unequal battle, and Haym saw the necessity of augmenting and further drilling his voices to get the required power from them: "It'll be the devil of a job . . . but it's got to be done."

The summer holidays put an end to rehearsals and the Haym family went off to spend the month of August in their newly acquired chalet in the Swiss mountains. In the middle of October Haym wrote again to Delius: "We are now rehearsing the Mädchentanzlied as well as Händel's Samson. An honour-able juxtaposition." He continued to put in a great deal of work on the score and marked various errors and points which he considered doubtful in red pencil in Delius's copy. It is perhaps worth mentioning that during the months of preparation for the performance Haym sent a flow of suggestions and queries to the composer. He had begun by asking Delius's opinion on who should sing the solo parts. More detailed questions on the score itself followed: "Why don't you augment certain harp passages with the *celesta*, e.g. the motif which first dies away on p.127?" "Is the 'ah' missing in the piano reduction & in the parts to be sung at the end of the Mädchentanzlied?"[7] He suggested dispensing with the doubling of some of the wind in the second half of this "Tanzlied"; trying to find a substitute for bells in the final chorus; and "on p.141 bar 2 you have the first violins playing spiccato—fine, but then clar. along with flute & oboe should also play staccato". "I keep on coming across inexact markings in the score which I should very much like to put in

---

[7] The missing two bars were supplied in a later edition of the vocal score.

order, in the parts too of course." And again: "Unfortunately I keep finding many such open questions, with which I don't wish to burden you, as it may possibly be all the same to you." For all the many rehearsals over a period of several months, at the end of November poor Haym was still nervous: "My hair still stands on end when I think that we shall be firing off a fortnight on Saturday!" Schillings, however, had visited Elberfeld shortly before and was able to reassure Delius: Haym was "fully prepared".

Delius arrived a few days before the performance and was able to attend the final round of rehearsals and clear up the various outstanding points Haym was waiting to talk about. Not for the first time, he stayed *en famille* at the conductor's home, idolised by the Haym children, who had grown up under the spell of his music and to whom he was a familiar figure. One of the two girls, Eva, had at the tender age of twelve been drafted into the women's chorus for the performance.

Emma Tester, Meta Diestel, Matthäus Römer and Charles Clark were the soloists at that performance on 11th December 1909, when the "Mass" was first given in Germany in its entirety. It was a great success and at the end the composer was given a standing ovation by an audience which almost filled the Stadthalle. Deferentially he ceded the applause to conductor and performers, particularly to the members of the choir, who had given the performance of their lives. The women's chorus had, in the event, sung brilliantly. As in London, Clark commanded the main solo role with assurance, although as Haym had feared his German was not equal to the occasion and it was with difficulty that the audience followed his enunciation. To German ears too his voice had a hollow ring—something which at the time was considered peculiar to English singers. Römer's fine tenor voice was well-known to Elberfeld audiences. It had a tendency to *vibrato*, but was deployed to supple and sensitive effect in the "Mass". The women were both excellent, with Tester, the soprano, projecting her voice high above choir and orchestra and taking pride of place among the four soloists. What was eminently clear was that Haym had imbued his enormous forces with tremendous enthusiasm. He had convinced them that this first performance in Germany of Delius's complete "Mass of Life" was a musical event of the first magnitude, and they had believed him and reacted accordingly.

It was not long before further performances of the "Mass"

were being projected in several European cities. One was particularly interesting in that it was attended by two of Delius's newer friends and admirers, Béla Bartók and Zoltan Kodály, both young men and relatively little known at that time. Bartók had first met Delius (and perhaps also Haym?) at the 46th Festival of the Allgemeiner Deutscher Musikverein in Zürich at the end of May 1910. Delius's "Brigg Fair" was one of the works played, and Bartók revelled not only in the music but also in being able to spend some time together with the composer himself. So much so that on his return to Budapest he wrote to Delius to tell him that this newly-found friendship had made his stay at Zürich "one of the most beautiful periods of my life", and he confided to a friend: "For us the most important impression was meeting Delius."[8] The performance of the "Mass" which he later attended was given in Vienna, under the aegis of the Committee for the Worker's Symphony Concerts, in February 1911. The work made a deep impression both on Kodály and himself, Bartók being especially moved by the fourth and sixth sections of Part II: "Der alte Mittag" and "O Mensch! gib Acht"!:

Do you too feel the same, I wonder? In their simplicity and poetry both these sections are intensely moving. Then we were greatly interested in the wordless choruses. We have never heard anything quite like this before. I think you are the first to have experimented in this way. I believe this field offers many possibilities—quite remarkable effects could be obtained.

To return to Elberfeld, Delius, as a result of the success of the "Mass", began to find greater favour in the town. "Sea Drift" was scheduled for the following season and was given in fact early in 1911 with Felix von Kraus, one of Haym's original suggestions for Zarathustra, singing the solo baritone role. Haym had tried hard, but abortively, to arrange a performance of the "Mass" in Berlin, with himself conducting, soon after its Elberfeld première, but in the event he did not have long to wait before undertaking the work again. It was agreed that the "Mass" should be included in a three-day festival to be held in October 1911 to commemorate the centenary of the Elberfeld Choral Society and the fiftieth anniversary

[8] Letter to Etelka Freund, Zürich, 31 May 1910, quoted in "Béla Bartók Letters", edited and annotated by János Demény (London, 1971). Translations from the original German of the six known letters from Bartók to Delius are also printed in this volume.

of the Concert Society. A 131-page "Festschrift und Programm" was brought out for the occasion, Haym contributing
an "Introduction to the Words and Music" of the "Mass",
with the full text following. This was later published separately
in booklet form, both in German and English. Containing sixty-
five short musical illustrations, it represents its author's
principal public utterance on Delius and as such should also be
considered, however briefly, in these pages.

Haym opens by reflecting on the attractions for composers of
the Masses of the Catholic Church—the "Missa solemnis" and
the "Missa pro defunctis"—and the human emotion with
which they were charged. Beethoven, Verdi and Brahms had
given us great religious works:

> And now we have a "Mass of Life"! A certain contrast to
> the "Missa pro defunctis" is implied in its very title. The
> composer would seem to say to us: "Many Requiems have
> been written to commemorate the dead, let us now dedicate
> a "Mass" to the living! Whole generations of artists have
> employed all the constructive imagination and warmth of
> feeling they possessed in order to depict the horrors of Hell
> or the consolations of Heaven; let us now sing a new song, in
> praise of our Life here on earth!"

A paragraph or two is given over to Nietzsche and the
background of his work, Haym reminding us that "Zarathustra" was conceived, in Nietzsche's own words, "in a state
of rapturous tension and inspiration such as I had never yet
experienced". Delius uses the text with complete freedom, as a
springboard for his musical imagination: "I should particularly
like to emphasise the fact", writes Haym,

> that the only proper standpoint from which to judge the
> work is the purely musical one. Delius has been put down
> as a programme musician whose strength lies in his use of
> colour. Nothing could be more erroneous. We may grant that
> here and there in his symphonic poem "Paris" (the chief
> work of his "Storm and stress" period) there are some very
> realistic outbursts of musical impressionism. Since that time,
> however, he has more and more consciously restricted him-
> self to a mode of musical expression, which, though it may
> not be the only one, is certainly the most important of all—
> the portrayal of human emotion . . . the outer world does not
> intrude on his world of sound, except in so far as it under-
> goes that mysterious process, by which all external impres-
> sions are transmuted subjectively into a vibrating medium,

into just that fluid psychic condition which we call mood.

Indeed Haym was already wide awake to this quality in Delius when he published an introduction to "Appalachia" in the *Täglicher Anzeiger*, shortly before he gave the first performance of the work in 1904:

He has a more acute ear than the rest of us and because of this he hears and writes down sounds which none before him has heard . . . Delius is a master of the art of lighting upon a mood, portraying it and letting it die away.[9]

Neither Haym nor Cassirer, as we have seen, professed any liking for academic analyses of musical works, least of all of Delius, and what follows Haym's opening remarks on the "Mass" and its textual subject-matter is perhaps best described as a very readable commentary on the individual sections of the unfolding work. Throughout he takes pains to emphasise the originality of Delius's inspiration: his use of the chorus as an orchestral instrument, the "remarkable intervals" in a phrase given to the female chorus (four bars before fig. 53). How, he asks, can one analyse the "half-mystical, half-naturalistic charm" of the setting of "Süsse Leier"? Indeed, to what end if "out of the mass of quaver passages seething with chromatic harmonies and suspensions, one only brings to the surface an unobtrusive little pair of figures" (one of which happens to be the bell-motif, recurring at intervals throughout the work). As for the "Mädchentanzlied", this is "one of the most original and harmonically complicated pieces of music imaginable". It is a movement which closes with an elegiac passage that is typically Delian, adorned with "the most haunting turns of melody, the most unexpected harmonies, and the tenderest touches of orchestral colour".

In the following movement ("Heisser Mittag") "the wonderful music in which the composer evokes the mood of silent noontide proclaims the unerring hand of genius. He is never at a loss for fresh nuances and refinements to express the sense of timelessness, of perfect happiness, of being withdrawn from the world". Finally, in the last two sections, "music here plays a

[9] An excellent example of this sensitive depiction of mood is the part-song written in 1907, "On Craig Ddu"—although this was almost certainly not known to Haym when he wrote his introduction to the "Mass". Here Delius distils from a six-line poem of Arthur Symons the very silence of the hills, in effect by turning away from the temptation to respond in musical terms to individual words or phrases—the response is solely to the mood of the poem in its finished form, and the result is a miniature of exquisite beauty.

fitting role as interpreter of things that cannot be put into words, and Delius has succeeded in writing an ending of solemn and monumental grandeur to his work". Haym had no doubt that the final long movement—containing the original "Nachtlied Zarathustras"—was "the crown of the whole work" and that "the pearl in the crown" was the "Mitternachtslied". Bartók said much the same thing in an article he published in the Hungarian journal *Zeneközlöny* in February 1911, "A Delius Première in Vienna", in which he takes as his theme the originality of Delius's use of wordless choruses in the "Mass" and in which he considers that "the three profound last numbers . . . are perfect from every point of view".[10]

Haym had also, as we have seen earlier, mentioned "Parsifal" in the same breath as the last movement of the "Mass". Was Delius then, for him, *the* great post-Wagnerian? This at least was implied in a letter he wrote to the composer, referring to the "Mass", on 20th July 1909: "I thank you for having written this work—I consider it the most significant to have been written since 'Tristan'." A little further back, on 1st January to be precise, Hermann Suter had expressed himself in similar terms, again on the subject of the "Mass": "I have to thank the profound soul of your musical language for the most powerful impressions I have experienced since I first became acquainted with Wagner." Haym, of course, was an absolutely committed Delian, and those who have a distaste for the Delius idiom are unlikely to be converted by the eulogistic tone of his commentary. It was never intended in the first place to be a critically analytical piece of writing. On the contrary, Haym himself would have seen it as an ideal vehicle for the kind of propaganda he had been making for years on Delius's behalf. For all that, it is a first-rate and original introduction to the "Mass".

The first concert of the Elberfeld Choral Society's centenary programme opened with a Bach motet, which was followed by "A Mass of Life". Given on Friday, 20th October 1911 in the Stadthalle, it was followed on Saturday by a programme of works by Franck, Wolf, Bach, Schubert, Beethoven and Brahms. The third and last lengthy concert consisted of works by Weber, Berlioz, Schumann and Brahms, concluding with a performance of Beethoven's Choral Symphony, with the same

[10] Reprinted, in English translation, in "Béla Bartók Essays", ed. Benjamin Suchoff (to be published shortly by Faber & Faber).

soloists who had performed two days earlier in the "Mass". The whole programme was a fair reflection of Haym's own tastes. Apart from conducting at all three concerts he undertook the piano accompaniment for the three sets of *Lieder* which were given on the second evening. Among the soloists at the Festival were Raoul Pugno, Eugene Ysaÿe and Pablo Casals— a reminder that since 1900 many first-ranking musicians had been attracted to Elberfeld: Richard Strauss, Schillings, Buths and others had conducted; among the pianists could be numbered Risler, Busoni and Schnabel (Grainger was to come later); Efrem Zimbalist, Elena Gerhardt—the list of distinguished musicians could be extended still further.

Only Römer of the soloists two years earlier sang in the 1911 "Mass". The newcomers were Felix von Kraus, who had distinguished himself in "Sea Drift" in the preceding season, Hedy Iracema-Brügelmann (soprano) and Adrienne von Kraus-Osborne (alto). All gave excellent performances. Felix von Kraus sang with power, in spite of a slight indisposition, and his interpretation of the baritone rôle was judged to be above criticism. It really does seem that Haym was able to improve on his splendid 1909 performance. His orchestra was augmented by players from Cologne and Wiesbaden and together with chorus and soloists produced a more polished sound overall than had been achieved on the earlier occasion. He himself, marvellously precise and with the penetrative understanding that had come from a closer acquaintance with the work than any other conductor, was the inspiration of them all. "A complete and brilliant success" was the verdict of one critic, who wrote of an orchestra "luxuriating in the beauty of sound".

This was Delius's apotheosis in Elberfeld. Ironically it seems that little more of his music was to be heard there. In 1914 however, on 7th March, there was a final landmark in Haym's performance of "Songs of Sunset", which the composer had in fact dedicated to the Elberfeld Choral Society. The work had been completed in 1908, although Haym's acquaintance with it seems not to be documented prior to March 1913 (his last extant letter to Delius being dated 28th April 1910). It was then (in 1913) that he recorded on a page of notes that with the "Songs of Sunset" Delius again brought tears to his eyes. "Who else besides Wagner has such powers of tragic expression at his command?" The rest of modern music—that is to say Strauss and his followers—offered nothing but empty

sounds "ohne Stimmung"; and the man who remained un-
moved by Delius was considered by Haym to have lost the
ability to distinguish and to experience all that was deeply felt
and moving in music.

How appropriate that the end of an era should be marked by
the poignant and haunting Dowson settings, "Songs of Sunset":
"They are not long, the days of wine and roses." Just as it
separated many friends, so the war separated Haym from
Delius. More than that it took two of Haym's sons away for
ever: Franz and Peter were killed on active service in France in
1918. Their brother Rudolf was more fortunate. Encouraged
by Delius, he had succeeded in persuading his father to buy
from the composer early in 1912 the remaining 140 acres of
Delius's former orange plantation, Solana (or Solano) Grove,
in Florida. Delius was anxious to be rid of the property, which
he was anyway not in a position to manage from Europe and
which was by then run-down and non-productive. He was
furthermore short of money and could ill afford to continue
paying the taxes which Solana Grove incurred. Haym paid
Delius's asking price of 500 dollars and the eighteen-year-old
Rudolf was despatched to America. He set about restoring
Delius's old house to something like its former condition, but
there was not much to be done with the plantation, and after
a few months he left to go further south. The property was
finally resold about 1919.

Remaining in Elberfeld during the war, Haym fell gravely
ill in 1918 and his old friend Julius Buths stepped in to deputise
for him at a performance of "The Seasons". He recovered
sufficiently however to conduct later concerts in the 1918–19
season, including what is said to have been a particularly
impressive performance of "Das Lied von der Erde". But
public life in Elberfeld reflected as in other towns the political
chaos of post-war Germany. The world of beauty and fine
manners which the surviving children remembered from the
early years of the century had disappeared. Those childhood
Sundays spent round the piano as father Haym played Bach,
Beethoven and Delius—an activity which replaced church-
going for the family—were an idyllic but distant memory.
Haym died at the age of sixty of 15th February 1921, having
retired only the previous year. His wife Cornelia lived on until
1953.

Something of Delius has been lost in the process of his

"anglicisation"—a process which began as early as 1906. He may have been born in Bradford, but his parents were German and the most substantial part of his purely formal musical education was undertaken in Leipzig. At the time he would have been most receptive to external artistic influences—say from the late 1870's to the beginning of the '90's—the musical language and tradition of Europe remained emphatically German. In his early days he drew from Scandinavia much of his subject-matter, particularly from Norwegian literary sources, and the essence of the cool, mountain landscapes of that country continued to be transmuted in his music throughout his life. His stays in America resulted in the addition of a distinctive exotic flavour to his harmonies and occasionally to his thematic writing. These elements were grafted on to the German stem, and Delius's basic musical make-up was completed.

The reviewer of Haym's first performance of "Over the hills and far away" made no mention of "Fritz" Delius's English origins, and "Paris", which came next in Elberfeld, is an even more Straussian effort, being no more "English" in idiom or instrumentation than "Heldenleben", its approximate contemporary. If we pursue this theme as far as the "Mass", which Haym performed in 1909, none of the works given in Elberfeld seems to owe much, if anything, either to Delius's English background or to the resurgent nationalist voice at the time discernible no less in English music than elsewhere in Europe.

What happened about 1906 was that Delius, aware that at last his music showed signs of being ready and sufficiently well-established to cross the Channel, if this is not too crude a way of putting it, aware too that friends there were tilling the ground on his behalf, was beginning to shed a part of his German self. He came to look more frequently to English themes—to the poems of Dowson and Symons, to English folksong, to English landscapes remembered from his youth. He now set English words more frequently than German ones. Some of his more Impressionist pieces, such as "In a Summer Garden" and "On hearing the first cuckoo in spring", give us an instinctive feeling that, wherever the inspiration may be rooted, an essentially English natural setting is being evoked. Not that the Nordic/Germanic ever completely disappeared in Delius. On the contrary, it broke strongly to the surface on occasion, most obviously in "Fennimore and Gerda" (1908-10), "Arabesk" (1911), "The Song of the High Hills" (1911-12) and "Eventyr"

(1917). It is almost as if Delius had said: "I have accepted the rôle of an English composer in spite of myself, but perhaps you will allow me from time to time to show you what I was and what perhaps I still really am."

As Delius became accepted in England, so at least in one sense did a performing tradition slowly wither and die. Germany, the country which had discovered him, gradually relinquished him and he is now virtually forgotten there. England, claiming him as her own and for a while enthusing over every newly-discovered work of his that was presented for her delectation, in time sat placidly back, content it seemed with a diet of "First Cuckoos", "Paradise Gardens" and "Hassan" serenades, while declining the doubtful and difficult pleasures of the large-scale works. But it was on the large-scale works that the Delius tradition established by Haym had been solidly based. "Over the hills and far away" is about the shortest and perhaps the least consequential orchestral work of his that the Concert Society presented—yet it requires Strauss's orchestra and the demands it made at the time on the Elberfeld band would have been considerable. Over the years, as we have seen, came "Paris" (twice), "Das Nachtlied Zarathustras", "Appalachia", the piano concerto, "Lebenstanz", the "Mass" (twice), "Sea Drift" and "Songs of Sunset". In this list, I think, may be discerned not just the tastes of the Elberfeld musical establishment (or perhaps more accurately the tastes of its pro-Delians) but also the personal preferences of Haym. And to take it a step further one may with reasonable justification assume that Delius encouraged Haym to perform those works which he himself felt to be the best and most typical of him. How interesting in the last few years to have seen such distinct signs of a revival in England of just that earliest German tradition. The work of Charles Groves in Liverpool recalls in its programming as well as in its loving attention to detail the dedicated professionalism of Delius's pioneer, Hans Haym.[11]

("Music and Letters", January 1973.)

[11] I am particularly grateful to Herr Rudolf Haym, of Wilhelmsfeld, and Mrs. Eva Haym Simons, of New York, son and daughter of the conductor, for both written and oral information given to me about their father; and I must especially acknowledge the invaluable and unfailingly helpful work of Frau Marie-Luise Baum, of Wuppertal, who has supplied me with much documentary material. My principal published sources are: Marie-Luise Baum, "Hans Haym" (biographical article published in "Wuppertaler Biographien", 9. Folge, Born-Verlag, Wuppertal, 1970); the "Festschrift und Programm",

published in Elberfeld 1911 to celebrate the centenary of the Choral Society and the 50th anniversay of the Concert Society; and Hans Haym, "Frederick Delius: 'A Mass of Life': Introduction to the words and music" (Universal Edition, No. 8256). My material is, however, largely based on unpublished letters to Delius from Hans Haym and others, now in the Archive of the Delius Trust, London; and on contemporary reviews in the *Täglicher Anzeiger*, Elberfeld. Since the completion of this article Marie-Luise Baum has published a further biographical note on Haym, together with a select list of works and a short bibliography, in "Rheinische Musiker", vii, pp. 42–3.

Delius as a Composer of Opera
by Christopher Redwood

The majority of commentators who have hitherto written on this subject have perforce judged mainly from the printed score. When the present writer prepared a thesis with the above title in 1965 there had been only one Delius opera produced in London in the previous thirty years. This was, of course, the famous "A Village Romeo and Juliet", a work mentioned in all standard reference books on opera, and by which the composer's contribution to the stage has usually been judged. In the ten years since then, however, the British capital has seen presentations of two other representative operas by Delius, one of them in two separate productions, and so the time is ripe for a reassessment of his achievements in this field.

Leaving aside 'prentice efforts (Bulwer Lytton's "Zanoni" and Ibsen's "Emperor and Galilean", sketches for both of which survive), there are six operas in all. "Irmelin" (1890–2) was not staged until Beecham brought it forward at Oxford in 1953, and "The Magic Fountain" (1893–5) has yet to see the light of day. "Koanga" (1895–7) was the first of his operas that Delius witnessed: at Elberfeld in 1904, and has subsequently appeared in London in 1935 and 1972 (the latter with leading singers from a production first given two years earlier in America). "A Village Romeo and Juliet" (1900–1) had its première in Berlin in 1907 and reached Covent Garden in 1910. It was revived there in 1920 and has subsequently been produced at Wiesbaden (1927), The Royal College of Music (1934), and Sadler's Wells (1962), and in America (1970, 1974 and 1975). "Margot la Rouge", a one-act melodrama, has never been produced, although the parts of the music that went into Whitman's "Idyll" makes us wish it could be. The last opera, "Fennimore and Gerda", (1909–10)[1] was first given in Frank-

---

[1] This is the date which appears on the autograph full score, although Beecham (p. 163) states that work on the opera was begun in 1908.

furt-am-Main in 1919, and has been produced in London in 1968, 1970 and 1979.

Before considering these works in detail it is instructive to examine the operatic influences of the composer's youth. Brought up in Bradford, he would have had little opportunity for seeing opera, but he attended college in Isleworth from 1877 to 1880, and we know that his first operatic experience, while still in his early 'teens, was a performance of "Lohengrin" at Covent Garden, which made a profound impression on him. Subsequently he made business trips for his father's firm which took him successively to Stroud, Chemnitz, Norrköping and St. Etienne. During this period he had several opportunities to visit opera-houses: while in Germany he saw "Die Meistersinger" and was bowled over by it. The abrupt termination of family employment was, however, followed by two years in America, where he is unlikely to have seen any opera at all. All the greater must his relief have been, therefore, to find when he reached Leipzig in 1886 that the opera-house there was rapidly attaining a reputation equal to any in Germany. The main reason for this prestigious position was once more the worship of Richard Wagner, and here he would have been able to hear the great Nikisch direct "Tristan".[2]

Wagner, however, was not the sole influence, for Beecham tells us that he was also taken with the later opera of Verdi,

". . . and envied a little, I think, several of the rousing effects and unerringly dramatic strokes of 'Aida'."

Throughout the first two years of his residence in and around Paris he was obsessed with the ambition to write an opera on some grand historical subject, involving the employment of large resources such as processions, pageants, and dancers."[3]

Besides the two early efforts for which some music was written Tiberius, Cleopatra and the Icelandic sagas were amongst many subjects considered. Yet his first opera, when it did come, had little by way of the devices Beecham mentions, nor did it show any of the sense of drama or musical intensity of Wagner or the late Verdi.

Written to his own libretto, it was based on two Norwegian legends, and chosen during a walking tour of the Jotunheim

[2] Sir Thomas Beecham: "Frederick Delius" (Hutchinson, 1959,) p. 35.
[3] ibid., p. 51.

region with Grieg and Christian Sinding (a fellow-student at Leipzig Conservatorium), so it is not unreasonable to suppose that the two Northern composers played some part in helping him to make the choice. Nils, the hero, has devoted his life to the search for a Silver Stream which flows to an unknown region where he will obtain his heart's desire. He is captured by a band of robbers who make him their minstrel, but escapes and is led by the Stream to the Royal Palace. Here he is mistaken for a Prince in disguise and ordered to sing at the nuptials of the Princess Irmelin, who is being forcibly married to a man of her father's choice after failing to find a husband in the six months allotted to her. While the King takes the guests hunting, Nils and Irmelin fall in love and elope. Ernest Newman found the music ". . . true Delius, immature but prophetic", but went on to add that the composer "lacked at that time the most rudimentary sense of stage technique . . . there is practically no action. Some of the naïvetés are staggering".[4] Nevertheless, it contains some beautiful music and does not deserve to be lost for ever. In his last years Delius, with Eric Fenby's assistance, compressed and modified the opera's prelude into a piece which has rightly become one of the most popular of his shorter works.

Nevertheless, the Wagner obsession continued, and in the summer of 1894 we find the composer writing to his mentor, Jutta Bell, ". . . I want to tread in Wagner's footsteps and even give something more in the right direction. For me dramatic art is almost taking the place of religion . . ."[5] A few months later[6] he wrote from Bayreuth, where he had seen "Tannhaüser" once and "Parsifal" ("magnificent: the finest work of Wagner") twice, and from Munich where he intended hearing "Der Ring", "Tristan" and "Die Meistersinger" three times each! Jutta Bell, an artistically-inclined Norwegian married to an Englishman, had been a neighbour in his days on the orange-plantation in Florida. Five years older than Delius, she would no doubt have had a number of interests in common with him, and one senses from his letters a strong spiritual affinity. At about this time she left her husband and went to Paris where she studied speech and singing with Mme. Mar-

[4] "The Sunday Times", 10th May 1953.
[5] Delius to Jutta Bell, 29th May 1894. These letters are in the possession of Jacksonville University, and are quoted with permission.
[6] The letter from Bayreuth is undated; that from Munich 12th August 1894.

chesi, preparatory to setting up as a teacher of elocution in London under the name of Jutta Bell-Ranske. It was in Paris that the paths of she and Delius crossed once more, and she agreed to help him with the libretto of his second opera. Predictably, the setting chosen was Florida, and the story that of Juan Ponce de Lion, the legendary Spaniard who is reputed to have been driven ashore there in 1512.

In the opera, entitled "The Magic Fountain", he is given the name Solano. (Delius's orange-plantation had been called "Solano Grove'). He is depicted as seeking after the Fountain of Eternal Youth, traditionally situated in Florida, and clearly in the composer's eyes a close relative of the Silver Stream sought by Nils in the first opera. Shipwrecked on the Florida coast, Solano is washed ashore and found by the Red Indian Princess Watawa, who leads him to the Chief to explain his quest. He is recommended to consult an old Seer and given Watawa as guide. On the journey he becomes infatuated with her, but she repels his advances as she has sworn vengeance on the white man. When they reach the Seer, Watawa leaves Solano outside his hut while she explains that she has a knife concealed about her, and asks whether she should kill Solano. The old man replies that it is unnecessary as the waters of the Magic Fountain mean death to all who are unprepared for them. As they proceed together, her feelings toward Solano gradually change, and when they reach the Fountain she confesses her plot to kill him, begging him not to touch the waters. Finding that he will not listen to her warnings, she throws herself into the Fountain, drinks, and dies. Solano realises his mistake, follows her example, and dies on her breast.

It is the final sting-in-the-tail which alone distinguishes this story from its predecessor. The phenomenon of similar stories being set repeatedly by a composer is not unusual to opera-goers; one immediately thinks of Puccini with his Eastern settings, his violence, and his religious moments; of Britten with his persecuted boys and father-figures. The most out-standing example is Wagner who, to quote Wilfred Mellers, "used opera as a medium for spiritual autobiography",[7] successively identifying himself as the Dutchman, as Lohengrin, as Tristan, and as Wotan. With Delius's declared intention to

[7] Harman and Mellers: "Man and his Music" (Barrie & Rockliff, 1962), p. 744.

follow in Wagner's footsteps it should not be at all surprising to find him, too, writing autobiographically.

Although "The Magic Fountain" has never been performed, there is evidence that it came near to production on more than one occasion. Philip Heseltine, Delius's first biographer, stated that it was accepted at Weimar in 1893, but later withdrawn by the composer after the libretto had been translated and the parts copied, because he had misgivings about the quality of his work. Heseltine's date must be wrong as the music was not completed by 1893, but Delius's letters to Jutta Bell show that the story may have been substantially correct. Referring to the opera by its earlier title of "Watawa", he wrote on 25th February 1896: "There is some talk of "Watawa" being given in Weimar." On 15th July of the same year he told her: ". . . 'The Magic Fountain' is, as it appears, on the list at Weimar: when it will come on I don't know." A third letter, undated but almost certainly written in December 1896, states: " 'Watawa' is at present in Weimar awaiting its performance—when? I don't know." At this point there is a gap in the correspondence and no further reference to the opera. At the same time we have letters from Sinding to Delius which suggest that the work was seriously considered by the authorities of the German opera-house in Prague. On 24th December 1895 he wrote to say that the music had arrived there, and on 10th January 1896 he passed on the intimation he had received from the director of the theatre to the effect that it would probably be performed in February. When that month arrived, however, he found it necessary to write again to ask what was happening, and added that Delius should obtain a contract with the director of the theatre, whom Sinding mistrusted. After this we have no more letters for over a year, and the opera is not mentioned again. To increase our mystification, attempts to verify the facts by Sir Thomas Beecham before the Second World War, and more recently by the present writer, both with full co-operation of the authorities concerned, have failed to produce a shred of evidence to support them.

Despite Beecham's enthusing over the work, "The Magic Fountain" does not appear from the score to be a great advance on "Irmelin". Staging would require very careful handling, as there is little action, and at the same time Delius's music had not yet reached the point of development where it could hold an audience by its sheer beauty and mask the fact that little is happening. There are several "borrowings" from the Suite

"Florida": the introduction contains the opening theme of the first movement, and this recurs when Florida is first sighted; the Indian war dance in Act II is taken from the third movement, as is also the transition to the scene in the glades at the end of Act II.[8] The first two bars of the theme which introduces Watawa were used again at "O past, O happy life" in "Sea Drift".[9]

While work on "The Magic Fountain" was proceeding, Jutta sent Delius a copy of a volume entitled "Gypsies". In acknowledging it he wrote:

"My intention is to write a musical work on the Gypsies that is why I wanted it. It was not for the present work: I have a vague idea of writing 3 works: One on the Indians, one on the Gypsies and one on the Negroes & quadroons. The Indians I am doing at present. But as I told you once, I always have another work which I think of in the entracte of the present one . . ."[10]

Here is a further Wagnerian scheme in which Delius crystallises, perhaps for the first time, one of the most frequently recurring themes in all his works: that of deprived people singing of lost days of happiness. Actually, we hear no more of the theme and, despite the prominent gypsy element in "A Village Romeo and Juliet", the trilogy idea seems never to have materialised. Nevertheless, he did proceed with the third part of the scheme, an opera concerning negroes, eventually lighting on George Washington Cable's novel "Bras Coupé" from "The Grandissimes", and by early 1896 he was well advanced on sketches for the libretto. On 9th February he wrote to Jutta: "I am not yet certain about the end—I must . . . make Bras Coupé kill himself & Palmyre or something of that sort." It is clear that he now found the liebestod an indispensable part of his apparatus. Later that month he sent her the libretto he had prepared, made the surprising admission that he had written the music and the words simultaneously, and. added: "It is more of an opera than the last one—with quartets, trios, quintets and chorus."[11] He asked her if she could find the time to work with him as she had done on the previous opera: revising the verses he had written as he sent them to her.

---

[8] Rachel Lowe: "A Catalogue of the Music Archive of the Delius Trust, London", (Delius Trust, 1974), p. 39.

[9] Beecham, op. cit., p. 67.

[10] Delius to Jutta Bell, 9th February 1896.

[11] Delius to Jutta Bell, 9th February 1896.

However, she was now extremely busy with her work in London and despite (or perhaps because of) the black American setting, she evidently declined the invitation to help. The next letter we have is dated 15th July 1896 and in it he wrote: "The text was rewritten by C. F. Keary, an English writer of much merit; and also a new friend who I value much." He had met Keary through his new acquaintance Jelka Rosen, and part o the attraction of working with him was the fact that he spent part of each year at Bourron, not far from Grez-sur-Loing where Jelka painted in the Marquis de Carzeaux's garden. One interest Delius and Keary had in common was Norway, for the writer had published in 1892 a volume entitled "Norway and the Norwegians". However, his experience of opera was very small and the libretto he produced was little short of laughable in places. A slave-driver rousing his charges by informing them that "The sun begins to gild the East" is one of the more frequently-quoted examples of his work, which was aptly summed-up by a critic in 1935 as "the wooden English of an old-fashioned opera translation".[12] (Not that Delius appears to have raised any objections; on the contrary, his invitation to Keary to collaborate again in his next operatic project would seem to indicate complete confidence in his friend.) There seems little doubt that the unsatisfactory nature of the libretto was a major stumbling-block in the way of performances of the opera, for when it was revived in America and England in the early 1970's with a revised text, audiences were surprised at the powerful impact it made.

The story, somewhat altered from the book, tells how Koanga (as the hero is now called) is brought from his West African home to work on a Louisiana plantation. Koanga, however, is a Prince, and refuses to submit to slavery. In order to overcome his recalcitrance, the owner encourages his love for the beautiful octaroon Palmyra, who is also his wife's half-sister and maid. The wife, realising she would lose her maid if a marriage to Koanga were to come about, prefers to conspire with the slave-driver—who also loves Palmyra—to prevent this happening. Accordingly, Palmyra is abducted at the pre-nuptual festivities, causing Koanga to fly into a fury, strike the planter, and rush off into the swampland. Here he invokes voodoo, causing the plague to descend on all those at the plantation. Returning to rescue Palmyra, he arrives just in time to snatch her from the

---

[12] "The Daily Telegraph", 25th September 1935.

slave-driver, whom he kills in the process. He is pursued back to the swamps, and here he meets his own death. When she hears of it, Palmyra offers herself as a sacrifice to her own gods by stabbing herself.

Musically, "Koanga" came at a time when the composer's nostalgia for his American days was strongest. He always spoke of the negroes on his plantation in the most friendly manner, and although there is some evidence to suggest that he regarded them in the inferior terms of the age he lived in, we have Percy Grainger's word that he had a black sweetheart in Florida.[13] Cecil Gray went so far as to suggest that he experienced "that which is known to mystics as 'the state of illumination' ", sitting on the verandah of his house one summer night and listening to the negroes improvising harmonies to their traditional melodies. Gray believed that the composer spent the rest of his life trying to communicate the rapture of this moment in his music.[14] A brief glance through the list of his early compositions shows how literally true this is. His first large-scale work, written in 1887 while he was a student at Leipzig Conservatorium, was an orchestral suite entitled "Florida". The following year came another suite, of which one movement was called "La Quadroône (Rhapsodie Floridienne)". At the time which we are now considering (1896) he had just composed the first version of a work which was to become (in a later revision) one of his masterpieces. This was "Appalachia", named after the old Indian word for North America. In this early draft, liberal use was made of such melodies as "Dixie" and "Yankee-Doodle", as well as other less well-known traditional tunes. Although "Dixie" and "Yankee-Doodle" were excised from the later version (to which was added a choral finale introducing a song which Delius had apparently heard sung in a Danville tobacco-stemmery[15]), he evidently felt that the use of traditional melodies had been sufficiently successful to warrant repeating the experiment. When he came to compose the music for "Koanga", therefore, he imparted unity to the first two acts by the regular appearance of traditional negro melodies, harmonised in the way he had heard them sung, and in a manner which exerted considerable influence on his own harmonic style. One of them, "He will

[13] See p. 122.
[14] Cecil Gray: "Musical Chairs" (Home and Van Thal, 1948), p. 191. (See p. 140)
[15] Beecham, op. cit., p. 73.

meet her when the sun goes down", bears a certain similarity
to the theme of the "Appalachia" variations, while another,
originally given the words "Come out, niggers come out to cut
the waving corn", is a tune which obsessed Delius for many
years. Snatches appear in the third movement of "Florida",
while one of the themes of the "Late Swallows" movement of
the String Quartet (1916) consists of the opening notes of this
melody with a different ending.[16] "I am keeping the whole in
the character of the negro melody" wrote Delius to Jutta.[17]
Once again, "Florida" provided a ready source of material:
the best-known excerpt from "Koanga", the Wedding-dance
"La Calinda", had formed the latter part of the first movement
of the suite. Now with vocal lines artfully added, it gained an
extra dimension.[18] Some time after the completion of the opera
it was decided to abandon the 3rd Act Prelude and substitute
in its place the prelude from the second act of "The Magic
Fountain".

There are no negro choruses in the third act of "Koanga"
(although there is a reference to "Come out, niggers" in the
orchestral interlude that leads to the epilogue). This is probably
one reason why the act seems less taut in performance. Separ-
ating its composition from that of the earlier part of the opera
came a return visit to Solano Grove. Whether the reason was to
escape from emotional entanglements in Paris, to seek the girl
he left behind him, to attend to business affairs, or to obtain
further inspiration for his opera, there is a certain disparity of
style apparent in the music that was composed after his return
to France. One possible explanation for this is that he was by
now living and working mainly in Grez-sur-Loing with Jelka
Rosen, and was about to embark on his period of most fruitful
creativity.

Large sections of the opera were first performed in concert
version at the composer's self-introductory concert in London
in 1899, and it seems to have been then that the decision was

[16] The connection between these two melodies, together with another from "The Magic Fountain", was demonstrated by Robert
Threlfall in a fascinating article entitled "Late Swallows in Florida"
in "The Composer", Spring 1974.

[17] 9th February 1896.

[18] It should be borne in mind that the composer had at this time no
thoughts of publishing "Florida"; this only took place when Sir
Thomas Beecham revised the suite some twenty years after Delius's
death.

taken to alter the Prelude to Act III.[19] When the work went into rehearsal at Elberfeld in 1904, it was found necessary to make simplifications to the libretto which took it even further away from Cable's story.[20] It was also necessary to insert a specially-composed aria for Palmyra to appease the soprano playing the rôle, who tended to develop a sore throat when she found that the costume Jelka Delius had designed for her was not to her liking! In the very last years of his life, Delius was still working with Jelka on improvements to the libretto in the hope that it would be performed in London before he died. Further modifications were made by Edward Agate and Sir Thomas Beecham for the 1935 publication, and a new edition was published in 1975. Whilst generally making the story more acceptable, this still contained such anachronisms as a slave-chorus with the line "I'm goin' to bring back so much money that your apron-strings won't hold"—hardly the sentiments likely to have been expressed on an eighteenth-century plantation, one feels! However, Delius himself, together with many subsequent commentators, seemed to overlook the vast difference in time and space between this setting and the Florida he knew a century later. In particular, the Calinda (which he was not likely to have heard on the East Coast) was a hysteria-inducing dance at one time banned on account of its violence and obscenity; the version we have come to know so well is positively balletic in its refinement.[21]

Although the "Gypsies" book which Jutta sent Delius in 1894 does not appear to have led directly to the composition of an opera, the remaining part of the trilogy was still in his mind at the end of the century. At what point he actually lighted on the story of "Romeo und Julia auf dem Dorfe" from Gottfried Keller's "Die Leute von Seldwyla" is not certain, but there is a letter in the Grainger Museum, Melbourne, from Delius to Jelka, dated 28th January 1898, which asks her to read the libretto of the opera he has sent her and give him her opinion.[22]

[19] See Robert Threlfall: "The Early History of Koanga" in "Tempo" No. 110, September 1974.

[20] For a detailed comparison see William Randel: " 'Koanga' and its Libretto" in "Music and Letters" Vol. Lii No. 2 (April 1971), pp. 141–156.

[21] See "The Dance in Place Congo" in "The Century Magazine" No. xxi (February 1886), p. 527; and "Historical Introduction to 'La Calinda' " by R. Nettel in "Music and Letters", No. xxvii (1946), pp. 59–62.

[22] Rachel Lowe, op. cit., p. 78.

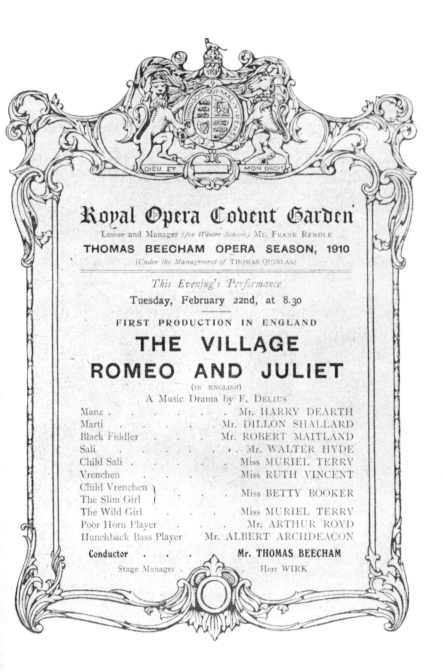

Programme of the first British performance of "The Village Romeo and Juliet" at Covent Garden, 22nd February, 1910.

Royal Opera Covent Garden

Proprietors . The Grand Opera Syndicate, Ltd.
Lessees . The Sir Thomas Beecham Opera Co. Ltd.

1920
THIS EVENING'S PERFORMANCE

Friday, March 19th, at 8.30

Delius's Opera

THE VILLAGE
ROMEO AND JULIET

Manz	. WILLIAM MICHAEL
Marti	. ARTHUR WYNN
Sali	WALTER HYDE
Vrenchen	. MIRIAM LICETTE
Black Fiddler	PERCY HEMING
Slim Girl	LILLIAN STANFORD
Wild Girl	KATHLEEN MOORE
Horn Player	SYDNEY RUSSELL
Hunchback	POWELL EDWARDS
Sali } Children {	. AMY SISSONS
Vrenchen } {	LILLIAN STANFORD
Conductor .	Sir THOMAS BEECHAM

Stage Director . GEORGE KING

Programme of the revival of "The Village Romeo and Juliet" at
Covent Garden in 1920.

There is further evidence that he discussed the project while in London for his 1899 concert, a letter from G. M. Karlyle suggesting that delicate handling would be necessary, and a different librettist from Keary. That Delius nevertheless first entrusted the task to Keary is proved by an undated letter from him which begins as follows:

"Dear Delius,

For the moment I am stuck with R. & J. I don't see this 2nd (or rather 1st) Act satisfactorily.—

I have written Act 2 (1) after a fashion; but I don't care for it; I put in an auction, because you said that it works well musically. It don't literally. Howbeit, I'll keep it, unless you think of something better —1st Vreli alone—voices from village girls and boys outside—then Sali & Vreli—then Manz (or Marti, I forgot who is father of Vreli) He comes in, threatens Sali—then some older villagers come in, are followed almost immediately by the **Maire** or other officials from neighbouring town with auctioneer—Manz's land sold by auction—then ?"

However, none of the printed editions of the score or libretto makes any reference to Keary, and Edward J. Dent, who attended the first performance,[23] credits Delius with having prepared his own libretto. It seems likely either that Keary withdrew from the project or that Delius took it over from him and completed it himself. Jelka, who certainly made the German translation, may have helped him with the dramatisation of the English version too.

Keller's original inspiration was a newspaper report of a true incident:[24]

"A youth of nineteen and a girl of seventeen fell in love. They were children of poor parents who, having long been bitter enemies, refused their consent to the lovers' marriage. On 15th August the two young people went to an inn where the poor folk of the neighbourhood were making merry, and stayed dancing there until one in the morning, after which they left together. The following day their bodies were found in a nearby meadow."

This simple idea he expanded into a delicate tale of the innocent love of two young people. The feud between their

[23] See p. 27.
[24] "Zürcher Freitagszeitung", 3rd September 1847. See introduction to Keller's "Romeo und Julia auf dem Dorfe" ed. Margaret A. McHaffie (Nelson, 1956).

fathers he imagined to have arisen over a strip of wild land which separated their two farms. Because the owner of it was illegitimate he could not (under Swiss law) claim his inheritance, so he contented himself with occasional visits punctuating the vagabond existence he eked out by playing his violin at public gatherings. The farmers surreptitiously purloined strips of the land until the inevitable mutual accusation occurred, leading to litigation which ruined them both. The children first met on the wild land, where they played together while their fathers toiled. An accidental confrontation when they grew up prompted them to arrange a further meeting on their old playground, and when the girl's father crept up on them the boy knocked him insensible. The father was taken to an asylum and his daughter forced to sell the farm. She spent the last night there in the company of her new lover, after which they decided to spend all their money on one happy day together at a nearby fair. When recognised they moved on to an inn haunted by the fiddler and his cronies. Finally, having decided that they could never be happy together on earth, they took to a deserted hay-barge from which the boy removed a plug, and drifted down the river into eternity.

At first glance it would appear that Delius followed this plot very closely, but a more detailed comparison reveals that he (or Jelka) modified it extremely skilfully to suit his purpose. The quarrelling of the parents, which takes up about half of Keller's story but which would not call forth the kind of music Delius wished to write, is reduced to no more than is necessary to provide an insuperable objection to the children's love. Then again symbolism, that most pungent ingredient of all romantic works and which is hardly present in the original, plays an important rôle in the opera. This is most apparent in the character of the Dark Fiddler who has turned from a minor, earthly figure into the central personality of the work. He makes his first appearance in the opening scene when the children are playing on his (unclaimed) land; when, as older children, they have their first romantic meeting, this also takes place on his land and it is not long before he appears again. When at the fair they are recognised and jeered at, it is the Fiddler who persuades them to accompany him to the Paradise Garden, and when they finally abandon that and their lives he is found "playing wildly on the verandah". This last episode is one of a number of interpolations by the composer, the Fiddler having faded from the picture by this point in the book. Another addition, and no less symbolic, is the following scene where the opera is brought to a close with the voices of unseen boatmen singing: "Tally-ho! Travellers we a-passing by!" Clearly this is the composer's final comment on the transitory nature of earthly happiness, and is a master-stroke of construction. Less successful is his "dream-wedding" sequence where, besides attempting to depict the ceremony in the musical strains of a religion he abhorred, he rather naïvely has the lovers share the same dream, whereas in Keller their dreams were merely simultaneous and not identical.

As will be mentioned later, Delius's operatic characters are most successful when they move as if in the control of some unseen power, and in this case the Dark Fiddler clearly represents the compelling force of evil in the lives of the lovers. Christopher Palmer has pointed out[25] that the composer would have viewed such a vagabond character with more sympathy than the essentially middle-class moralist Keller, and suggests that Delius found a parallel with his own character.

"He, like the Fiddler, was in a sense an outcast, spiritually isolated, cosmopolitan in outlook and temperament but basically stateless; for routine morality and the standard ethical code of the society into which he was born he cared not a fig."

If this is so, then we have a further example of the composer projecting his own personality into his operas. Mr. Palmer also points out that Delius added considerably to the scenic descriptions, particularly in the cases of the wild land and the paradise garden—each lush and overgrown (like his own Solano Grove) in the way that appealed to him so strongly and so regularly. Furthermore, he twice introduced a mention of snow-mountains, invariably linked with horn-calls in the orchestra. These nowhere appear in Keller's story, but we know them to be important motivating features of Delius's compositions.

The music of "A Village Romeo and Juliet" is not quite that of Delius's maturity. The influence of Greig is still apparent, and there are moments of pure verism which any composer of the period could have written, such as the ending of the scene where the boy strikes the girl's father. The harmonic idiom is certainly chromatic, but it is surprising to find upon examination

---

[25] "Delius and Poetic Realism" in "Music and Letters", October 1970.

that the important themes are essentially diatonic. The exhilarating opening melody, for instance, simply consists of an incomplete scale descending from tonic to tonic, with an answering phrase which repeats the procedure in the opposite direction. The opera makes use of a number of leitmotifs, a procedure which it is somewhat surprising to find Delius had not employed previously.[26] The most famous excerpt, "The Walk to the Paradise Garden", which is so often said to "distil the quintessence of the opera" is simply a highly-professional working together of these leitmotifs. The interlude was certainly composed after the rest of the opera, probably to cover a long scene-change.

We now come to the most curious of Delius's stage-works, the melodrama "Margot la Rouge". As is well known, he composed it for a prize competition organised by the Italian publisher Sonzogno to rival that held by Ricordi; twelve years previously it was won by Mascagni's "Cavalleria Rusticana".[27] The story, although written by a French authoress, Berthe Gaston-Danville,[28] contains a sufficient streak of verism to satisfy an Italian publisher. It is set in a Paris café, where the clientèle is discussing the latest amour of Margot la Rouge. A group of soldiers enters and they begin light-hearted banter with the girls. The sergeant, however, abstains, as he recognises in the description of Margot his former sweetheart. When she enters they embark on an impassioned love-duet, but this is interrupted by the arrival of her current lover, and a quarrel develops. She tells him that she hates him, and he attempts to stab her. The sergeant, however, interposes and receives the fatal wound himself. In retaliation Margot kills her lover with the sergeant's bayonet, and the curtain falls as she is arrested. Most writers seem to have assumed that because the story is not obviously in the Delian vein the composer could not possibly have made a success of it. However, the central love-scene (more than a quarter of the opera) *is* in this mould, and in fact contains some of the loveliest music he ever wrote. The story

[26] "Koanga" has one leitmotif, associated with appearances of the hero.

[27] But not, it would appear, sufficiently well known, for both Beecham and Jefferson ("Delius" in Dents' "Master Musicians" series, 1972) transposed the publishers' names.

[28] The identity of the librettist, who wrote under the nom-de-plume of "Rosenval" has been uncovered by Lionel Carley in "Delius: the Paris Years" (Triad Press, 1975).

itself is slow to come to life, (nothing of real significance happens until halfway through), but it is possible that with our present understanding of Delius we could make allowances for this. Beecham is rather less than fair to the work, saying of the central scene: ". . . he apparently found himself incapable of inventing the right sort of music to meet the needs of the situation, fell back upon the use of a little figure already exploited in 'Paris' and worked it almost to death." The figure to which he presumably refers is one of those triplet fingerprints which we meet so frequently in Delius's music, yet which always manages to sound different in a fresh context. Actually, setting apart, there is little here to remind us of "Paris".

Rather more than one third of the music was used thirty years later with great success in Whitman's Idyll "Once I passed through a Populous City". This does not necessarily imply that the remaining two thirds is bad music: much of it is concerned with the more macabre happenings and is not characteristic of the composer, but need be no more objectionable than the corresponding moments in "A Village Romeo and Juliet". Other parts are taken up (as one might expect, considering the object) with the Puccini-esque device of parlando recitative against fragments of orchestral melody. The biggest obstacle in the way of performance is the loss of the full score, but even this could be reconstructed from the orchestration of "Idyll". When we reflect that the work was composed between "A Village Romeo and Juliet" and "Sea Drift", there is every reason for a performance to be desirable. Lithographs of the vocal score, prepared by Ravel, are extant and Philip Heseltine's, now in the British Museum, contains revisions. One wonders whether he considered mounting a production— perhaps as part of his ill-fated opera scheme during the First World War.

Beecham tells us that after completion of "Margot la Rouge", Delius began negotiations with Oscar Wilde's executors to make an opera of "Salome". It is difficult to envisage any other composer treating this subject in view of the opera Richard Strauss subsequently made of it, but one cannot imagine Delius matching the sensuality and lust of the story. The Strauss opera appeared in 1905, and within six months came a ballet on the same subject by Delius's friend Florent Schmitt.

With the completion of "Margot la Rouge" in 1902 Delius may be said to have bid the world of conventional opera farewell. One work was yet to come, but as will be seen it was an operatic experiment—not entirely unsuccessful, but never-theless not repeated. He was at this time in his early forties, mentally in his prime, and living with the woman he loved in the house which he loved. With hindsight we are able to add that he had just embarked upon his most fruitful decade of composition; in front of him lay the greater part of twenty years before his final incapacity, and more than a decade before the outbreak of hostilities which some maintain to have destroyed the world he loved and the atmosphere of which he sang. Why, then, was he to complete only one more opera ? The main reason, it would appear, is that his harmonic style was be-coming increasingly chromatic, and therefore demanding an intimacy of atmosphere and a subtlety of interpretation which are not suited to the bright lights and bold strokes of the opera-house. Taking this argument one step further we see the dichotomy which now faced Delius as a composer of opera. Having discovered what he wanted to say in music, he was faced with the unarguable fact that this could only be said when there was a state of virtual inaction on the stage. When he found it necessary to produce action, his writing became un-characteristic. "A Village Romeo and Juliet" strikes the optimum balance between these opposing forces, but after that date he was no longer prepared to compromise. Any new stage work had to be a departure from traditional form, and logically could only present the drama as a series of more or less static tableaux. A second reason is that with increasing confidence and experience he no longer needed words as a framework on which to build his musical edifices.[29] One must also consider that he may have been disillusioned; behind him lay five completed operas, the greater part of thirteen years' work, and none of them so far performed. However, Delius showed extraordinary resillience to the vicissitudes of success in the musical world—that he persevered until he was nearly forty before receiving any sort of recognition bears witness to the fact—besides which, we should have expected the successful staging of "Koanga" in 1904 and "A Village Romeo and Juliet" in 1907 and 1910 to have spurred him on to greater achievements in the operatic field if this explanation held.

It is interesting to observe that the score of "A Village Romeo

[29] Professor Arthur Hutchings pointed out, in a lecture to the Delius Society, London, on 16th January 1975, the considerable proportion of Delius's compositions using words before 1904 compared with works written after that date.

and Juliet", published after the British première in 1910, is headed "Oper in sechs Bilder" ("Opera in six pictures"). Early versions of the vocal score, including those lithographed at the composer's expense in Paris and used at Berlin and Covent Garden, are headed "Oper in einem Prolog und drei Akten" ("Opera in a Prologue and three Acts"). It would seem to be indicated that some time between the production of the two scores the composer altered his view of the work, although the point is only of academic interest at this stage to the observer, who sees no difference from traditional form. Nevertheless, the observation is of significance in relation to Delius's last opera. The designation of "six pictures" might be taken as indication that he would have liked the work to be played without an interval; if so, he was once more treading in Wagner's footsteps, and the word "Bilder" is also that used by Wagner to describe the scenes in his own works. Even more likely, however, is the influence of the theatrical technique of Strindberg, who had been acquainted with the composer in Paris in the '90s. As an enthusiast of Scandinavian literature, it is impossible that Delius could have been unaware of Strindberg's work, and he may well have seen some of his plays presented by the Théâtre de l'Œuvre in Paris. Inspired somewhat by Reinhardt's "Kammerspielhaus" ("chamber-playhouse"), which was functioning in Berlin at the time of the first production of "A Village Romeo and Juliet", Strindberg opened his own chamber-theatre in Stockholm the same year. Curtain-drops were abolished, scenery confined to a few props, casts reduced to two or three persons, and the action concentrated into a brief time-scale.

Now Delius had written to Jutta in 1896: "I don't believe in realism in opera",[30] and many years later he wrote to Philip Heseltine: ". . . realism on the stage is nonsense, and all the scenery necessary is an impressionistic painted curtain at the back, with the fewest accessories possible."[31] In an interview given at the time of the first production of "Fennimore and Gerda" he said:

"Ninety minutes to two hours is long enough for any opera, and by reducing intervals, as I have done in my own work, to three minutes instead of the usual half-hour necessitated

[30] Delius to Jutta Bell, 25th February 1896.
[31] Delius to Heseltine, October 1916, quoted by Beecham, op. cit., p. 178.

by ponderous realistic decoration this limit can easily be preserved."[32]

It might seem therefore that, notwithstanding his "processions, pageants and dancers" phase, he had been a life-long champion of the very ideas that Strindberg was aiming at.

In choosing "Fennimore and Gerda", Delius was returning to one of his favourite Scandinavian authors, the Danish Jens Peter Jacobsen, some of whose poetry he had already set, and whose "An Arabesque" was to provide the inspiration for a later extended composition. Since it is only a small part of the novel "Niels Lyhne" that was used for the opera, it is worth summarising the book briefly. It begins with the somewhat unfulfilled marriage of the hero's parents, then traces Niels's various love-affairs, beginning with a teenage passion for his consumptive elder sister, followed by a shy infatuation with a well-connected widow. Throughout we see Niels as a vacillating dreamer, in contrast to his more masculine friend Erik Refstrup who sows the seeds of atheism in his mind. When the opera opens, the two young men are staying with Niels's uncle, who has a daughter Fennimore. She sings them a yearning love-song, and each believes that it is he who is being addressed. A snatch of conversation overheard by Niels, however, makes it clear that it is Erik whom she loves. Before long the two are married and Niels returns to Copenhagen. But Erik's career as a painter does not go well; his marriage, too, seems empty, and he takes to drink. He sends for Niels, but instead of this helping matters it only serves to fan the smouldering love between the latter and Fennimore into flame. Niels moves to a house across the fjord and a liaison is established. The climax of the drama comes one autumn evening when Fennimore, alone and eagerly awaiting a visit from Niels, receives instead a telegram informing her that Erik has been killed in a road accident whilst out with his drinking companions. When Niels arrives Fennimore, instead of turning to him for comfort, rails at him and dismisses him from her life for ever. After this the novel tells of another unsuccessful love-affair, this time with a tempestuous opera-singer, which does not appear in the opera and so need not concern us here. Instead, Delius moved straight on to the following episode where Niels, having taken over his parents' farm, falls in love with Gerda, the teenage daughter of a local councillor. They are married and the opera ends on a happy

[32] Interview with G. M. Stevenson-Reece in "The Evening News", 1919.

note—something which has not occurred, incidentally, since "Irmelin". The book, however, ends very differently, both Gerda and their infant son meeting early deaths, and Niels himself dying of wounds received in the Dano-Prussian War. The subject of his atheism plays a large part in these later chapters, and was apparently originally intended to be the central theme of the story. Doubtless this was one of the features which attracted Delius to it. Abandoned sketches show that he first intended to follow the story through to its conclusion, but he probably preferred to end with his favourite theme of nature's eternal renewal. After a series of pictures which progress through the seasons, the final scene takes place significantly in the spring (as do the final movements of "North Country Sketches" and the Requiem).

Experimenting on Strindbergian lines, Delius reduced the story to a series of eleven pictures connected by short instrumental interludes: "short, strong emotional impressions given in a series of terse scenes"[33] was his own description. It is worth noting that although he was still friendly with C. F. Keary at the time he began work on "Fennimore and Gerda", he eschewed further collaboration, preferring to prepare his own libretto. The idea of an opera constructed of scenes from a novel, compressing a diffuse time-scale into a short entertainment was quite new at the time, and needed careful handling if it was to succeed. One of the work's shortcomings is its length (about one hour) which makes it less than a full evening's entertainment, and there is difficulty in finding a suitable companion-piece. There is a further drawback in the common streak of restlessness and indecision in the make-up of all three main characters, which makes them difficult to define. Perhaps this is what Beecham had in mind when he passed his damning verdict: ". . . three rather dreary people who have nothing to sing".[34]

"Fennimore and Gerda" came at the end of Delius's period of most successful compositions, and already there is a discernible change in his musical style. The beauty is still there, but it is presented less unremittingly and in a more subtle manner.

---

[33] *ibid.*

[34] Beecham, op. cit., p. 164. It must be admitted, however, that Beecham was inclined to be partisan in his judgement of the later compositions of Delius of which he did not direct the first performance. Although "Fennimore and Gerda" was dedicated to him, he never conducted it.

There are discords which we do not remember in earlier compositions, and which we do not meet again until the Requiem of 1914–16. It is only in the final two pictures (whose introductions have been conjoined to form the popular Intermezzo from the opera) that we see a return to the essentially diatonic style of "A Village Romeo and Juliet" and, in the singing of Gerda's sisters, the la-la-ing of the maidens in "A Mass of Life". It is almost as if the composer was relieved to have completed the psychological drama of the first nine pictures and felt himself on happier ground when dealing with the simple love of Niels and Gerda. Once again, there is a parallel with the Requiem: the composer is always least successful when trying to express philosophy in music. (In his earlier settings of Nietzsche, while he agreed with the sentiments expressed, it was the portions of greatest *poetic* appeal that he selected.)

Earlier in this essay the view was propounded that the operas of Delius have certain similarities of plot. What are these similarities? There are usually two persons concerned, both seeking after some high ideal. However, the spectator feels that somehow the quest is doomed to failure from the start, almost as if the characters are in the control of some unseen, superhuman power. In the first two operas the object is a tangible one, namely the Silver Stream and the Fountain of Eternal Youth respectively. Subsequently the object becomes the intangible, in each case the search for earthly happiness. In "Irmelin" it is only Nils who is seeking his heart's desire (although the Princess Irmelin's six months' wavering over her suitors might be said to betray a similar state of the unconscious mind), and one of the main sources of dramatic weakness is the lack of that feeling mentioned above, that the characters appear to be unable to control their own destinies. This feeling becomes stronger in "The Magic Fountain" through the conflict of racial tension; in "Koanga", on the other hand, it is barely present at all. All control over the fate of the two principals clearly lies in the hands of their white overlords, and the work is the closest to a conventional opera that Delius came to write. In "Fennimore and Gerda" the feeling of doom is made more obvious firstly by the restless, neurotic character of Fennimore, as made clear in the very opening pages, and later by the illegality of the love between her and Niels. It is only in "A Village Romeo and Juliet" that we have this feeling without any obvious signs of manipulation of the plot. The controlling factor seems to lie in the hands of the Dark Fiddler whose presence is never less than plausible, and it has been rightly pointed out that, while the obvious parallel between Sali and Vrenchen lies with Tristan and Isolde or perhaps with Pelléas and Mélisande, there is also an element of Hänsel and Gretel in their make-up, inasmuch as they present a naïve innocence that promises catastrophe.[35]

The atmosphere necessary for such a story to succeed is very much aided if the setting is long ago in time, and it will be observed that Delius's operas become progressively more modern. This is not of such great importance in "A Village Romeo and Juliet", where the story itself has a particularly timeless quality, but the more up-to-date setting of "Fennimore and Gerda" puts an almost intolerable burden on the three main characters.

Arthur Hutchings[36] listed three requirements necessary to "composers such as Wagner and Delius" in an opera libretto. These were:

1. A legendary story, charged with romantic atmosphere.
2. "A tale which provides scope for the voluptuous and ecstatic . . ."
3. "A story in which some scenes present either the distances and horizons of seascape and landscape or the romantic appeal of nature . . ."

To these three we might add that for Delius the following are also essential:

4. A story which deals with a quest after the unobtainable.
5. Characters who move as if in the control of some unseen power.

Finally we should consider briefly the two subjects that Delius evidently considered after "Fennimore and Gerda". Heseltine, whose biography was published when the composer was not only still alive but still healthy, mentions "Deirdre of the Sorrows" and "Wuthering Heights". Clare Delius[37] adds that he had the whole scheme of the latter outlined in his mind during the First World War and explained it to her. The treatment was to be a series of pictures as in "Fennimore and Gerda", but she gives no further details. There can be few

[35] Peter Heyworth: "Lovers in an Alpine Landscape", in "The Observer", 8th April 1962.
[36] "Delius" (Macmillan, 1948).
[37] "Frederick Delius: Memories of my Brother" (Ivor Nicholson and Watson, 1935).

books which have such a diffuse time-scale and one would have thought that this alone would have proved an insuperable problem, although one can see the theme of yearning, lost love appealling strongly to the composer. The other story is also the kind of subject that would have suited Delius, although one would have expected a result more on conventional operatic lines. It is certainly a matter for regret that he did not repeat the experiment he had once essayed, foreshadowing the chamber-operas of later in the century. Had he done so with success, and other composers followed his lead, it might indeed have been "possible for opera to become the supreme vehicle for the expression of the finest and subtlest psychological ideas".[38]

[38] Interview with G. M. Stevenson-Reece.

The Early Versions of Delius's Piano Concerto
by Robert Threlfall

One of the most fascinating aspects of musicological study is that devoted to composers' own revised versions of their works, whether undertaken for perfectionist or practical reasons. Although Frederick Delius is not usually considered to belong to either the practical or the perfectionist category, a fair number of his major works exist in versions subsequently substantially revised. The early *Appalachia* without chorus; the various scores finalised as *Life's Dance*; the version of *In a Summer Garden* which the composer himself first conducted—all these show considerable differences from the later definitive scores. The *Paris* that we know appears to be a conflation of different earlier elements; whilst *Eventyr*, too, according to Beecham—under whose roof it was first sketched—became a larger work when the composer returned to it a few years later. Most striking of all, however, in both the scope and nature of revision, are the transformations which the *Pianoforte Concerto in C minor* underwent. Resisting the temptation to stray further among those earlier scores above-mentioned, let us concentrate on the last-named work for the present.

Warlock's pioneer volume on the composer refers (pp. 137, 164, first edition; pp. 122, 202, second edition) to a first version of the Piano Concerto in three movements, material from the third movement of which was subsequently used in the Violin Concerto; when the work was later cast into a continuous scheme, this third movement yielded its place to the recapitulation of the first movement. Beecham, too, in his book on Delius, not only refers to the three-movement version (p. 99), but gives some further detail of the original third movement (without, however, referring to any later transplant to the violin work) as well as describing the re-casting into one movement at a date not given but deduced to be 1906 (pp. 132, 135–136). The first performance, given at Elberfeld in the autumn of 1904 by Julius Buths, conducted by Hans Haym, is always stated to have been of the original version; the performances on 22nd October, 1907 (Queen's Hall, London, conducted by Sir Henry Wood) and subsequently by Theodor Szántó (to whom the work as published is dedicated) being in the revised "three-in-one" movement form, in the solo part of which Szántó is known to have had one hand, if not two. "The present printed score, however," Eric Fenby assures us, "is as Delius intended" (despite, presumably, the virtuoso pianistics of, for example, the last page; which undoubtedly form Szántó's signature as much as the carefully-fingered chromatic thirds of earlier sections).

There the matter seems to have rested, despite confusions caused by differing copies of the published score and orchestral material and by the appearance of Delius's misleading date of 1897 on most printed copies; but though presumably true in essence, the story as told so far is far from complete: let us now examine the further evidence currently available.

The exhibition of "Deliana" staged in Bradford and London in 1962 under the auspices of the Delius Trust provided a basis for fresh speculation, inasmuch as a score described as a *Fantasy for Piano and Orchestra* (Catalogue of Exhibition, item 82) was displayed, this being opened furthermore at a page in no wise resembling any part of the Concerto we know! This score was said to be signed and dated 1897, so it already seemed likely it was of a version unknown to or ignored by all previous commentators—as, in fact, it proves on examination to be. To clarify the position, it seems advisable to tabulate forthwith the various manuscripts still known to be extant, following this later with a similar listing of the various editions published to date.

Manuscripts (in the archive of the Delius Trust).

(aa) Arrangement for two pianos (in a copyist's hand) in three movements, *viz.*: 1. Allegro ma non troppo; 2. Largo (D flat major); 3. Maestoso con moto moderato 5/4—Molto tranquillo 4/4. (Third movement defective: only five pages survive, though Beecham, in his description, speaks as though he were familiar with the content of the whole movement.) Dated "Spring 1897".

(B) Full score in Delius's hand of *Fantasy for Orchestra and Pianoforte*, in one continuous movement of several sections. Orch: 3.2.2+BsCl.3—4.2.3.1—Timp.—Strings—Piano solo. (The piano solo part appears at the foot of this score.) Dated "1897". Bound.

(b) A solo piano part basically agreeing with that in score (B); in a different copyist's hand from that of (aa), but with Delius's own overwriting, alterations and additions, especially to the Largo section and the final cadenza.

Note: the manuscript sent to the original publisher (Harmonie-Verlag) remains at present untraced.

The musical contents of these manuscripts may be summarised as follows: (aa) exhibits a conventional three-movement form; the first movement of which agrees in substance with the first 15 pages of the published edition, followed by a short further development and recapitulation of material similar to pp. 28–36 *ibid.*, leading to a two-page coda ending fortissimo in the major key. The music of the second movement agrees closely with the D flat largo section known from the published scores, but here also coming to a full close and equally self-contained; however, the details, especially of the piano writing, and the distribution between solo instrument and orchestra differ in both these movements, often very considerably, from what was later printed. What exists of the third movement moreover has no resemblance to any portion of the published work. On the other hand, MSS. (B/b) show the conflation of the original movements 1 and 2, which is such a characteristic feature of the published version, by inserting the largo section after the development and before the recapitulation section of the original first movement material. This resemblance to the published work in outward shape does not extend, however, to particular details: the key-scheme of the exposition is different, the second subject appearing here in A flat instead of the relative E flat; and the development, though more extended than that of the version (aa), still differs greatly from the published version; until a somewhat similar double pedal and diminuendo link to the largo section, here shortened by the omission of the matter occurring after cue 19 in the printed score. After the recapitulation which then follows but which here omits the solo version of the second subject matter, this work ends with a climax and pause and a ruminative cadenza, partly accompanied. At the very end, the opening motive of the whole work appears in the orchestra leading to a quiet close in the major key. As in the case of (aa), both layout and distribution of the solo part differ greatly from parallel passages in the published work.

At first glance, it might well seem, then, that the Fantasy-version of the Concerto post-dates the three-movement one, the latter called the original version by all previous writers. As the revision by the composer before publication entailed the recasting of his work into one movement, it would appear likely that the Fantasy was his first attempt in this direction; for it seems illogical, to say the least, that Delius should have extracted a concerto in the three conventional movements from a one-movement Fantasy: doubly so, indeed, if he subsequently returned to the Fantasy form before publication. This tentative conclusion, however, is shaken by a number of circumstances of varying weight, of which the most important are as follows:

The manuscript full score of the Fantasy (B) is pencilled over in a number of places with matter which on close inspection is seen to be such as otherwise only appears in the three-movement version, (aa). The start of the development section in the first movement of the latter, the piano obbligato part in the slow movement, the climax of this same slow movement, all these passages and other details too can be dimly recognised among the pencillings into spare staves of the score of B. All these changes are "one-way": they all favour (aa) and no alterations in the opposite direction are to be discovered. Once identified, these pencillings are hardly explicable save on the supposition that the Fantasy score *preceded* (aa); when this conclusion is accepted, most of the other details fall into place. It is next to be noted that the final published version is always much closer in music and figuration to (aa), although in outward form of course it resembles rather B.

A few inconsistencies remain, though none is sufficiently serious to challenge this opinion. Thus, B ends with a cadenza in which appears a figure otherwise occurring in the 'cellos at the commencement of the (later-rejected) third movement of (aa). This same figure is pencilled into the very ending of the score of B. It seems curious to introduce an entirely new such figure in the final cadenza—although distinguished precedent is to be found in no less than Schumann—whereas were (aa) earlier than B the prominent use of this same figure therein would have given more point to its subsequent use in a closing cadenza. In fact, this little fragment must have had some special value to Delius; for though it is excluded from the Piano Concerto as printed, it finally achieves its destiny in the cadenza of the *Violin* Concerto (one bar after cue 20)—where it is at least as unprecedented as it was in the piano Fantasy! A few bars of this very passage are to be seen in a sketchbook (now in the Grainger Museum, University of Melbourne, Australia) whose contents are otherwise chiefly devoted to works of the period around 1916, such as "Late Swallows" and the two "Songs to be sung of a Summer night on the water", where we catch the composer in the very act of reminding himse'f of this earlier motive at the time of the composition of his Violin Concerto.

Besides the manuscript score of B, it will be recalled that a separate piano part has survived. In places, this appears to be a slightly earlier state of the solo part than that in the full score; and its writing resembles the hand of the copyist who prepared a vocal score of *Koanga*, being also on similar oblong paper. This latter vocal score did not originally contain Palmyra's aria in Act II, nor the transplant from *The Magic Fountain* in the prelude to Act III; and hence it may date from the late '90s rather than from the early 1900s. This solo part of the Fantasy, then, may likewise be of similar date. One wonders indeed why this solo part should exist at all if the version B was never publicly performed, as is Mr. Fenby's opinion— unless perhaps it was the version played with Henry Falke in the Paris salon mentioned by Beecham (without date) on page 99 of his book? The apparent non-survival of the manuscript full score of (aa) is equally remarkable, for this must have existed for use at the performances known to have taken place. Was it subsequently "cannibalised" by Delius, or by Szántó, or by both, when work on the published version took place? (Scores of rejected versions of the other works named above have survived in the Trust's archive). Incidentally, proof of (aa) being the version first performed by Julius Buths under Hans Haym at Elberfeld in 1904 is independently established by the review in the Elberfeld *Täglicher Anzeiger* dated 26th October, 1904, and by a letter from Haym dated 6th August, 1904, in which he states "The 5/4 time will not be exactly easy for the orchestra". Only in (aa) does that passage in 5/4 time occur. Finally, if indeed (aa) "was played frequently in Germany between 1904 and 1907", as Beecham says, there was hardly time for B to intrude between (aa) and publication.

However unlikely it may first have seemed that Delius should have extracted a conventional three-movement concerto from his Fantasy, it is not impossible; and the internal evidence now offered, taken as a whole, seems convincing. The Fantasy was Delius's natural form into which he first cast his work; it would have been remodelled perhaps under German influence into the conventional three movements and subsequently restored to his first overall conception, but using material gathered during the production of his intermediary version, (aa).

On 20th April, 1906, Julius Buths, writing to Delius, asked how matters stood regarding publication of the Piano Concerto, which he had been the first to play in public in 1904 in Elberfeld. "In any case, another thorough revision would be necessary beforehand", he said. That the work was at that time still intact in three movements is proved by a letter to the composer from Marie Geselschap dated 2nd April, 1906, asking "whether you want the Third Movement . . . very slow, and whether you want to leave the *Cadenza* at the end as it is and have it played quasi impromptu ? (Evidently this version—aa—whose finish is now sadly lacking in the only apparently surviving manuscript, terminated in similar fashion to the earlier score B.).

Later, in September of that same year (1906), correspondence takes place between Delius and Theodor Szántó, who now first appears on this scene. The question of alterations to be made in the piano part is mentioned; and in the early months of 1907, sending the score to Szántó, Delius points out that the closing bars are incomplete and that Szántó will probably want to end with a flourish, which Delius asks him to supply on the basis he indicates. From another letter in mid-January it appears that it was at this time that Delius had been working his way through the score, presumably recasting the piece into its present overall shape—a date confirmed by Max Chop. In April he reports having spoken to Henry Wood, who will have the work included in the next Promenade Concert season. At the end of May the score is sent to the publishers, Harmonie-Verlag, and the contract duly signed shortly afterwards. By August difficulties arise with them because of the corrections and changes called for, as a result of Szántó's continued working at the piano part. Small as these changes seem to the composer, all the material is affected; and what guarantee is there that Szántó will not find other things he wishes to alter, say the publishers ? However, on 22nd October the performance takes place in London as planned, and is a great success.

The next chapter opens in June 1908, when Szántó announces that he has prepared a "supplement" to the piano concerto, "indispensible for both conductors and pianists", he says; he thinks there are also a few places which need altering in the orchestral part. Delius asks him for these alterations but it is late September before they reach him; and then he receives what is presumably a completely new score with "a few compositional alterations" also "examined and revised" by one Glenck, a friend of Szántó's. Delius then writes at length: on 28th September he thanks Szántó and Glenck for their work, of much of which he approves; but he makes a number of very practical criticisms of some of the changes and says they do not all meet with his agreement. By October, however, his attitude is hardening. On the 17th he writes both to Szántó and to Harmonie stating that the work is not a spectacular piano piece with a subordinate orchestral accompaniment, as Szántó apparently feels, and maintaining that he was quite satisfied with the effect of the score as he heard it in London. Although the altered version is well done, the whole character of the work has been changed. Harmonie having defended Szántó's efforts to make "your otherwise impossible work performable", as they said, Delius rejects these remarks as "completely unworthy" and blames Szántó for his attitude in calling the work "a thankless task in the old version". Only two performances (in late October, 1908, at Halle and Leipzig) in Szántó's latest version are permitted by the composer, who promises to take legal action against any other such performances. He only allows Szántó these two performances, he tells him, because he knows the pianist's intentions were good (and presumably because it was too late to do otherwise). "Of ordinary concertos there are already enough", he ends, "without my adding to their number; and as you know, I would not take a single step to achieve a mere popular success".

Argument continues during the rest of the year, as Szántó has another performance booked for January, and also the question of a new impression from the publishers is ahead. Finally, retaining some of the proposed alterations, Delius is told by his soloist that the score "now has the appearance I always wished (except in one place)". This one place may concern the four bars of scales at cue No. 23, which Delius rightly called "boring and empty" and wanted omitted. Szántó's justification for them was that they gave colouring and added tone, and he did not insert them just for virtuosity. The principal reason for the revision, he now says, was the many mistakes in the original version: instrumentation was only the second reason! Finally, however, on 1st April (1909) Delius is able to tell his publisher to proceed with the new impression using his latest altered score.

It is obvious from this brief summary of a very lengthy and detailed correspondence that Szántó's revised score involved many changes, pianistic, orchestral and compositional, which the composer subsequently rejected, as well as some other suggestions which he accepted. The differences between the unpublished three-movement version and the printed edition reveal clearly the capable pianistic improvement Szántó achieved, presumably before his original London performance of October, 1907: there is no doubt that the work as published now incorporates a cogent and well-wrought piano solo part, far firmer than the composer's originals, interesting as they are. Even if the pianistic additions seem in questionable taste in some places, it is well to remember that, for example, the last page—Szántó's applause-raiser!—was in fact developed or added to by him at Delius's request. Perhaps we should there-therefore agree to one of his other requests, and omit the four bars of scales at cue No. 23, "then the entry after the gap will sound much better", as he rightly said.

To conclude, let us now list the different printings of the published version of the work.

Published Editions

(H) Harmonie-Verlag, 1907; no publisher's number. Full score, lithographed. "Theodor Szántó gewidmet." Orch· 3.2.2.3—4.2.3.1—Timp. Cymbals—Strings.

(hh) Harmonie-Verlag, 1907; No. 180. Arranged for two pianos, four hands by Otto Singer (printed by Röder), pp. 38, "Klaviersatz bearbeitet von Theodor Szántó".

(h/u) Copies of this two-piano publication are also to be found in U.E. covers. (The note about Szántó does not appear on all U.E. copies: it appeared on the old U.E. title-page and was later added at the head of the first page of the score, but *after* the introduction of the new title-page.)

(uu) Universal-Edition, ?1921; No. 3903. Arranged for two pianos (as above, but printed by Breitkopf and Härtel).

(HU) No full score was engraved by U.E., but copies of the Harmonie score, with alterations pasted over, and in Universal-Edition covers, No. 3901, are in circulation. (That these alterations date from as early as 1914 is established by a copyist's copy from that date, a photograph of which is in the Delius Trust archive). Orch: 3.2+CA.2.3—4.2.3.1—Timp. Cymbals, Bass Drum—Strings.

(TB) Boosey & Hawkes, 1951; No. 8864. Full score, engraved and printed by Lowe and Brydone. Revised and edited by Sir Thomas Beecham. Orch: as in (HU).

(tbi) Boosey & Hawkes, 1975: No. 8864. Pocket score (HPS 895) reduced from the above, incorporating a few corrections.

(tb2) Boosey & Hawkes, 1975; No. 20214. Arranged for two pianos as above; but re-engraved, and incorporating Beecham's editing.

The differences between H/hh and HU/uu are far too numerous to list in their entirety, but as a rule concern details rather than the overall plan. Among the most significant discrepancies may be mentioned the change from C to 2/2 at one bar after cue 9 (this change occurs 8 bars after cue 9 in TB!); extensions of one bar into two before cue 20; and insertion of a bar (two bars in full score HU) at cue 26, where again a change of C to 2/2 occurs. Likewise, a number of detailed performance directions, in many cases bilingual, appear first in (uu).

All these publications (except TB) carry the date 1897 under the composer's name, thus causing (hh) in particular to have been referred to at times as the "first version". The full score was first engraved for the Beecham edition; which, however, contained one aberration in the erroneous inclusion of a part for double basses (at an incredible altitude) in written unison with the 'cellos for six bars at cue 19. Essentially, the notes of this score agree with the patched-up Harmonie-U.E. version (HU), upon which Beecham's characteristic editing of dynamics, etc., is superimposed.

There perhaps we may leave this confusing and confused story, upon which it is hoped these notes will not have piled confusion worse confounded. At least it seems a pity that a work over which so much trouble was taken by the composer and his first interpreters should have now all but disappeared from the repertory as also from the affection of apparently even his most loyal admirers.

("Musical Opinion", August 1970 and October 1971.)

Delius and Form: A Vindication
by Deryck Cooke

I

"In fact...the intellectual content of Delius's music is perilously thin."—Peter Heyworth, *The Observer*, 4th February 1962.

"For Delius, admittedly, form was unimportant."—Rollo Myers, letter to *The Listener*, 15th February 1962.

"In fact" . . . "admittedly" . . . these statements sound very authoritative; they seem to be offered as no less than the simple truth. But if we really *are* after the truth in musical criticism we can reach it only by establishing real facts, which do really have to be admitted. *In fact*, the pretended facts quoted above are mere expressions of groundless opinion. I intend to prove this, and to establish the actual facts of the matter, which are actually undeniable.

This may sound arrogant. But after all, we must all be tired by now of the never-ending stream of uninformed opinion, masquerading as authoritative judgement, which constitutes so much musical criticism (and even more musical journalism). If we are ever to put musical criticism on a basis of truth, we shall have to work from the startling but once-for-all definition of "certainty" given by the great American philosopher Charles Sanders Pierce: "In sciences in which men come to agreement, when a theory is broached, it is considered to be on probation until agreement is reached; after it is reached, the question of certainty becomes an idle one, *since there is no one left who doubts it*" (my italics).

So I want to stress, firmly, that I offer these two essays, not as a personal point of view, to be commended, condemned or waved aside in vague journalistic phrases, but as a reasoned aim at the truth, which must either be *proven wrong* by hard factual reasoning, based on firm technical grounds, or else accepted as conclusive. In short, it is intended as a first attempt towards a scientific musical criticism; and it concerns Delius because of all composers he stands most in need of rescuing from the confusion of fashionable dogma and loose journalistic opinion.

Fact No. 1. The classical method of analysis, while able to demonstrate the existence of a definite form in professional works using classical methods of construction, is so imprecise that it cannot establish *incontrovertibly* whether that form is adequate or inadequate. *Proof:* Musicians with professional analytical equipment disagree amongst themselves about the formal adequacy of even certain highly-regarded works, a notorious example being Schubert's Ninth Symphony.

Fact No. 2. The classical method of analysis has so far proved incapable of demonstrating even the *existence* of a form in works which do not use classical methods of construction, such as those of Debussy and Delius, let alone of establishing whether it is adequate or not. *Proof:* There are no writings in which the classical method of analysis has succeeded in throwing any light on the forms of works of this kind. *Consequence of Facts* 1 *and* 2*:* In the existing state of analytical knowledge—*i.e.* that based on the classical method of analysis—the statement that "the intellectual content of Delius's music is perilously thin" is not a fact, but an opinion.

Fact No. 3. The application of the term "intellectual content" to Delius's music begs the question how large a part the intellectual or rational faculty plays in different types of composition. In the forms of works written to a *strict* pre-formulated scheme, such as canon, the intellectual faculty plays a large part; in the forms of works written to a *flexible* pre-formulated scheme, such as fugue or sonata, the intellectual faculty plays a fair part; but in the forms of works written to no pre-formulated scheme of any kind, the intellectual faculty plays no part at all. *Proof:* Debussy and Delius—the chief composers of works of this kind—both disavowed the use of the intellectual faculty ("ingenuity") in composing their music.

Fact No. 4. The faculty which builds up the form in works not written to a pre-formulated scheme is the imagination, controlled by an intuitive sense of satisfactory shape. *Proof:* No formal proof is possible, but in the absence of the intellectual faculty, no other explanation exists. The utterances of Debussy and Delius give support to this explanation. *Consequence of Facts* 3 *and* 4*:* The term "intellectual content" is inapplicable to the music of Delius, as to that of Debussy.

Fact No. 5. The proportion between (1) concern with the form as such, and (2) concern with the form as extra-musical expression, varies from composer to composer. *Proof:* Wagner's writings about his own works are almost entirely concerned with extra-musical expression, Stravinsky's almost entirely with form as such.

Fact No. 6. Even composers who are most concerned with extra-musical expression are also preoccupied with form. *Proof:* Wagner, although so concerned with extra-musical expression, evolved new formal methods of his own.

Fact No. 7. No composer of any standing is not concerned with form. *Proof:* Delius, of all composers the most purely concerned with extra-musical expression, was aware of the need for a technical command of basic structural devices, as the following of his remarks indicate: "Towards the end of my course with Ward—and he made me work like a nigger—he showed great insight in helping me to find out just how much in the way of traditional technique would be useful to me. . . . A sense of flow is the main thing, and it doesn't matter how you do it, so long as you master it." *Consequence of Facts 5, 6 and 7:* The statement "For Delius, form was unimportant" is false, as it would be of any reputable composer.

Fact No. 8. From about 1850 onwards, the formal methods of all reputable composers differ so fundamentally—whether they use classical methods or not—as to be personal to themselves; and the methods of one are no standard for understanding those of another. *Proof:* It is impossible to understand the form of Wagner's music according to the methods of Brahms, or of Debussy's according to the methods of Richard Strauss.

Fact No. 9. It has been necessary for critics to make a new act of understanding for each of these composers, in the matter of their formal methods; and general critical understanding has only arrived after a specialist has studied the composer concerned and publicly explained his formal methods. *Proof:* There was general critical bewilderment over the formal methods of Wagner, Debussy, Strauss, Stravinsky, Bartók, Schoenberg, *etc.,* until a growing body of literature appeared in each case which elucidated the formal methods of the composer concerned.

Fact No. 10. No one has publicly explained the formal methods of Delius. *Proof:* The extant writings on Delius either ignore the question or apply the classical method with inevitably fruitless results.

Fact No. 11. It is only possible for a critic to offer a helpful judgement of a composer's formal methods when he has become familiar with that composer's works and analysed them carefully. *Proof:* The only helpful judgements we possess of any composer's formal methods, by a critic, are those by one who has made a special study of the composer concerned, such as Ernest Newman in the case of Wagner—in which event the critic no longer functions as such but becomes a specialist; critical judgements made without a study of the composer's music—such as those of Hanslick on Tchaikovsky—invariably contain demonstrable errors of analytical fact. *Consequence of Facts* 8, 9, 10 *and* 11: Since the critics quoted at the head of this article neither know Delius's music intimately nor have studied and analysed his works, their pretended judgements concerning his form are mere groundless opinion.

Fact No. 12.   A new method of analysis has come into being of recent years—two different examples of it being Rudolf Reti's "Thematic Process" and Hans Keller's "Functional Analysis"—which, by examining meticulously the bar-to-bar organisation of music, can demonstrate the presence of a form in works not written to any pre-formulated scheme. *Proof:* Reti succeeded in demonstrating, in Debussy's apparently amorphous *La Cathédrale Engloutie*, a clear monothematic structure. *Consequence:* This type of analysis should be applied to Delius's music, to see whether it can explain his formal methods; and until this has been done, and the results carefully examined and assessed by those professionally equipped to do so, journalistic opinion should be suspended on what is still a matter of idle conjecture.

II

"One can't define form in so many words, but if I was asked, I should say it was nothing more than imparting spiritual unity to one's thought. It is contained in the thought itself, not applied as something that already exists."—Delius.

"It has always been my opinion that Delius had a well-nigh perfect sense of form for what he had to say."—Eric Fenby.

"Delius lapsed into rhapsody."—Peter Heyworth, *The Observer*, 25th March 1962.

In the previous essay I tried to prove conclusively that Delius's formal methods are *terra incognita*, and that all wholesale journalistic condemnation of his music on structural grounds is so much idle opinion, based on ignorance of the true facts. I also suggested that, since the classical method of analysis has proved powerless to judge the formal adequacy of a given professional work, and especially of works by composers with such personal formal methods as Debussy and Delius, the only possible solution of the problem is to apply to one of Delius's works the new analytical methods, stemming from the writings of Schoenberg, which have come into being recently; and I indicated that there is hope of success, since Rudolf Reti, by means of his "Thematic Process", succeeded in demonstrating a taut formal coherence in Debussy's apparently amorphous *La Cathédrale Engloutie.*

Some people have been amused at the idea of applying to the "rhapsodic" Delius methods we know mainly from Hans Keller's use of them in his "Functional Analysis". "You can't really be serious?" I have been asked. Indeed, I am: in this article, I want to make a main onslaught on the hitherto un-broached question of Delius's handling of the formal element of composition, by applying the new method, in my own way, to his Violin Concerto.

> *"Seeing that the principles of classical structure are utterly foreign to Delius's nature, we may admit that the finest music in his concertos is the most purely rhapsodic; therefore the violin concerto is better than the others. Even in this work, Delius cannot write one coherent rhapsodic flight of lyricism from start to finish. Who could? He is forced to find substitutes for the variety and contrast of classical ritornello, though he did not know the fact in such terms. Denied advancement by metabolism, germination, or apotheosis of themes, he uses sudden adventitious changes of time and texture . . ."*—Arthur Hutchings, *Delius.*

It is small wonder that present-day musical journalists, finding Delius's music somehow distasteful owing to its fluidity, and being unable to discern any form in it, should fall back on the word "rhapsody" as a blanket term of disparage-ment (it has been much bandied about as such in this centenary year)—since Delius's admirers, who find the music much to their taste, seem equally unable to discern any form in it and have fallen back on the word "rhapsody" as a blanket term of approbation. In his book on Delius, Professor Hutchings, himself an adept at the classical method of analysis, seems to have been so hypnotised by Delius's singularly fluid outpouring of beauty as to have lost his analytical faculty altogether: after the introduction to the Violin Concerto quoted above, he devotes only one page and two music examples to what is one of Delius's most concentrated structures, and does not even attempt to describe its overall shape (as Harold Rutland does succinctly in a few lines in his sleeve-note for the Pougnet-Beecham recording), let alone its subtle interior organisation.

In any case, what on earth does "rhapsody" mean? If it means anything concrete at all, it must mean an undisciplined outpouring of ideas with no inherent connection, which are not organised into a coherent form. But the idea that such a thing can exist, except in music of such feebly amateur quality as to be beneath consideration, is a chimera. It is certainly inapplicable to Delius's finest works, except as a mere metaphor to evoke that wonderful spontaneous poetic flow of his, that miraculous freedom (akin to Debussy's) from all the clanking machinery of traditional formal methods. The truth is that where Delius does indulge in rhapsody is in his very worst works, which are indeed so amateurish as to be beneath consideration. The Violin Concerto, on the other hand, is a superb example of germination and rigorous thematic development, but of a uniquely plastic kind, far removed from the traditional hammer-and-chisel type.

Let us see how far the classical method of analysis will take us in understanding the work. It will certainly make clear the main outline of the form. The work is continuous, but falls into five sections:

1 With moderate tempo (sonata exposition)   93 bars
2 Slowly ("slow movement"="development")   73 bars
3 Ad libitum (accompanied slow cadenza)   30 bars
4 Tempo I (sonata recapitulation)   61 bars
5 Allegretto (scherzo/finale, referring back to 1)   83 bars

Judged simply as an overall plan, this is a highly original solution of the problem of compressing the four movements of a normal sonata work into a single movement which develops the initial material throughout. It can be schematically expressed as follows:

1 *Sonata-form first movement*, the exposition and recapitulation being separated by (a) a development section which is the:
2 *Slow movement*, and (b) a cadenza, bringing the recapitulation (see 1), which leads to the:
3 *Scherzo*-theme, which turns out to be the main material of the:

4 *Finale,* the second theme and coda of which refer back to
(2) and (1).

But of course, a plan is one thing, carrying it out another.
However, still using the classical method of analysis, we find,
surprisingly enough, that it can demonstrate the existence of a
very complex form, in detail, stage by stage:

1 **EXPOSITION** (93 bars):

Introduction (orch) (2 bars)	2 bars 4/4
First Group (38 bars):	
A (vln)	6 bars 4/4
B (vln and wind)	5 bars 12/8
C (vln and wind)	3 bars 12/8 (1 of 6/8)
dev. of B and C (vln and orch)	5 bars 12/8 (1 of 4/4)
A1 (orch ritornello)	2 bars 4/4
dev. of A (vln)	4 bars 4/4
D (vln)	2 bars 12/8
dev. of A (vln)	10 bars 4/4
reference to B (orch)	1 bar 12/8
Transition (37 bars):	
New version of D (vln)	6 bars 12/8=4/4
D (vln)	2 bars 12/8
dev. of A (vln)	7 bars 4/4
reference to D (orch)	1 bar 12/8
dev. of B (vln)	3 bars 12/8
A1 (orch ritornello)	2 bars 4/4
dev. of D (vln and orch)	14 bars 12/8
A1 (orch ritornello)	2 bars 4/4
Second Subject (16 bars):	
E (brass)	5 bars 4/4
dev. of B (orch and vln)	3 bars 12/8 (1 of 6/8)
E (orch)	3 bars 4/4
reference to A (vln and wind)	5 bars 4/4

2 **DEVELOPMENT—SLOW MOVEMENT** (73 bars):

Statement (38 bars)		
(*i*) F (A and B fused) (vln)	14 bars 6/4	
(*ii*) G (vln)		4 bars 4/4
dev. of F in 4/4 (vln) 24		16 bars 4/4
G (oboe and vln) bars		4 bars 4/4
Restatement (35 bars):		
(*i*) F (vln)	13 bars 6/4	
(*ii*) G only (vln and orch)	22 bars 4/4	

3 ACCOMPANIED SLOW CADENZA (30 bars)

> 30 bars 4/4 (1 free; 1 of
> 6/4; 1 of 7/4)

4 RECAPITULATION (61 bars):
Introduction omitted
First Group (39 bars):

same as exposition until 28th bar, with slight rescoring, harmonic tonal changes:	27 bars 4/4 and 12/8
then contracted—	
dev. of A (vln and orch)	9 bars 4/4
D (wind)	2 bars 12/8
reference to B (orch)	1 bar 12/8

Transition (11 bars):

New version of D (vln)	6 bars 12/8=4/4
D (vln)	2 bars 12/8
dev. of A (vln)	3 bars 4/4

Second Subject (11 bars):

E (brass—wind—tutti)	11 bars 4/4

5 SCHERZO-FINALE (83 bars):
Statement (30 bars):

(*i*) Scherzo-Theme H (orch)	8 bars 12/8
(*ii*) Second theme J (vln) (new form of G) 22	7 bars 4/4
dev. of J in 12/8 (vln) bars	6 bars 12/8 (1 of 6/8)
J (vln)	9 bars 4/4

Link (vln) (1 bar)   1 bar 12/8

Restatement (52 bars):

(*i*) H extended (orch)	24 bars 12/8 (1 of 6/8)
(*ii*) Coda, based on A (vln)	28 bars 4/4

What does this broad analysis tell us? Four things, which are of crucial importance. First, that Delius, far from indulging in rhapsody, was concerned with evolving a very original and intricate, but entirely clear form, involving nine main ideas, with thematic cross-references. Second, that the work was written with a strong feeling for rightness in the proportions, since the balance of the various movements and sections, in the matter of numbers of bars, cannot be faulted. Third, that Delius was aware of the need for reshaping and compression on

restatement (compare exposition—93 bars—and recapitulation —61 bars). Fourth, that the rhythmic organisation is most original, alternating 4/4 with 12/8 or 6/4 throughout.

But the classical method of analysis can take us no farther. If it is powerless to demonstrate the adequacy of the form in works constructed on classical patterns, it is even more helpless here: in the sonata movement, as can be seen, Delius does not keep his themes neatly distinct from one another, but while he is developing one he introduces another in the middle of that development, and so on; moreover, it is useless to attempt to work out the tonal scheme on classical principles, since Delius, like Debussy, does not use tonality to oppose themes against one another in a dynamic perspective, but to create an "impression-istic" flow of changing atmospheres. The only way of trying to demonstrate any true coherence in the form of the Violin Concerto is to use the new methods of analysis, which can at least demonstrate a logical connection in the sequence of A, B, C, etc., and their various developments, by scrutinising closely the bar-to-bar evolution of the thematic argument.

In applying the new methods (in my own way), I shall ignore Delius's wonderful harmony, and confine myself to the thematic and rhythmic elements. This will not only save much-needed space in the matter of music type, but will also give the lie to the following recent statement by a musical journalist: "Delius is not a particularly interesting melodist . . . his most natural rhythmic state is inertia . . . the one field in which he claims our attention in his use of lush, chromatically-sliding harmony to evoke a haze of dreamy, motionless musing."

1 EXPOSITION. The orchestral introduction is a motto of two 4/4 bars, out of which the whole work grows. In this (and only one other case), I shall give the harmony, since it indicates the weight given to the motto, and contains an element which eventually becomes thematic. The motto is given in Ex. 1, together with its abstracted thematic shape (Shape I) and its abstracted rhythm (P). The essence of this rhythm is the characteristically Delian syncopated accent on the second beat.

Idea A of the first group (Ex. 2) enters immediately, also in 4/4: in its second bar it swings into the rhythm P, with the falling second which opens the motto. The falling second is the basis of the descending scale-pattern of A. In the fifth bar of Ex. 2, the violin takes up figure *x* from shape I to rhythm P, in a new form; in bar 6, it appears to go off into rhapsody if one does not notice that the orchestra supports it with a repetition of *x* in its new form (Ex. 3, which underpins bar 6 of Ex. 2). In any case, the violin's bar of "rhapsody" is a free variant of A.

A, in using the rhythm P in its second bar, superimposes on it a new rhythm Q to a thematic figure y (Ex. 2, bar 2, and Ex. 4): this figure will be pervasive, and its rhythm (a Delius "fingerprint") even more so.

At the end of Ex. 2, the two-bar development of x implies two further bars to complete the period of two four-bar phrases, but Delius contracts here by weaving in immediately a second idea in 12/8 (B)—see Ex. 5. As Professor Hutchings says, Delius "knew the need for such duality"—but on the other hand the change of time is not "adventitious": it begins the opposition between 4/4 and 12/8 (later 6/4) which is the individual rhythmic basis of the work. Also the new theme B grows out of what has gone before: it is at once a new fluid form of shape I and a new fluid form of rhythm P (Ex. 6). In rhythm P, the second note is emphasized by both syncopation and length; in its new form in B by syncopation only, marked by an accent in Ex. 6.

After the threefold statement of B in Ex. 5 (a contraction of an implied fourfold one), the melodic line proceeds immediately by developing B in a different form, B1, which gives a new thematic shape in three different versions—shape II (i), (ii), and (iii)—see Ex. 7.

After this two-bar development of B in Ex. 7, the melodic line continues immediately by weaving in a third idea, C— which is a quicker form of shape II (i); as with B, its implied fourfold statement is contracted into a threefold one, its half-bar length necessitating the single bar of 6/8 (see Ex. 8). The one bar of apparent rhapsody which follows, concluding Ex. 8, can be seen to be thematic, since it continues C's version of II (i).

After this single bar of "rhapsody", the melodic line continues immediately with one statement of B, a one-bar contraction of C in 4/4 and resumed development of B in 12/8 in another new form (Ex. 9). This shows the extraordinarily subtle organic coherence of Delius's apparently wayward flow.

So far I have illustrated my analysis from the beginning, bar by bar, to show how closely Delius pursues his thematic argument, but from now on I shall take this for granted, since, for the sake of space, I shall have to confine myself to illustrating only the turning-points of the form. A score would help the reader at this point.

The development of B continues for three bars, culminating

in a new forceful form of A—a two-bar contraction of it over a dominant seventh on B flat, which acts as an orchestral ritornello A1—see Ex. 10. (Professor Hutchings regrets that the opening "eschew(s) the chance of germination, by cross-reference and interplay, possible only when introductory material is ritornellic": the introductory material is certainly not—it is germinal—but the first theme, A, is clearly used as a ritornello in the forceful form A1 over its dominant seventh on B flat.) The violin responds by developing A1 (see Ex. 10 again).

This development continues for four bars; then a fourth idea, D, is woven in (Ex. 11). This is a new brooding version of *x* as developed in Ex. 2—see Ex. 12. D is set out as a new thematic shape (shape III) in Ex. 13. After this, the development of A is resumed (see bar 3 of Ex. 11) and continues for ten bars; then a quiet reference to B brings the first group to an end.

The transition opens with an apparently new idea which, being in fact a flowing transformation of D, may be called D1 (Ex. 14); after six bars of this, D itself is reaffirmed. Then eleven bars of development of A, D and B bring back the orchestral ritornello A1, with its dominant seventh on B flat, more forcibly. Finally, another fourteen bars of intensive developmeny of D bring the third and climactic statement of the orchestral ritornello A1, still with its dominant seventh on B flat; this time it goes straight into the powerful second subject, E (Ex. 15). But E is a highly contrasted and contracted re-fashioning of D, or shape III (see Ex. 16—the F natural which opens A1 in Ex. 15 is retained by the harmony throughout the two bars before E enters). Also E's rhythmic shape is a new dynamic version of the basic rhythm P (see Ex. 16 again).

Modified repetitions of E are interrupted by lively references to B, and followed by quiet references to A, which end the exposition by glancing back to its beginning.

Obviously, sonata-form is merely a way of explaining what happens in this work: the music can in no way be said to be *in* sonata-form (in the normal sense)—it is an example of Delius's free yet thematically coherent formal method of evolving a form out of an initial idea. The concentration of his formal organisation should be clear at this point; from now on, for reasons of space, I shall merely indicate the derivations of the new main ideas.

2 DEVELOPMENT = SLOW MOVEMENT. Since the exposition has itself contained so much thematic development, the development section takes the form of a slow movement devoted to lyrical (but closely organised) treatment of new transformations of the exposition's main material. The main idea of the slow movement, F, takes up shape II (ii) and continues with shape I to a fusion of rhythms P and Q (see Exs 17, 18 and 19). In its second bar, the strings accompany the violin's version of shape II (ii) by a version of shape I, with its second group of three notes inverted; this interpretation is confirmed when in the fourth bar the violin itself has I in its original shape (see Ex. 18).

At the end of the fourteen-bar statement of F, notes three, four and five of shape I are treated as a separate thematic figure, z, which generates the second idea of the movement, G (see Ex. 20). The rhythm of G is yet another, drawn-out form of the basic rhythm P (see Ex. 21). The whole slow movement is made up of alternation and interweaving of F and G (see general analysis above) and nothing else.

3 ACCOMPANIED SLOW CADENZA. The slow movement ends with dying references to G, and the cadenza begins with a characteristic piece of violinistics (Ex. 22). If anywhere, a composer might be forgiven for "lapsing into rhapsody" in a cadenza; strange, then, to find Delius meticulously picking up thematic shape II (i) from the end of the slow movement as a starting-point for his "free" passage-work (see Ex. 22 again). The cadenza itself, however, is not built out of shape II (i). The ascending arpeggios of Ex. 22 are followed by falling ones, and the cadenza takes this pattern as its basis, in the form of a "new" figure, consisting of one bar of ascending and one bar of descending arpeggio (Ex. 23). Delius used to improvise *harmonically* on the violin, in *arpeggios outlining chords*, and this cadenza is no doubt a formalised example of the fantastic and wonderful harmonic arabesques he used to draw from the instrument. For formalised it is: its arpeggio pattern is a taut fusion of idea A (with the rhythm P) and shape II (iii)— see Ex. 24.

The cadenza is built entirely out of fourteen beautiful variations on this basic idea, to sustained wind or string chords. Three times it is expanded into a three-bar pattern, by extending either the ascending or the descending arpeggio to two bars; but more interesting, in the case of this "rhapsodic" composer, is that it is twice contracted into a single bar (as in Ex. 25). The final descending arpeggio takes the form of excited woodwind figures, which waken the music from its musing for a powerful orchestral statement of A, which opens the recapitulation.

4 RECAPITULATION. There is no need to analyse the recapitulation in detail. As indicated in the general analysis above, for twenty-seven of its sixty-one bars it restates the process of the exposition exactly, with modifications in the scoring, the harmony, and the tonal disposition, after which it drastically compresses the remainder. The second subject, E, uninterrupted this time, works up to an fff climax, heralding the final stage of the work.

5 SCHERZO-FINALE. The main scherzo material, H, begins by taking up, in more lively form, shape II (i) as at the end of the slow movement and the beginning of the cadenza (Ex. 26—compare Ex. 22). This is a subtle stroke: the recapitulation is "ignored", as it were, since in the implied *four-movement* form, the Scherzo-Finale *continues after the slow movement and cadenza*, not after the end of the first movement. This interpretation is confirmed by the fact that the whole shape of H is implicit in certain phrases of the cadenza (see Ex. 27).

In this scherzo theme, Delius uses for the first time regular sequences of four-bar periods, and each bar has the four-square rhythm of H. This may be regarded, perhaps, as the one weak spot of the work. Even so, not for the reason given by one musical journalist—that this section shows how "deadly" Delius is when he "tries to be animated", that the attempt to dance here is "depressingly languid". On the Pougnet-Beecham recording, the music has the delicately lilting movement of an English country dance, and we do not ask more from Delius, since we do not expect him to burst suddenly into the electrifying rhythms of Stravinsky or Bartók. Even the four-bar periods can be defended, as characteristic of many dance-movements of great composers. Nevertheless, it has to be admitted that when this theme is extended, on its second appearance, to twenty-four bars, the effect of the continuous repetition of the rhythm of H, together with the persistent pattering of the soloist's *moto perpetuo* semiquaver accompaniment, does become a little wearisome; and that Delius's one attempt to stave off monotony —a "fading-out" of the rhythm in bars 11–13 together with a contraction to a "half-bar" of 6/8 in bar 12—does not really achieve its purpose. However, this is a single and comparatively slight flaw which should not unduly worry those who can respond to the strange charm of the music itself.

The second idea of this movement, J, introduces the finale

261

element, and also brings the threads of the work together: it is a refashioning of shapes II and I and of the rhythm Q, as an urgent version of the main idea of the slow movement, F, which itself goes back to the thematic origins of the whole work (see Ex. 28—compare Ex. 17). After the recurrence of the scherzo material H (the twenty-four-bar extension mentioned above), J does not return, but instead there is an extended coda of just over the same length, which is a concentrated summing-up, in Delius's most exquisite elegiac vein, in the form of an intensely chromatic treatment of the first two bars of A; it dissolves, at the end, into an unclouded F major, with added sixth. Since J was concerned with elements of A, the coda, recalling A itself, is a perfect equivalent for the expected restatement of J, and a perfect ending for the work, looking back to its beginning.

In the closing bars, woodwind references to the pervasive rhythm Q make a final unifying comment. In Ex. 29b, the first clarinet figure is a version of shape I, ignoring the shape's third note (the repeated D) and taking A as the fifth note instead of C. This is confirmed by the clarinet's second figure in Ex. 29b, which uses for its fifth note not A but A flat—the crucial harmonic inflexion of the fifth note of the original motto (see Ex. 29a and Ex. 1). But the flute's imitation of the clarinet figure in Ex. 29b is a version of the second bar of the concerto's first theme—A. So A itself is ultimately derived from shape I, not only by transforming the motto's initial falling second into a descending scale, and incorporating into its second bar the rhythm P, but also by refashioning the motto itself as the pervasive little melisma y to the rhythm Q (Ex. 29c).

In other words, the whole material of the work, thematic and rhythmic, is evolved out of its initial two-bar motto—with what *entirely unrhapsodic, rigorously organic* mastery I believe to have demonstrated conclusively.

("The Musical Times", June and July 1962.)

THE CONTRIBUTORS

RUNCIMAN, JOHN F. (1866–1916). English critic and musicologist who was from 1894 until his death music critic of "The Saturday Review". He was also editor of "The Chord" and "The Musician's Library", and correspondent of "The Musical Record" (Boston). His attacks on several composers ended in libel suits. His works include "Old Scores and New Readings", and lives of Purcell and Wagner.

CUMBERLAND, GERALD (1881–1926). English critic and writer on music and a prolific contributor to English and American papers. His *Set Down in Malice* (1918) and *Written in Friendship* (1923) caused mild stirs in their day.

DENT, EDWARD JOSEPH (1876–1957). English musician and Cambridge Professor of Music, composer, critic, teacher and author, who shared Delius's atheism and anti-clericalism. Author of standard books on Alessandro Scarlatti and Busoni, he will also be remembered for the part he played in founding the International Society for Contemporary Music, and by his several still current English translations of opera libretti.

KLENAU, PAUL VON (1883–1946). Danish composer and conductor who founded the Copenhagen Philharmonic Society. He was noted for his performances of the music of Delius in Vienna and Central Europe. He conducted a concert in honour of Delius's sixtieth Birthday in Frankfurt-am-Main, and gave *A Mass of Life* in both Vienna and London in 1925.

CAPELL, RICHARD (1885–1954). English music critic and author. Music critic of the *Daily Mail* and then (1933–1954) of *The Daily Telegraph*, Capell was on active service during the First World War and a war correspondent during the Second. His masterly book on the Schubert songs (1928) remains his most important contribution to musical literature.

OYLER, PHILIP (1879–1974). Practical expert in self-supporting farming enterprises and communities who lived at Grez-sur-Loing around 1930 while managing a nearby farm

263

estate. He became acquainted with Delius and devoted a chapter to him in his best-known book *Sons of the Generous Earth* (1963).

ORR, CHARLES WILFRED (b.1893). English composer of fine songs. His influences are his admiration for the Lieder of Hugo Wolf and the poetry of A. E. Housman, and also his personal friendship with Delius which lasted for nearly twenty years.

BEECHAM, SIR THOMAS (1879–1961). Arguably the greatest British conductor, Beecham became the principal interpreter of Delius's music from the time he met the composer (1907) until his death more than half a century later. He organised Delius Festivals in 1929 and 1946, and recorded a large part of Delius's output.

LAMBERT, CONSTANT (1905–51). English composer, conductor and writer on music, who holds the distinction of being the first British composer to be commissioned to write a ballet for Diaghilev. He was the most prominent champion of the music of Delius among the generation which followed Beecham.

EVANS, EDWIN (1874–1945). English critic. He succeeded Richard Capell on the *Daily Mail* and Edward J. Dent as President of the I.S.C.M. A fine linguist and a man of wide artistic interests, he enjoyed the friendship of some of the most famous composers of his time, and was an ardent propagandist for their music.

CARDUS, SIR NEVILLE (1889–1975). English music critic and author, Cardus, who wrote over a long period for *The Manchester Guardian* and its successor *The Guardian*, was known equally for his writings on cricket. He never concealed his deep affection for Delius's music.

ELGAR, SIR EDWARD (1857–1934). English composer, Master of the King's Music. Initially as much an outsider to the British musical establishment as Delius, Elgar became its chief ornament.

NEWMAN, ERNEST (1868–1959). The most widely-read English music critic of his day, and author of a standard life of Wagner (1933–1947), Newman had occasion to write about Delius's music over a long period, as Music Critic, successively, of *The Manchester Guardian*, *Birmingham Post*, *The Observer* and *The Sunday Times*.

HARRISON, MAY (1891–1959). Eldest of the Harrison sisters, three distinguished instrumentalists, May was an Auer pupil greatly admired by Kreisler, as well as by Delius who wrote his Double Concerto for her and her sister Beatrice. May gave the first performance of Delius's Third Violin Sonata (1930) with Arnold Bax, with whom she also recorded the first sonata.

ARNOLD, CECILY (1896–1974). English singer and teacher of singing, harpsichord and viols, Cecily Arnold gave the first performance of Delius's song "Avant que tu ne t'en ailles" in 1932.

NICHOLS, ROBERT (1893–1944). English poet and writer who served in France from 1914 to 1916, thereby qualifying for inclusion as a War Poet, and later became Professor of English Literature at Imperial College, Tokyo. His friendship with Delius led to his selecting the words for the Idyll "Once I passed through a Populous City" from Whitman's verse, which was set, with Fenby's collaboration, to music from the unpublished opera *Margot la Rouge*.

GRAINGER, PERCY ALDRIDGE (1882–1961). Australian composer and pianist, a pupil of Busoni and a disciple of Grieg, both friends of Delius, whose close friend Grainger, his junior by twenty years, became. His collection of the folk-tune "Brigg Fair" (1905) and his six-part *a cappella* setting of it (1906) were directly responsible for Delius's composition of *Brigg Fair, An English Rhapsody* (1907).

GRAY, CECIL (1895–1951). Anglo-Scottish critic and composer. Close friend and musical associate of Philip Heseltine, Gray is remembered more for his important study of Sibelius 1931, revised 1934) and memoir of Peter Warlock (1934) than for his compositions.

SIMON, HEINRICH (1880–1941). Editor of the *Frankfurter Zeitung*, he wrote eulogistically of Delius's *Fennimore and Gerda* on the occasion of its first performance (Frankfurt, 21st October 1919), and became a close friend of the Deliuses. He gave an illustrated lecture-recital on *Fennimore and Gerda* in London on 11th October 1936. As an influential Jewish refugee from Hitler's Germany, he embarrassed the Nazis who caused his assassination in Washington D.C. on 6th May 1941.

RANDEL, WILLIAM. A Maine resident, Professor Randel has taught at universities in Minnesota, Florida, and Maine in the U.S.A., and in Europe at Helsinki, Athens and Bologna. His published works include *The Klu Klux Klan, Huxley's American Visit, Centennial: American Life in* 1876 and *American Revolution: Mirror of a People*.

LOWE, RACHEL (RACHEL LOWE-DUGMORE). Rachel Lowe is a former archivist to the Delius Trust and author of *Catalogue of the Music Archive of the Delius Trust* (1974). She is currently engaged on research involving Delius, Grainger and their period at the University of Western Australia, where she recently assisted with the Australian première of *Hassan*.

CARLEY, LIONEL (b.1936). Dr. Carley studied languages at Nottingham, Strasbourg, Uppsala and Stockholm. He has been archivist to the Delius Trust since 1966, and has published one monograph, *Delius: the Paris Years*, and several articles on the composer. In preparation are a life and a volume of letters; also, with Robert Threlfall, a pictorial biography.

REDWOOD, CHRISTOPHER (b.1939). Educated at Christ's Hospital and Trinity College of Music, where he presented a thesis on "The Operas of Delius". Lecturer and author of several articles on related topics; editor since 1973 of *The Delius Society Journal*. Director of Music at Parmiter's School, London.

THRELFALL, ROBERT (b.1918). Educated at Wimbledon College, he subsequently studied piano-playing in London under Solomon. For several years he was Assistant Archivist, and is now an Adviser, to the Delius Trust. He has lectured and written on different facets of Delius's work, and is also the author of a monograph and other articles on Rachmaninoff.

COOKE, DERYCK (b.1919). Musicologist and author, Deryck Cooke, long a member of the music staff of the BBC, has become widely known for his *The Language of Music* (1959) and his completion of a performing version of Mahler's Tenth Symphony.

INDEX